ANOINTED FOR BURIAL

Todd and DeAnn Burke

New Covenant Commission
Oklahoma City, OK

All Scripture references are taken from the *New American Standard Bible*, copyright 1973, by The Lockman Foundation, unless otherwise noted.

To the glory of God—whose right it is to receive
all the praise.

To the Khmer Church—the ones who are
walking in the way of Jesus to eternal
life, and would tell this story if they could.

Here is a modern miracle story right out of the book of Acts! A burning spirit house, people raised from the dead and miraculous healings are told about in this true story. Not since the revival in Indonesia has there been such an exciting wonder-work of God as that which occurred in Cambodia during the dying days of the last regime. Bloodied and persecuted the church still survives through the grace of God.

Todd Burke is a young man called of God to a unique ministry of what properly can be called a pioneer, apostolic work. Strange things happen to him for which there is no explanation but God. Todd exercises a risky, daring kind of faith which God honors. Some of the incidents are truly incredible—but then you need to read the book.

Charles Farah, Jr. Ph.D
Professor of Theological
and Historical Studies
Oral Roberts University

FOREWORD

This exciting book is worth reading for at least three reasons: First, because it is the highly unusual story of a brave young couple working in a far away place at a critical time; second, because it sheds light on the contemporary history of Cambodia, a little country which has suffered much with little notice by the rest of the world; third, because it underlines God's way of operating under circumstances of spiritual crisis, even including demonic warfare.

As personal testimony, the story is not unlike those of many other intrepid missionaries who have struggled on the frontier of evangelism. The names and places are different, but the sense of dedication and faith are the same.

As history, the story makes no attempt to analyze the politics or sociology of the place where it happens. But it reveals a great deal about the thinking and motivation of the people—Christian and non-Christian.

As an example of spiritual principles, the story is at its best. It demonstrates that God is at work in today's world—and that His activity can accelerate and intensify wherever there is stress and challenge, never discouraged by human imperfection.

Naked faith is still the way to see results in the kingdom of God. Without denominational structure, without organized funding, without even much advance planning, a spiritual harvest in Cambodia came about on a scale far beyond what could have been expected in a "normal" missionary crusade. And simple faith still brings His miraculous help. God remains more interested in attitude than in aptitude.

Todd and DeAnn Burke are missionaries who will leave a mark not just on Southeast Asia, but on the world. Their vision is large, their faith undaunted, their personal spiritual lives of a sort that makes it possible for God to speak to them directly and often. As you read, you will be reminded of the book of Acts. And you will thank God for fresh, glorious evidence that His Holy Spirit is still alive and well on planet earth.

John Garlock
Director, Christ for the
Nations Institute

CONTENTS

ANOINTED FOR BURIAL

CHAPTER 1

The Door Opens

"According to this visa, you have only one day left in our country." Even before the interpreter translated the statement from Cambodian to English, the atmosphere crackled with tension and I sensed the official's suspicion as he thumbed through the pages of my passport. His eyes lifted, narrowing as he watched me. I felt uneasy under his searching glare.

The tasteful surroundings told me Mr. Dy Bellong was an important man. But I would have been even more nervous had I realized I was standing in the office of President Lon Nol's minister of foreign affairs.

"You're right, Mr. Dy Bellong," I replied through the interpreter. "This is another reason I have come to you. I have many friends among your Khmer people, and I want very badly to stay in your country." I knew that, short of a miracle, I would be forced to leave Cambodia the next day.

When I had first entered Dy Bellong's office, I presented one of my visit cards to his aide. My name immediately stirred their suspicions. Somehow a rumor had reached them that I had been expelled from Thailand.

"I've never even been to Thailand," I had assured them and handed them my passport, knowing they would not find any immigration entries from Thailand.

That's when they noticed I had only one day left on my visa.

Mr. Dy Bellong laid my passport on his desk while I quickly stated my purpose for coming. At this point I had nothing to lose by being straightforward.

"How do we secure permission to use the indoor arena of the Stadt Olympic?" I asked. He seemed astonished by my request. I explained that we wanted to have a public concert with a musical group from the United States, sharing the message of Jesus with the Khmer people.

He bristled slightly and said, "The Khmer people already have their religion. Why do you want to give them another?"

I had never before been confronted with that question, but I took a deep breath and responded boldly, "I agree, Mr. Dy Bellong, that your people don't need another religion. But they do need Jesus." I paused while his aide interpreted my words. Dy Bellong looked at me curiously.

"Religion," I continued, "is man trying to climb to God—hoping to attain salvation. But Jesus is God coming to man—bringing salvation as a free gift. Salvation cannot be bought, earned or stolen; Jesus paid the price. It is a gift we can only receive by believing on Him. Even Christianity as a religion in its many forms is to no avail. Only Jesus can save. We just want to share Jesus with your people."

He quietly considered my words for a few moments, then his eyes shifted back to my passport. Pondering, he gently closed it and slipped it into one of the many pockets of his safari suit. After speaking in a low tone to his aide, he instructed me to return in three days. We exchanged the traditional *sam peah* gesture greeting of respect and I followed Kai Wan out of the office.

Once outside, Kai Wan exploded with excitement. "God will help us!" I was puzzled as to why Dy Bellong had kept my passport, but Kai Wan's joy was contagious. Unlike Kai Wan, I didn't yet realize that the strong Buddhist influence, complicated by the war situation, made it highly improbable for anyone to secure a resident visa for the purpose of preaching the gospel. Later I recalled Tom Cornwall's discouragement when he forewarned me, "They won't let you stay, believe me, I've tried." And here, my Christian friend had cut through all the hierarchy of immigration officials by taking me to the top man.

2

I hung on to his belt as he steered his motorbike through the crowded streets. "Why didn't you tell me you were taking me to such a high official?" I spoke loudly in his ear.

He turned, a broad, confident grin spread across his face. His dark eyes twinkled, but there was no reply.

As we jostled through the maze of traffic I reflected over the incredible events of the six short days I had spent in Cambodia. Leaving Japan on September 3rd, I had stopped over in Hong Kong to secure a visa for Cambodia. All they would give me was a seven-day tourist visa. My wife, DeAnn, stayed behind in Okinawa since it was predicted that Cambodia would fall to the Communists in a matter of weeks. I didn't know what to expect.

When I stepped off the airplane at Phnom Penh airport the first thing I heard was a rumbling in the background. "I wonder what that noise is?" I asked another deplaning passenger. "It sounds like thunder."

Before the man answered he looked at me as if to say, Boy, do you have a lot to learn. Then he answered, "That's the sound of war, young man."

His response sobered me and I felt a chill go down my spine. The sound of distant bombs and rockets was to become familiar to me in the days ahead.

I was fortunate to find an English-speaking taxi driver who drove me the eight miles into the city. All I had was an address, 81 Nehru Boulevard, where a missionary couple, Tom and Louise Cornwall, had been living before their departure. As we approached the city, the ravages of war became more and more noticeable. The delicate beauty of this one-time paradise was now marred with barbed wire and sandbag barricades. Most buildings had guards at the entrance. Refugees lined the sidewalks, sheltered by sheets of plastic draped over poles. I realized there was a lot of difference between just reading about a war and actually being in the midst of it.

My driver pulled up in front of a three-story building and cut the motor.

"This is it," he said, directing me to get out.

3

I had hardly stepped out of the taxi before I found myself engulfed by a crowd of people. They acted as if I was the first white man they had ever seen.

"*Barrang, barrang, barrang!*" the children yelled excitedly, as they pushed their way through the crowd towards me. (I later learned *barrang* means "foreigner.") Just then the iron front door of the building opened and a short Cambodian man came out to chase the crowd away. He greeted me humbly and began carrying my bags inside the building as if he had been expecting me.

Once inside, I learned his name was Kuch Kong. He explained that he, his wife San, and their five children had fled from Siem Reap, 150 miles to the north, when it was overrun by the Khmer Rouge (the Cambodian Communists). Late one night when his city was under attack, a rocket crashed through a wall in Kong's home and stuck in the rafters just a few feet from their heads—without exploding. A few days later Siem Reap was evacuated, and the Kuchs had come to Phnom Penh seeking refuge in this building.

San cleaned a room for me on the third floor next to the auditorium and brought a plate of green oranges to eat. This isn't so bad, I thought to myself, flipping the dials to operate the huge overhead fan. I had barely gotten things put away in the room when a young man came to see me, carrying several sheets of paper in his hand. With a beaming smile he told me his name was Sam-Oeurn.

"Are you Jesus' servant?" he asked me.

"Yes, I am." I smiled in return, never having been asked such a question as that before.

He thrust the papers into my hand saying, "God showed me you were coming. This is my testimony. He told me to write it and give it to you."

I concealed my surprise and accepted the papers. As I read his testimony I felt myself drawn to this young man, a refugee from Takeo, who was about my age. He had once been a Buddhist monk, but became disillusioned with shaving his head, walking around barefoot in orange robes, and begging food as a means to salvation. He had come to know the Cornwalls before they had to leave Phnom Penh. He said he believed in God and wanted to learn

4

more about salvation in Jesus Christ.

I talked for a long time with Sam-Oeurn and late that afternoon he took me to where he lived—a one-room apartment shared with four other families. They were refugees too. I decided to invite Sam-Oeurn to come live with me in the building. He could handle the cleaning and maintenance as well as help guard the entrance. I sensed we would need a guard after Tom Cornwall told me a bomb had once been planted there by some who didn't care for their presence.

Both Kong and Sam-Oeurn spoke some English, so they were my best sources for learning Khmer. Until I grasped the language, they would serve as interpreters.

I explained to them that at present I only had a seven-day visa. "I don't know how long the Lord will allow me to stay in your country, but I want to use effectively what time I do have. What could we do to start a work for the Lord?" I asked them.

Sam-Oeurn promptly suggested I teach English classes. "My people, especially those of college age, are hungry to know English and they like to study with Americans. You could teach English and use the Bible for your textbook."

We agreed the classes would begin the next day. Early on the morning of my second day we put a sign on the front of the building announcing an afternoon and an evening English class with an American teacher. I was amazed to see that by noon we had enrolled more than twenty in each session. Sam-Oeurn was right. I figured that was a good beginning, so we took the sign down. Those who enrolled were required to purchase gospel portions from us, and classes began that same day.

I started out by teaching the Gospel of Luke in the afternoon class and the Gospel of John in the evening. Each lesson period was to last about an hour, but it often lengthened into two. I discovered my students loved to sing, so at the beginning of each session I taught them a chorus in English. The volume of their singing aroused curiosity in the neighborhood, and new ones began coming in.

We would go through a chapter verse by verse, then Kong or

5

Sam-Oeurn interpreted, explaining the meanings of the words. As we discussed these words we sowed the seed of the gospel and by faith planted the message of Christ.

After covering passages telling of Jesus healing the sick and delivering people from demonic power, I stressed, "Through the power of the Holy Spirit, the same Jesus we read about here still walks the earth today, performing signs and wonders. The miracles you read in this book can happen in your homes, your places of work, on the street—if you believe the words of Jesus, they can happen anywhere!"

There were many questions and discussions after class and I sensed that some of them were receiving the message. Day by day I saw their interest change from the study of the language to the Lord. Their spark of new life kindled a wildfire of interest until we lost control of the numbers. On the fifth day of classes we had ninety in the afternoon session and ninety-four in the evening. We didn't have benches for all of them, but they came and sat on the floor.

Kong and Sam-Oeurn were busy from early morning to late at night instructing and counseling new believers, in addition to their other tasks. As the people accepted Jesus as Savior, God began confirming His word by working miracles in their lives and families. When I first arrived I scarcely knew how to begin to reach the people. Now, only a few days later, we were shepherding a nucleus of new believers whom God would later use to spread the gospel in Cambodia. Already a number of them wanted to be baptized. Things happened so fast I felt as if I were moving in God's jet stream.

During these days I had tried unsuccessfully to have my visa renewed. It seemed everywhere I turned there was more red tape. Every time I thought I had fulfilled all requirements, an immigration official would tell me of some other document I had to have. It seemed hopeless, and I was running out of time.

To make matters worse, two policemen had appeared one morning to interrogate me about the prospect of my staying in Cambodia. They flashed some impressive-looking badges, then curtly demanded to see my passport.

I handed it over reluctantly, wondering what this was all about.

"Maybe you can stay," the heavyset one said, "but it will be very difficult to arrange." The two of them exchanged dialogue in Khmer while I stood there growing more impatient by the moment. It was beginning to dawn on me that these were the two fellows Tom Cornwall had warned me about. "Watch out for those birds," he cautioned. "You can never pay them off once and for all. When they need money, they'll be by to see you."

The Lord had already taught me that this was His money, and I wasn't about to use it to pass a bribe under the table. I took my passport out of the man's hand and said crisply, "I'm sorry, gentlemen, but I am too busy to spend any more time with you this morning."

They seemed a bit agitated, but they left, promising to return.

Watching them leave made me consider the impending expiration of my visa once again. I wondered how many other people they had pressured into meeting their demands. My staying in Cambodia was in the Lord's hands, I reminded myself. He would have to overrule if He wanted me to remain here.

In driving to and from the immigration office I had passed a beautiful stadium in the center of the city. It had outdoor olympic facilities as well as an indoor arena seating about eight thousand. I could envision a great gospel crusade within those walls. I knew an American singing group called the Luminaires was scheduled to be in southeast Asia at about this time. Rev. Arthur Chesnut, whom I had just left in Okinawa, hoped that I could schedule some meetings for them in Phnom Penh. A week ago I had dismissed the proposition as being too far-fetched to even consider. Now, I could see there might be a possibility.

Gradually my daydream brought me to the question, Why not? I had never seen a crowd of people in the arena. Surely it must be available, I mused. No one had yet told me that public meetings had been banned because of the war. The government felt there was too much danger of terrorist activity if large crowds were permitted to gather. Not knowing this, I pursued my daydream.

7

I learned that there were only four other missionary couples in Cambodia at the time of my arrival. One of these couples, Tim and Barbara Friberg, were Wycliffe missionaries working among a tribal group called the Cham. We became good friends and they were quite helpful with their advice those first few days. The other three couples were with a mission board that had been working there for fifty years. I thought their experience would be helpful so I called on them to see if they would be interested in working together to rent the Stadt Olympic for a crusade. In my naivete I thought they would be enthusiastic about the idea. Their cold response hurt me. They made it clear that they would not participate in such an effort. To me, they seemed satisfied that I wouldn't be around long.

So with only one day left on my visa, and my hopes dwindling, I met the afternoon class and tried to appear confident. "You know the things that are happening in your lives—the way God is confirming His salvation through Jesus to you?" With smiling faces, they all nodded.

"At the end of this month a Christian singing group from America will be coming to Phnom Penh," I continued. "If somehow we could get the Stadt Olympic arena we could have a crusade where thousands of your people could witness the things you've experienced, and taste of your Lord's salvation. Would you like that?"

They shouted their enthusiasm, waving their arms in the air. But my next question brought a solemn hush.

"How does one go about securing permission to use the arena?"

No one had a suggestion. Then one well-dressed man stood and said he wanted to read a Scripture he had discovered in the Bible that day. He read in halting English, "Therefore I say to you, all things for which you pray and ask, believe that you have received them, and they shall be granted you" (Mark 11:24). What better answer than that could I hope to receive? The man asked the class, "Do you believe God can give us that arena to have a crusade?"

They nodded agreement, and we prayed accordingly in Jesus' name. In their childlike faith they fully expected God to answer their prayers. They were excited to watch and see how He was going to do it. So was I.

When class was over, I was introduced to Kai Wan, the brother of Kong's wife, San. A handsome, middle-aged man, he spoke English quite well and immediately offered to take me to see someone who might help us get the stadium for a crusade.

What an immediate answer to prayer, I thought to myself. Less than an hour after the students had prayed, I was standing in Mr. Dy Bellong's office. I grinned to myself, thinking how surprised DeAnn would be if I could tell her all that had transpired in the few days since my departure from Okinawa. I knew she was anxiously awaiting word whether she should fly to Phnom Penh. In three days I would have the answer.

As Kai Wan's motorbike approached our building I was jolted back to reality. It would soon be time for the evening English class. I looked forward to sharing with them how God had already begun to answer the prayers of the afternoon students. I thanked Kai Wan for his help and hurried to my room to prepare for class.

On the morning of the third day after my visit to Mr. Dy Bellong, I returned to his office to find out his decision. By this time my visa had already expired. I was first greeted by his aide, who took me right in to see Dy Bellong. He received me warmly.

"I've arranged for you to have the stadium." His first words left me in mild shock. I had been praying for that answer, but it took a few moments for the full impact to set in. This meant we could have the crusade!

Then he informed me that large gatherings had been banned because of terrorist activity, but they were making an exception for us and would give us military protection and a police escort during the three days of our meetings.

My mind was clicking fast. "What will be the charge for our use of the arena?" I asked, remembering I had a little less than $200 left.

He smiled and answered, "There will be no charge." He went on to say that whatever we needed—platform, microphones, speakers—they would supply all equipment for us.

9

But I barely heard the rest. As he continued talking through his interpreter, I realized I didn't even have definite confirmation that the Luminaires would come. But I knew that if the Lord could provide the use of the arena, He would also see that the Luminaires arrived on schedule.

In the excitement of discovering we could have the Stadt Olympic rent-free, I had momentarily forgotten the matter of my visa. My thoughts were suddenly interrupted when Dy Bellong handed over my passport.

"I have also taken care of your visa for you," he smiled compassionately.

I thumbed through the passport and found a new entry had been made, but I couldn't read it. The aide showed me I had been given a diplomatic multiple entry visa, valid for one year, with renewal guaranteed—provided the government could hold off the Communist siege that long.

My heart raced and almost burst with thanks to God. With the Khmer *sam peah* gesture, I expressed my gratitude to Mr. Dy Bellong. I could hardly contain my excitement at realizing I would be able to stay in Phnom Penh and have the crusade. Dy Bellong smiled as I left his office. I felt I had a new friend. My heart was full of praise to God, for I realized only He could have arranged these amazing events.

CHAPTER 2

A Royal Welcome

I had read about how God parted the Red Sea for Moses and the children of Israel, but now I was seeing the hand of the Lord part the sea of red tape for me. I felt like Job when he said to God, "I have heard of Thee by the hearing of the ear; but now my eye sees Thee" (Job 42:5). It was awesome to see God at work in matters which, by human standards, seemed insoluble.

After leaving Dy Bellong's office I took a taxi straight to the central Postal, Telephone and Telegraph building to wire the good news to Okinawa. I wanted DeAnn to come immediately. Also, I had to confirm final arrangements with the Luminaires.

Upon arriving at the P.T.T. office shortly before noon, I learned that it was possible to phone Okinawa until 12:30 P.M. I decided talking to DeAnn would be much better than sending a wire, so I gave the number to the operator. As I looked around at the rather primitive equipment and heard the Khmer operator bickering with one in Hong Kong, I wondered if the call would ever go through. Just before they had to close down the circuits, the operator made contact with Okinawa. She told me my party was on the line.

The connection was so bad I could hear only fragments of sentences, but it was exciting to realize I was actually talking to DeAnn. I told her to come to Phnom Penh immediately and to contact the Luminaires telling them to plan to arrive no later than September 27th. The crusade was to be September 28th through 30th. The call was very frustrating because I had no assurance DeAnn could hear all my instructions. Her voice was coming

11

through to me only intermittently. So I sent a wire and a letter to be sure she had the information in writing.

When I walked out of the post office, the streets were almost deserted and all the shops were closed with their heavy iron doors bolted shut. It was siesta time. This Khmer custom was very difficult for me to adjust to. It seemed just as the day was getting well under way, everything ground to a halt for siesta from noon until about three o'clock. Sometimes I would pace the floor looking at my watch, and wonder, When are these people going to wake up? I've got things to do!

But today my body was telling me I was kicking against the goads. The afternoon heat was beginning to sap my strength and I couldn't seem to shake a touch of pneumonia I had picked up while in Okinawa. Maybe an afternoon siesta wouldn't be so bad after all, I thought.

I spotted a cyclo in the shade of a nearby tree and found the driver eager for a paying customer. A cyclo is a type of bicycle with two wheels in front supporting a carriage for the passenger, powered by the driver who does the pedaling. As I relaxed in the passenger seat with the sun beating down on my head, my excitement subsided and I realized how weary I was. I was glad when the cyclo rounded the last corner toward home.

I slowly climbed the stairs to my second-floor office and was surprised to look up and see the two policemen who had visited me a few days earlier. I guess they figured during siesta time I was almost sure to be there. Forgetting my weariness, I remembered their attempt to collect a bribe on their first visit. Their self-assured smiles told me they were confident of getting their money this time.

But I had reason to be confident, too. I opened the door to my office and they strutted in like two proud peacocks. I cut the formalities short and asked, "Why are you here, gentlemen?"

In broken English they asked to see my papers once again.

I paused a moment, walking behind my makeshift desk, then asked coolly, "May I please see your papers, first?"

They looked at one another in surprise. Reluctantly, they

showed me the same badges they had displayed on their first visit. I quickly copied down the information on their badges while they looked on in surprise.

"Now," I said, "would you like to see my passport?"

I took the passport out of my pocket, turned to the page where the new visa was stamped, and handed it to them across the desk. I announced my new friendship with Mr. Dy Bellong and explained that he had not only taken care of my visa, but had arranged other favors for me as well. They looked at the diplomatic visa in my passport in stunned unbelief. Then they nervously looked over at the pad of paper where I had made note of the information on their badges. In a matter of seconds their whole attitude changed and they quickly cut a trail for the door. I never saw them again.

As I closed the door behind them, I realized how serious that confrontation could have been had they come that morning when I didn't even have my passport in my possession. I couldn't help smiling and thinking, Well, Lord, your timing is perfect. You are never late, but you are not early, either!

During the Bible classes that day, I shared with the students the news of the upcoming crusade. As far as I was concerned, my getting a diplomatic visa was a greater miracle than obtaining the use of the arena, but the students couldn't comprehend immigration problems since they had never been outside their own country. However, their excitement over the crusade was electrifying, and they assured me they would do everything they could to contribute to its success.

We advertised the crusade as "The Way To Life" and printed thousands of posters and handbills in the Khmer language. The publicity read: "Bring your sick, blind, and lame and believe God for healing." Ordinarily, I would have been reluctant to say something like that, much less print it and post it all over the city. But seeing God's evident hand in all the arrangements up to now, I felt the boldness of faith to publicize the crusade in this way.

At last I received a telegram saying DeAnn would be arriving in Phnom Penh on September 17th. The students were anxious to meet her. They had asked endless questions about her and many of them wanted to go with me to the airport. I realized I might as well forget any thoughts of a private reunion!

Since I had no transportation of my own I arranged to borrow an old Peugeot. The day DeAnn was to arrive I worked feverishly around the building, cleaning and getting everything in good order. The Cornwalls had left a few home furnishings, including kitchen items, towels and sheets, and two small waterbeds equipped with mosquito nets. (I had quickly learned that the mosquito nets were indeed necessary.) At the market, I selected some things for our first meal together in Cambodia.

When the time came to go to the airport, the old Peugeot was packed with students, while others were lined up behind the car on motorbikes and bicycles. As the procession started off in a cloud of dust, amid the stares of people from the surrounding neighborhood, I chuckled when I thought about how surprised DeAnn was going to be when this welcoming party greeted her.

The plane touched down about noon and I searched the faces of those getting off the plane. My heart skipped a beat when I saw DeAnn start down the loading ramp, her brown hair shining in the sun. She was wearing a colorful new dress she had bought in Hong Kong. As she caught my eye and waved a greeting, I realized how much I had missed her. Finally, after she had cleared the immigration and customs checkpoints, I could kiss her hello. She was overwhelmed by the smiling faces of the many students who had come to welcome her to their country, and I could see she instantly liked these enthusiastic young people.

Riding the eight miles into the city, DeAnn asked all the same questions I had asked on my arrival, about the "thunder" in the background, the barbed wire and sandbag barricades, the pitiful refugee dwellings, and the amazing variety and modes of transportation. But in spite of the tragedies of war and the nauseating smells, the natural beauty of the country had captured her; she was falling in love with Cambodia and its people just as I had.

When we arrived at the building we found a message had come from Dy Bellong inviting us to join him for dinner in his home that same evening.

"You are really getting a royal reception to Cambodia!" I told DeAnn. We barely had time to get her baggage into the room and get ready to go. Our visiting would have to wait until later.

Deep blue monsoon clouds formed in the west, appearing as legions of warriors on horseback attacking the setting sun. Drops began falling just as we set out for Dy Bellong's home, and by the time we arrived we were engulfed in a terrific downpour. His home was quite a distance from our building and DeAnn felt pity for the cyclo driver who had to pedal all that distance in the rain.

At Dy Bellong's home we were greeted by one of the servants at the gate. Judging by all the vehicles outside I assumed a host of dignitaries were present; inwardly I felt a little out of place. Well-dressed guests were milling around on the veranda, enjoying the oriental strains of minor-key musical played by the Khmer orchestra Dy Bellong had hired for the affair. A multitude of odd-shaped instruments were being played and we immediatley were attracted by the beautiful woman soloist who performed. After a few numbers the music seemed to our ears to have a certain monotony about it. Each song could begin at almost any point or end at any point without it making a great deal of difference.

Servants rushed to and fro, keeping various serving tables well supplied with hors d'oeuvres and assorted carbonated beverages. We drifted among the guests, meeting Americans, Australians, Britishers and others, all of whom were actively involved in some sort of humanitarian aid or embassy work. Soon, the guests were escorted upstairs to the elaborately decked dining room.

Food was served buffet style and we helped ourselves to ample portions of everything—to our later regret. Dy Bellong made the rounds to see that his guests were well taken care of, then seated himself at the head table.

"What's that he's eating?" DeAnn whispered to the sophisticated woman seated beside her.

"Roasted pig, I think . . . mostly fat!" she replied with a grimace.

His plate was heaped high with cubes of pig fat and we watched in disbelief as he shoveled it down as if eating ice cream. Meanwhile, I had been picking at my food in search of some tasty morsel of meat—finding none. I nonchalantly scraped the remains to the side and even deposited some on DeAnn's plate, so as not to appear wasteful of the delicacies. Still hungry, I went back through the line, concentrating on finding "lean" meat and selecting from the vegetables and fruits that were provided in abundance.

The evening was pleasant for us, being serenaded and having the opportunity to meet so many important people in government work. But we went home almost as hungry as we had come.

During her first week De Ann observed in the classes and tried to make herself familiar with the new surroundings. She was astonished to learn of all that had happened in the short time we had been separated. She began helping me in the sessions, taking over the music portion of the class, and the students immediately loved her. They hadn't seen many women playing guitar before, so this added a special delight to each meeting. The following Monday she began teaching a morning Bible class, starting with fifteen students. She tried to offer a little more English for the sake of those students who already had a fair command of the language. This proved to be a great asset to the work, for in time, many of the older and well-educated Khmers were attracted to the Lord through her.

Having her with me was such a blessing. Our living quarters needed her touch to make it home. A few pieces of furniture, new linens, and a grass mat completed the list of additions to our one-room apartment. Working in the kitchen was quite frustrating for her after having been so used to modern conveniences in the States. Preparing a meal seemed to take all day, so Kong's wife, San, performed most of this necessary task, leaving DeAnn free for teaching and secretarial duties.

As soon as posters and handbills for the crusade had been printed, we organized teams of volunteers to go around the city and surrounding villages, posting the advertisements in public places. We strung up large banners across the main streets of Phnom Penh and advertised in the newspaper and on the radio. When the government television network heard about the Luminaires they wanted them to sing on television, which opened a door to reach the upper-class citizens of the country. Later we found out that the three days we had scheduled the crusade were also Buddhist holidays. That meant all the shops would be closed and people would be free to attend the meetings.

It seemed the Lord was putting the details of the crusade together in a miraculous way; yet one problem remained. We had not yet found an interpreter. Kong and Sam-Oeurn had only a limited knowledge of English, though they did well with what they knew. I felt surely the Lord could supply someone else and I had been earnestly praying about the matter.

When I asked the other missionaries for help they only discouraged me. They insisted it was impossible to prepare for such a big meeting in so short a time, citing examples to prove their point. I asked Son Sonne, the director of the Bible society, if he would be willing to help, but because his work was closely involved with the other missionaries, he was afraid of losing their support if he cooperated with me. He was sympathetic to my problem, but he had too much at stake. I understood his situation and appreciated his honesty. He did offer literature, gospel portions and all the tracts we could use. But I still needed an interpreter.

Kai Wan dropped by one morning to tell me he had visited one of the churches sponsored by the other missionaries. He said he overheard the leader warning the people to stay away from me by saying, "You have to watch out for these young Americans. Many of them are Communists and come to countries like ours under the guise of religion."

I couldn't believe it. Kai Wan also learned this was the same man who had reported to government officials that I had been expelled from Thailand.

Their antagonism toward me was disturbing, though I veiled my feelings for Kai Wan's sake. I hoped this would be the end of the conflict, but sensed it was to be but the first prick of a sharp thorn in my flesh.

The very day after I heard this news from Kai Wan, one of the

17

missionaries came to see me. I felt he was there to interrogate me for some reason. "Why did you come to this country?" he asked.

"Because God sent me," I answered sincerely, assuming surely that another missionary would understand that response. But he looked dubious. I went on to relate some of the unusual events that had brought me to Cambodia and had allowed me to remain in the country thus far. I shared with him about the new believers in our group and how God was performing miracles in their lives, but everything I said seemed to make him feel more threatened. Finally I suggested we have prayer together, and we parted on good terms. But I was still baffled by the attitude of these missionaries.

Before going to bed that evening I went to my knees in prayer for an interpreter. But instead of asking, I simply praised Him. "Thank you for giving us the best, Lord. You gave us the best visa, the best arrangement for the crusade, and I believe you for the *best* interpreter."

The next morning I hadn't yet gotten out of bed when I heard a knock on the door of my office. I jumped out of bed, jerked on my pants, and climbed through the window that separated our bedroom from the office. Opening the door, I found a handsome Khmer man about thirty years old standing with briefcase in hand.

"Are you T.L. Osborn's representative?" he asked in perfect English.

"No, I'm not," I said, fumbling for an answer to his unexpected question. "Uh . . . but my wife worked as a secretary at his foundation in America. Why do you ask?"

"My name is Nou Thay," he answered. "I was in Vietnam recently and brought back to Cambodia two of Brother Osborn's miracle films I had seen there. I thought you might have a projector so I could show these here in Cambodia."

"Here," I motioned toward a chair, "please come in and sit down."

Nou Thay began telling me about the miracles he had seen in the films, and how he yearned to see the power of God work like that in the lives of his fellow Khmers. Hearing him speak in almost

18

flawless English, I sank back in my chair and wondered if this was the interpreter I'd prayed for the night before.

Picking up one of the handbills on my desk, I interrupted him, "Do you know about the crusade we are having here in two weeks?"

"Yes, I heard about it," he replied. "But I wasn't sure who was sponsoring it." I watched his face as he read the handbill through. When he reached the bottom, where I had urged people to "bring the sick, blind and lame . . ." his eyes brightened. "Praise God! Elijah's come!" he exclaimed.

I protested and assured him I was not Elijah.

"No," he explained, "I don't mean you are Elijah. It's just that I have been praying that God would send someone like Elijah who would challenge our Buddhist country with the power of God as Elijah challenged the prophets of Baal. I believe God is answering my prayer."

I told Thay about my problem of finding an interpreter for the crusade. "How are you at interpreting?" I asked him suddenly.

Caught off guard, he stammered a bit and said, "Well, I can't speak for myself."

"Yes, you can," I said. "You know whether you're good or not. Just give me your honest opinion."

He was silent as he glanced around the room, then looked down at the floor. Cracking a smile, he responded timidly, "Well, I'm probably the best!"

A warm excitement rushed through me. I felt that the Lord had caused him to say that just for me. "Then you'll do it?" I challenged him.

Without hesitation he agreed, adding that he would help with the crusade in any way possible. We continued talking and he shared how he had come to the Lord. His father was a Christian so he had been among missionaries all his life and had thus become very proficient in English. He sang well and could play almost any musical instrument.

I told him our work was charismatic in nature, and I wondered how he felt about that. The term was new to him, but he quickly understood what I meant. He confessed he had not been baptized with the Holy Spirit, but he did accept our teaching concerning the gifts of the Spirit. I perceived he was a sincere Christian who genuinely wanted more of God's power in his life. I learned later that his hunger for the Lord and his blunt honesty had put him at odds with the other missionaries, and Christian workers.

Our hearts were knit together as we became better acquainted. But as soon as word of our friendship reached the ears of the other missionaries, they invited me to their homes and tried to discourage me from working with Nou Thay. They reported him to be a deceptive opportunist and cited several incidents to support their point of view.

At first I was disturbed by these stories, but when I checked them out one by one, I found they were based on untruths or misunderstandings. So I decided to disregard their advice. I had prayed for an interpreter, and God had sent me one who also became my friend.

CHAPTER 3

With Signs Following

The two weeks of preparation for the crusade raced by all too quickly. On September 27th, the Luminaires arrived and we found room in the building for them to lay out their sleeping bags. I had never taken part in a big evangelistic crusade before, much less try to organize one, but John Guest and the Luminaires had conducted a few in their travels, so their suggestions were helpful.

The meeting was to begin at two o'clock on Friday, September 28th. We were rushing around, still making final preparations, when people began entering the arena. Military guards frisked everyone at the door, checking for concealed weapons.

As the hour approached, we took our seats on the platform under the large banner, "The Way To Life." People were still flooding into the arena and the choice seats were already filled. Others crowded the exits and massed behind the platform on a second-level terrace. Children swarmed around us, chattering and watching the Luminaires in their colorful outfits. It was no doubt the first time most of them had ever seen American performers.

Though we had tried to prevent them, vendors made their way through the crowd hawking sliced sugar cane and pineapple chunks on sticks. Over the public-address system I tried to bring order out of the chaos, but finally decided just to sit down and pray with Nou Thay and the Luminaires about the problem. We agreed in prayer that the Lord's will would be done in the meeting; after all, He had made the whole thing possible.

"Shouldn't we go ahead and begin?" I asked Thay.

21

"No," he answered. "They're still arriving at two o'clock, Cambodian time," he smiled and explained. "That means any time between two-thirty and three."

"But shouldn't we try to get the people to sit down?"

"No," he said with assurance. "When the Luminaires begin to sing they will all quiet down and find seats."

He was right. As soon as Jimmy Carothers sat down at the upright piano and the Luminaires gathered around the microphones, the crowd settled down and listened intently. They weren't all in seats, however. Many were sitting on the floor and others stood against the walls. It reminded me of a rock concert back in the States.

Before each song, one of the group would give a testimony and explain the lyrics of their next number while Thay interpreted. Just as David's singing drove the evil spirit from Saul in ancient times, so the music of the Luminaires seemed to cleanse the oppressive atmosphere and prepare the crowd for the preaching of the word.

About five thousand people were in the audience, most of them middle and lower class people. Among them was a large number of refugees. Seated to my left was a whole section of soldiers dressed in battle fatigues. Many of them had been wounded or had suffered the loss of a limb and I was touched by the look of hope written on their attentive faces. Before the meeting I overheard a reporter interviewing one soldier who was leaning on crutches near the platform. He had lost his right leg in combat. "I don't understand what this is going to be about," he said, "but maybe this Jesus can help to relieve our pain and sorrows." That was my prayer, too.

The crowd was captivated by the songs and testimonies of the Luminaires. "His name is Jesus," Diane Dix told the crowd. "He's changed my life and given me peace and hope where I had none before. He can do the same for you today if you will begin by inviting Him into your life."

The Luminaires continued to share for over thirty minutes. As the time drew near for me to speak, I began praying for God to anoint me with the Holy Spirit. I needed His power to proclaim the Lordship of Jesus to these people who had never heard His message. How can I prove to these people that Jesus is any better than Buddha? I wondered to myself.

I thought of the Apostle Paul telling the Corinthians, "My message and my preaching were not in persuasive words of wisdom, but in demonstration of the Spirit and of power" (1 Cor. 2:4). I knew it would take more than just a few persuasive arguments to shake the Khmers out of their religious traditions and superstitions. It would take more than just my witness. It would take a powerful demonstration of the Holy Spirit.

While reading through the gospels in preparation for the crusade, I had been drawn to the story of the four men who brought the paralytic man to Jesus. Unable to reach Jesus because of the crowd, they removed the tile roof and with ropes lowered the crippled man to Jesus. I saw in this story a way to convey the truth of Jesus as the only way to salvation—the only way to the Father.

When the Luminaires finished their last song, I stepped to the microphone beside Thay. "Many of you are wondering why we are here," I began. "It can be said in one word: Jesus. We've left our country to share with the world the salvation all people can have in Him."

Thay was interpreting phrase by phrase and we seemed to have the people's attention. "I can't prove to you that Jesus offers more than you have in Buddha or in any other religion. Only Jesus can prove that to you as He did in the days when He walked the earth."

Then I began to relate the story of the paralytic man who had been healed by Jesus. During Thay's interpretation I prayed silently that the Holy Spirit would breathe life into those words and cause them to pierce each individual heart.

I related how Jesus' statement to the man—"My son, your sins are forgiven"—made the people present very upset. "The four men who had brought the paralytic were disappointed," I explained. "They didn't care about having their friend's sins forgiven. They wanted him to be healed! And the religious leaders were enraged because they thought Jesus was blaspheming. They cried, 'Who can forgive sins but God alone? Who does this man think He is?' "

The conflict captured the attention of the Khmer people. They loved hearing a dramatic story.

"But Jesus didn't end the scene there," I added confidently. "He had a reason for not healing the man immediately. Jesus asked the people, 'Which is easier? To tell the paralytic his sins are forgiven, or to say to him, "Arise, take up your bed and walk"?' Jesus turned to the paralytic, and commanded him, 'Arise, take up your bed and walk.' "

The confidence I felt radiating from Thay as he interpreted encouraged me that the Khmers were really comprehending what we were saying. Holding up the Bible in my left hand (as I had seen Billy Graham do on TV many times), I pointed to it and said, "Jesus proved who He was by what He did. When Jesus spoke, that paralytic stood up, picked up his pallet and walked out before the eyes of everyone. The people, including the scoffing religious leaders, were amazed and glorified God, saying, 'We have never seen anything like this!' I pray you will be making this same statement before you leave this place today."

The Luminaires were behind me on the platform, backing up every sentence with prayer and amens. Their support was invaluable.

With a sweeping gesture taking in the whole crowd, I said, "Every one of you has come here with a problem in his life. But there is one here who is greater than your problems, who loves you and wants to forgive your sins. It is Jesus. He can heal your bodies and bring peace and joy to your lives, even in the midst of this war that is tearing apart your country. Give Him a chance to prove to you that He is Lord and Savior."

With a silent prayer, I continued, "All of you who would like to know whether Jesus is Lord and has this power to save you and to heal you, please raise your hands." They went up all over the stadium; an air of restlessness crept over the crowd.

"Now," I shouted into the microphone, "put your other hand on the area of your body where you may need a healing. Or place your hand upon your heart if you want to have your sins forgiven and to find a new life in Christ."

With their eyes fixed on me, those with their hands in the air waited for further instructions. "I am going to pray with you now and ask Jesus to show you who He is by what He does in your lives today."

Slowly I prayed a simple prayer so Thay could interpret every word clearly. Behind me the Luminaires were praying softly in their heavenly languages and I felt a surging confidence that the Holy Spirit was doing a mighty work at that moment.

I raised my head and looked out over the crowd, hesitating a moment because I was not sure what to do next. Then a thought came to me, Why not ask those who feel they've received a touch from God to come forward and share what had happened to them?

I made this appeal over the microphone, expecting that a few would leave their seats. At first there was silence, then laughter broke out here and there. I was bewildered.

"Maybe they don't understand," Thay suggested. "Let me ask them once again."

After he made the appeal again, a few began walking toward the front. Then it seemed as though someone had lifted a floodgate; hundreds streamed down the walkways. I looked on in amazement, wondering, could all these have been healed?

The Luminaires brought a woman onto the platform who said she had been healed of blindness. Thay listened to her story, then told me excitedly, "She's been totally blind for many years, but found she could see clearly right after we prayed!"

I was awestruck as I looked at her beaming face. She was so thin, dressed in a long black *samput* ("skirt") and simple white blouse. A young girl stood by her side, evidently her daughter. "Ask her to tell the people what happened," I suggested to Thay.

"Yes, that's a good idea," he affirmed, pulling the microphone from it's stand. He spoke in Khmer, urging her to be bold about her healing. Her name was Somontha. She had been blind many years due to cataracts. Her youngest daughter had accompanied her everywhere and had brought her to the crusade.

As she talked, I told Thay of my idea to test her sight before the people. He retrieved the microphone and explained to the audience and to the woman what we wanted to do. "How many fingers do you see?" I asked her. As she counted my fingers perfectly, reporters rushed up with cameras. Her testimony was firmly established, and a mood of excitement filled the arena.

I heard someone shouting from my left, and turned to see Khemara, one of our new students, escorting a man toward the platform. Thay beckoned him to the microphone, and he told how he had been carried into the meeting lame. After prayer he sensed strength coming to his limbs. Stepping out, he found to his amazement that he could walk again. He strutted, did some knee bends and ran across the platform to everyone's delight.

The crowd clapped in approval and pressed closer to the platform. People, desperate for healing, mobbed the Luminaires who had moved down front by this time. The attempts of the police to control the crowd were fruitless.

Meanwhile, some of my students began distributing booklets and tracts at the side of the platform. I had made the mistake of offering literature to all who came forward. It was sheer bedlam. Young people began grabbing for everything they could get their hands on. I shouted for my students to box up the literature and save it for the next day.

In spite of the chaos, many miracles had taken place; lives had been touched and changed by the power of God. Jesus had confirmed His word with signs following. We encouraged everyone to return the next two days and to spread the news about the crusade.

The meeting had lasted four hours. We dismissed the crowd several times but there were many inquirers who wouldn't leave until they could talk and pray with someone about the things they had seen and heard. About forty of my students, the nine members of the Luminaires, DeAnn, myself and Thay worked among the people who remained. We prayed with them and gave them tracts and gospel portions.

When we finally got back to the building that evening we were completely exhausted and full of mixed emotions. On one hand we were thrilled with the healings and miracles we had seen; on the other hand, we were sad and bewildered because so many had come looking for a miracle and had been disappointed. I thought of the lady who had brought her baby daughter to me, asking prayer for her leg to be healed. "Dear Jesus," I prayed, my heart in anguish as I viewed the twisted limb that was deeply scarred. It had been mangled by shrapnel during a rocket attack by the Khmer Rouge. I put my hands on her little leg and prayed for her, but nothing seemed to happen. Her parents' pleading eyes begged me for what I couldn't perform. I felt uncomfortable, but tried to offer encouragement. "Pray to Jesus and He will help you," was all I could muster.

As our team shared the evening meal together, all of us realized we had had similar experiences that day. We knew that miracles were not an end in themselves, but we still felt a personal sadness over such encounters. After dinner, John Guest, Thay and I discussed things we might do to overcome some of the difficulties we had experienced that day. Then we wearily went to bed.

Early the next morning we met at the arena to rope off certain areas and talk to the police about controlling the crowd. We locked all gateways except the front entrances and changed the speaker system, hoping to improve the acoustics. Calling the Khmer students together we assigned specific posts throughout the arena to help keep order among the people. We decided to pass out literature only to those who stayed after the meeting for prayer and counseling.

The second meeting, following the same format as the first, went much more smoothly since we were now able to maintain order. We ministered with confidence, feeling certain the Holy Spirit was at work in the hearts of the Khmers to confirm what they were hearing and seeing.

When we had prayer with the people, so many miracles took place we couldn't record them all. As people were healed they came forward to testify of what God had done for them. The listeners grew more and more excited as the stream of witnesses continued. Soon the people were clapping and shouting their approval after each one.

I looked at my watch. "Almost 5:45!" I exclaimed. The Luminaires were scheduled to appear on the local TV station at six o'clock, so we had to rush them from the arena to the studio. We loaded everyone into the Volkswagen van that had been loaned to us during the crusade and headed for the outskirts of town. A power failure just as we arrived gave the group time to seek the Lord for what they should say on this national telecast. It was a unique opportunity to reach the middle and upper class citizens, especially since this was Cambodia's only station.

Moments later, the power returned and they were before the cameras. They sang several songs, then their spokesman shared this message:

"We realize there is war going on in your country, and we have prayed for peace. One of these days, and we pray it is in the near future, all swords will be beaten into plowshares and spears into pruning hooks. Then there will be no more wars. But this cannot come until the Prince of Peace shall come, who is Jesus Christ the Lord!"

Since there was no live audience we had no way to judge how the message was being received. But just as we were leaving the studio, a phone call came from Marshal Lon Nol, the president of Cambodia. He expressed that he had been deeply stirred by the group's message in word and song, and thanked them for their words of comfort.

When we finished at the TV station we barely had time to rush home before the nine o'clock curfew. We were so exuberant over the day's events we scarcely noticed the police patrols at every intersection. At one point I was so involved in conversation that I drove through a curfew checkpoint, forgetting to slow down and switch off my lights. Hearing a burst of gunfire behind us, I looked in the rear-view mirror and saw guards motioning for me to back up. Everyone fell silent as I shifted into reverse and slowly backed the van to their checkpoint. Several guards, heavily armed with machine guns and grenades hanging from their belts, encircled the van and peered in through the windows. The commander of the checkpoint stepped briskly to my open window and snapped a salute. Then he broke into a smile and motioned for us to go on our way. "That was a close one!" John Guest remarked.

Before going to bed we gathered for prayer, thanking God for what had already happened, and for the greater things we expected the next day. Everyone shared a highlight of the meeting that had touched him most.

Thay was bubbling with excitement. "In my whole life," he declared, "I've never seen such things!" Because of the language barrier we actually had to depend on him to find out much of what was going on. He and Sam-Oeurn were in personal contact with everyone who testified to healings. I smiled to myself, remembering my first encounter with Thay when he had said, "Elijah has come!" We were all thrilled to see that the God of Elijah was indeed showing himself to be alive.

Despite our excitement, we knew we had to get to sleep in order to have strength for the closing meeting the next day. As we parted, I stopped Kong and asked whether he had seen Sam-Oeurn. I had missed him since the close of the meeting that afternoon. Kong checked and found him in his room, praying and reading his Bible. Satisfied he was in, I locked all the iron doors of the building and went upstairs to retire.

I had been asleep about an hour when a sudden pounding on the door startled me. "Just a minute," I called, gradually gaining consciousness. At the door I found Kong with a look of terror on his face.

"Come quickly!" he shouted. "Sam-Oeurn have demon!"

He stunned me with his frightful expression. I frantically groped in the darkness for my pants and pulled them on. Hurrying down three flights of stairs, I could hear whispering voices and unintelligible shouting coming from Sam-Oeurn's quarters. As I rounded the last flight of steps I saw several members of the Luminaires gathered at the bottom of the stairs.

"Isn't it wonderful!" one explained as I passed through the doorway.

There was Sam-Oeurn, sitting on the edge of his bed with hands raised, tear-stained face beaming, speaking in tongues at the top of his voice. Kong was still agitated about what was happening, but one of the Luminaires wisely counseled, "Don't bother Sam-Oeurn; he's having a good time with the Lord." Then he tried to explain to Kong that this was similar to many experiences recorded in the Bible—not the work of a demon, as Kong feared.

"How did all this happen?" I asked the young people.

"I don't know for sure," answered Joseph Clark, "but I think it began during the crusade this afternoon. I was praying in tongues for someone when Sam-Oeurn interrupted me and asked what language I was speaking. He asked me, 'Don't you pray in English?' I told him I prayed in English but that I also can pray in a special language the Lord has given me. I explained to him that I didn't understand the language, but God did. Then I directed him to some passages in Acts and Corinthians."

"Then what happened?" I asked.

"I don't know," Joseph responded. "That was the last I saw of him. I guess he came home, read about it in his Bible, and asked God to give him this gift, too."

"Boy, did he ever get it!" I exclaimed.

Sam-Oeurn arose early the following morning. It was evident he was a changed man. It was Sunday and he was eager to share his experience in the morning service that would be held in the building. We were just as anxious to hear what God had done for him.

He had always been rather quiet and shy, but that morning he exploded with boldness. I couldn't yet understand the Khmer language well enough to catch all he was saying, but by his enthusiasm and the captivated faces of his listeners, I knew something was coming across loud and strong.

Following the service, a group of inquirers followed Sam-Oeurn to the prayer room on the roof of the building. Many had already professed faith in Christ and I had already baptized new believers.

30

But as of yet, I had not given them much instruction on their need to be baptized with the Holy Spirit. I wanted the Lord to do it when the timing was right. It looked now as if the door of heaven was opening for the dove to descend.

I left Sam-Oeurn to counsel with the seekers while I went to the airport to retrieve a piece of the Luminaire's baggage lost during their flight. About an hour later I returned to the building to find that during a time of prayer with DeAnn and the Luminaires, Thay had been baptized with the Holy Spirit. As they were praying Thay had fallen to the floor speaking in other tongues and continued speaking for more than half an hour.

At the same time, Sam-Oeurn had prayed with a twenty-nine-year-old school teacher, Saran, who had been coming to our meetings. He broke forth speaking in tongues when Sam-Oeurn laid hands upon him, and from that day on Saran was mightily used of the Lord. I was overwhelmed with praise and rejoicing.

Well, I reminded myself, Jesus described the Holy Spirit as being like the wind—we can't see where He is coming from or where He is going. But, praise the Lord, we can see His effects!

We left for the stadium about an hour early in order to set up everything for the last meeting that afternoon. On arriving we were surprised to find reporters and photographers rigging up lighting equipment, taping their recording mikes to our microphones, and setting up two movie cameras. They saw me walking toward the platform with a concerned look on my face and quickly assured me, "Oh, don't worry about us, we'll stay out of your way."

"But who are you?" I asked the reporter nearest me.

He introduced himself as a free-lance photographer. "And the rest," he turned, pointing to the others, "he's with The Associated Press, those two are with the *Washington Post*, and the tall fellow with the red hair is with CBS. We're working together to cover this crusade."

"But why are you filming us?" I asked incredulously.

"This is the biggest story in Cambodia," he answered. "When we heard what was happening in the crusade and saw the banners

31

and posters, we started pulling some of our equipment and personnel off the battlefield. This is a real scoop.''

The red-haired fellow with CBS introduced himself as Haney and wasted no time in scheduling an interview with me. He impressed me as being a youthful Walter Cronkite. ''We're planning to make this a spot on the news program '60 Minutes,' '' he informed me.

I could scarcely believe my ears—our crusade in Cambodia appearing on TV in the States! But then I began to wonder whether this was a blessing or a curse. What kind of things will these reporters write about us? I wondered. Should I let them do this?

As I watched them set up their equipment, I realized I really didn't have much say in the matter. I just sat down in a chair on the platform and prayed that the Lord would keep them from doing anything to hinder the crusade. The Luminaires and Thay joined me on the platform and we united in prayer before beginning the meeting.

This was the largest crowd of the crusade. The newsmen estimated more than eight thousand were in the stands and on the main floor. As the service got under way I noticed the presence of the cameras and newsmen seemed to have a sobering effect on the crowd. Everyone was quiet and attentive.

The photographers moved about snapping shots while the Luminaires sang. Even during my message they roved in front of the platform, but they did not seem to disturb the meeting.

Nearing the end of the message, I noticed people were already moving toward the front. Why are they coming already? I wondered. Have they been healed while I was speaking?

John and Dean Guest signaled for some of our students to find out what was going on. Sam-Oeurn, Saran and Khemara moved down front to receive those who were coming, and a few members of the singing group joined them to help minister to the people. Some were coming for prayer, but most of them had been healed already.

I quickly ended my message and prayed with the entire audience, as I had done the two preceding days. When Thay invited people to come to the front and testify of what God had done for them, the response was incredible. For several hours, hundreds of people streamed across the platform as we watched in amazement. The photographers moved in close to capture the joyful faces on film. DeAnn was down front with a camera trying to get as many pictures as she could.

When the procession was finished, Thay asked the remaining audience whether they believed Jesus had proven himself to be the Lord. They roared their agreement and then applauded spontaneously.

"How many of you want to receive Jesus as your Savior and Master?" we then asked. A sea of hands raised before us. Our students and workers moved into the crowd to pray and counsel with as many as they could reach, handing out tracts and gospel portions and instructing people where they could go to learn more about Jesus. On a large banner we had posted the address of our building where Sunday services were held; also several other churches in the city were mentioned.

For months afterward we continued to hear the results of those three days. One man, we learned, was carried from a neighboring village the last day of the crusade. Totally lame, he hadn't walked for years, but he was completely healed during the meeting. He became a new creature in Christ and started a church in his home. His fellowship continued to grow and we sent workers out to minister to them weekly. They named it Messiah Church.

Several days after the crusade a young soldier came to our building to see me. "I want to know more about this Jesus who has healed me," he said. Then he related how he had been totally deafened in his right ear while fighting in the war. He was loading ammunition in a cannon and was standing too close when it fired. The intensity of the noise had destroyed his right ear drum and doctors had told him he would never hear again with that ear.

"I followed your instructions at the meeting," he told me. "I placed my hand over my right ear and after the prayer I suddenly found I could hear perfectly." There was a look of amazement on his face as he recounted the experience.

"Several times I read the leaflet your workers gave me at the meeting," he continued. "But then I lost the address of your building. I just kept walking the streets and asking directions from people until I found you."

As we all prayed with him, this young soldier gratefully dedicated his life to Jesus. It was hard to tell who was happier—the soldier, me or the group of students.

We continued to receive reports from other churches in the city saying many had come to their meetings wanting to know more about Jesus and what the Bible teaches, because of the miracles they had seen.

Considering that the population of Phnom Penh was more than two million, the crusade had touched relatively few. But it had fired a fresh nucleus of Khmer believers with a new vision, and had demonstrated the power to see that vision fulfilled.

CHAPTER 4

The Call

DeAnn and I began thinking of Cambodia in the spring of 1971. We were finishing a one-year Bible school course in Oklahoma City and had begun to seek a place of ministry when we heard Jonathan Wakefield, an old friend, was in town. Knowing that he had just returned from a round-the-world evangelistic tour, we invited him over to share his experiences.

"What are the opportunities for overseas ministry?" we asked eagerly. "Are there any places left in the world that aren't overrun with missionaries?"

"The first place that comes to mind is Cambodia," he answered. "I wasn't able to go there on this trip, but I understand it is one of the few places left in the world that is still predominantly virgin soil for the gospel. Only a few missionaries are in the country, and there is no charismatic ministry or emphasis on the work of the Holy Spirit."

We looked up Cambodia in a reference book and learned that it was a land of eight million people. DeAnn and I both felt immediately drawn to this country. Jonathan gave us the address of Arthur Chesnut in Okinawa, a man interested in launching a work in Cambodia. We immediately wrote him for more information and sent particulars about ourselves, along with recommendation letters from others. But nothing developed.

Meanwhile, another couple in school with us also felt a call to Cambodia. They immediately began presenting their call to various churches and fellowships in order to raise support. A few

friends advised us to do the same, but somehow I didn't feel I was
ready to try to raise money in this way. At that time DeAnn and I
had only known the Lord for one year, and I was doing well to be
able to pray in public, much less preach. I had heard of people
having dreams or visions when they received a missionary call, but
we had nothing particularly miraculous to share. Once I thought I
had a vision of some people with slanted eyes—but then I learned
the Cambodians' eyes are round! Nice try, I grumbled to myself.

Other friends suggested we apply to a denominational mission
board. Although many fine missionaries go to the field by this
means, we didn't feel it was the thing for us to do. Many such
groups require years of education and training, and once a
prospective missionary has met their qualifications, he is often sent
where they need him, not necessarily where he feels called.

We talked with our pastor, who himself had been a missionary in
Africa for eighteen years, and he gave us some wise counsel. After
considering our ages—DeAnn was nineteen and I was
twenty—and the fact we were only one year old in the Lord, he
smiled and read to us from Isaiah 40:29-31:

> He giveth power to the faint; and to them that have no
> might he increaseth strength. Even the youths shall faint
> and be weary, and the young men shall utterly fall: But
> they that wait upon the LORD shall renew their strength;
> they shall mount up with wings as eagles; they shall run,
> and not be weary; and they shall walk, and not faint. (KJV)

He had no need to say more. *Wait* was the word, and we received
it. We continued our education at a local junior college, and
ministered to young people who were coming to the Lord out of the
drug scene and the occult. The other couple left for Cambodia as
we watched enviously. They promised to write and keep in touch.

The following months brought a severe trial to our faith. The
pastor who had been shepherding us fell into sin, divorced his
wife, married again and left the ministry. He was God's midwife
who had caught us when we were first born into the kingdom, and
the Lord had used him to bring great stability to our lives. It was

almost impossible to believe this could happen; yet through the experience we came to understand Paul's statement, "I buffet my body and make it my slave, lest possibly, after I have preached to others, I myself should be disqualified" (1 Cor. 9:27). Painful as the situation was, we were learning invaluable lessons that had eternal significance in terms of our future ministry.

In January 1972 I was accepted as a student at Oral Roberts University, so we moved to Tulsa. After one semester I was granted a full academic scholarship. By giving full attention to my studies, including a summer study tour to Israel, I was able to cover three years of a B.A. degree in about a year and a half. During this time, DeAnn worked as a secretary at the T.L. Osborn Foundation.

As I entered my last semester of study in January 1973, we began to think about what we would do upon graduation in May. The call to Cambodia had been shelved for almost two years, but it had never left our hearts. Several times we had written to the couple who had gone on to Cambodia, but there was no response.

Then one day on the ORU campus we met Larry and Jean Romans who had news about what had happened to our missionary friends. The difficult conditions they had encountered in Cambodia had magnified personal and other problems, leading to the husband's nervous breakdown. They had been in Cambodia only a month before having to leave, and the man had not yet recovered. This news, along with reports of increased fighting in the country, made us wonder if our call would ever be realized.

But we could not ignore the urgency we felt about going. And Jean Romans turned out to be the daughter of the Chesnuts to whom we had written—so our interest was kept alive.

Then we had a visit from a missionary named Tom Cornwall who planned to set up an organization for building schools in Cambodia.

"This is a plan whereby missionaries can be self-supporting on the field," he explained. "The schools operated by the government cannot accommodate everyone who wants to go to school, so there is a real need for private schools. The tuition paid by the students will provide for hiring Cambodian teachers and will support the missionary couple administering the school. There will be plenty of opportunities for ministry to the students, as well as outside the school. The plan is working well in Japan."

"We like the idea of being self-supporting," DeAnn and I responded. "When will the schools be ready?" We were excited about the prospect of working in such a program.

"We're leaving for Cambodia right away," he told us. "My wife and I will write and keep you informed."

Time passed quickly, and as graduation day drew near we considered the alternatives open to us. Tom Cornwall's plans for building schools in Cambodia were still far from being firmly established, so it looked as if our call might again have to be delayed.

As we considered the different paths that lay before us, I found I had qualified for a Fulbright Scholarship to pursue graduate studies. Then two financially secure positions were offered which involved ministry among charismatic groups. Yet Cambodia remained at the top of the list of our priorities.

My parents had no objections to my going into the ministry, but the idea of going to Cambodia was difficult for them to accept. Somehow they felt my going to a country in such an unstable political condition was a waste. And they had heard reports of missionaries in Vietnam (which borders on Cambodia) being imprisoned and tortured, or even killed. DeAnn's mother was equally upset about the idea of our going to a country that was in the midst of war. "Why would you want to waste such a good education?" they asked.

But whatever path we chose, we knew it would mean moving from our almost-new mobile home, so we decided to put it up for sale and see what happened. We didn't run an ad or put up a sign; we just asked a few friends to spread the word around that it was for sale.

In a few days a fellow student at ORU came to see our home and said it was exactly what she wanted. She was planning to get married that summer, and her fiance wanted to transfer to ORU. "Could you possibly hold it for us until we have word that he is accepted at ORU?" she asked.

"That could take months," I replied. "We may have to leave before that." She smiled and said, "If God wants us to have it, He will hold it for us." I agreed and she left.

One week later she called to say her fiance had been accepted at ORU, even though his transcript and other documents were not yet in hand. Her father had loaned them some money and she was ready to come by and write a check to secure the transaction.

DeAnn and I were elated that our home had sold so quickly, but we were a little scared when we realized that we had to make a decision during the final month of school that remained. Just an hour after word came that our mobile home was sold, we decided to go share the news with Larry and Jean Romans and ask them to pray with us. They knew of our great interest in Cambodia, so we wanted to tell them first.

We had barely seated ourselves in their apartment and told them the news, when their telephone rang. It was Jean's father, Pastor Chesnut, calling from Okinawa. After an exchange of greetings he said, "Jean, I need to know how I can get in touch with a young man named Todd Burke."

With a look of amazement on her face, she said, "Well, he's right here, dad. He and his wife just walked in the door."

Two years had passed since we had written Pastor Chesnut, and now he was calling us long distance, at his daughter's apartment, just as we walked in the door!

I picked up the phone and Pastor Chesnut said, "Is this Todd Burke?"

"Yes," I answered.

"Todd, how soon can you be in Okinawa?" he asked.

Taken aback, I stuttered a reply, "I-I-I don't know, sir. Why do you ask?"

"Well, I'm going to be leaving the work here on Okinawa for three months. I have to be in the States for the summer, and I need someone to come and take over while I'm gone. I understand from my friend Tom Cornwall that you want to go to Cambodia—is that right?''

"Yes, I do," I answered, still in a daze.

"Well, you can look upon Okinawa as a stepping stone, and be on your way to Cambodia when I return at the end of the summer. How about it?''

My mind was racing at top speed and I was quivering with excitement. Finally I responded, ''That's only a little over a month away! Maybe we should pray about it.''

"No time for prayer, Todd," he said briskly. "I need a yes or no answer *now*!''

I felt that word *now* reverberate through my being. DeAnn was looking at me with inquisitive blue eyes, wondering what was going on. Our future depended on what I said next.

Gathering myself together, I stammered out a reply, ''Y. . . Y. . . Yeah, we'll come. The Lord just sold our home for us an hour ago. You called from Japan to find out how to reach us just as we walked in Jean and Larry's apartment. This matter has to be from the Lord. We will go!''

In the midst of these events taking place all at once, we seemed to hear the Holy Spirit saying to us, "Join this chariot" (Acts 8:29). Sometimes, I mused, the Lord's chariot moves pretty fast!

It was June 8th, 1973, about a month after I had graduated from ORU with honors, and over the loudspeaker a voice was saying, "Ladies and gentlemen, we are beginning our descent into Tokyo International Airport. . . .'' I had been trying to catch up on my diary, and the events of the past few weeks seemed too fantastic to believe. We were aboard a huge 747 jet, about to land in Tokyo and make connections for Okinawa. My mind was already racing ahead to our plan to go to Cambodia at the end of the summer, but ministry on Okinawa was the first step.

I had normal fears about our ministry there. First, I didn't know anybody. Secondly, all my experience had been with informal Bible study and prayer groups, and I expected this would be a more formal type of ministry. With that in mind, I had gone out and bought one dress suit just before leaving the States. I hope they don't despise my youth, I thought.

DeAnn's voice interrupted, "Todd, you'd better fasten your seat belt."

As the plane lost altitude we looked out the window at the massive expanse of city that was Tokyo. I put my writing materials back in my briefcase and spun the digits to lock it. All the money we had was in that briefcase, so I wanted to make certain it was secure.

Inside the terminal we learned there were no connecting flights to Okinawa that day, so we found a hotel about an hour's drive away and phoned Pastor Chesnut to tell him of the delay.

"Boy, does it feel good to lie down," I exclaimed after reaching the hotel.

"I think I could sleep for ten hours even on this hard, narrow bed," DeAnn remarked. But to our surprise, we were wide awake in only a few hours, and it wasn't even daylight yet. Jet lag was something we hadn't counted on, and it took us a week to adjust to the time change so we could sleep at night and stay awake during the day.

The following afternoon, Pop and Mom Chesnut met us when we arrived in Okinawa and briefed us on our assignment for the summer. They had last-minute things to get done before their departure, so we were immediately thrust headlong into the ministry.

I was to be the interim pastor of a group made up primarily of U.S. military families who were stationed on the island. My main preaching responsibilities were on Sunday morning and Wednesday night. A young lady evangelist, Pat Pierce, was also on the church staff. She had charge of the Sunday evening meeting and also worked as a youth leader. She became a dear friend to DeAnn and me during that summer.

Only a few days after our arrival, I was to take charge of a teen camp, and DeAnn and I both were to teach in the camp. "I don't know how I'll teach them Child Evangelism," DeAnn complained. "I don't even have any materials to work with. Had I

41

known, I could have brought some things from home."

"Well, teach them something else," I encouraged. "Necessity is the mother of invention, you know."

The truth was, I didn't feel terribly well prepared myself, but my pride wouldn't let me admit it. We enjoyed the opportunity to work with the young people and the time passed quickly. But throughout the week I had a nagging feeling that something was wrong. The business manager and associate pastor of the church, Jim Sharpe, also served as a counselor at the teen camp. He seemed to assume authority whenever he could, and I had the feeling he resented the fact I had been assigned to do the preaching in the Chesnuts' absence. I had a peculiar feeling about Jim. DeAnn and I discussed the problem, but we couldn't come up with anything conclusive. "Maybe I'm just imagining things," I said, trying to shrug it off.

When teen camp was over, regular duties at the church occupied much of my time. Though I had studied a great deal about how to construct messages, this was my first experience of preparing and preaching sermons on a scheduled basis to the same congregation. The Bible became more and more alive as the days went by, and I enjoyed spending much time seeking the Lord in prayer.

The church's main outreach was among G.I.'s on the various bases scattered over the island. Each Saturday evening a team from the church led by Jim Sharpe drove north about thirty miles to a coffeehouse they sponsored, and spent the evening singing and witnessing to the military guys who came by. Then they would return with a busload of G.I.'s who would spend the night at Jim's home, staying over Sunday for a day of food, fellowship and worship. I was able to join the group a couple of times, and it was a blessing to be able to witness to some of these desperate men in the marines. But I couldn't help noticing Jim's strange behavior which at times appeared effeminate.

I had been on the island only a month when my uneasiness about Jim was explained. Late one Saturday night, just as I was about to go to bed, two marines, Gary and Chuck, knocked at our door.

I was surprised to see them. "What are you doing out so late?" I asked. "Aren't you supposed to be staying the night at Jim's?"

"Brother Todd, that's what we wanted to talk to you about," Gary said with pain in his voice. It was obvious something was wrong. They both faltered, searching for words.

"What is it?" I probed gently. "You can tell me."

Gary looked up with tears welling his eyes. "I've known about it for several weeks but I was afraid to say anything . . .Jim is a homosexual."

"What!" I exclaimed. "Are you sure?" I searched their faces in disbelief.

"We're sure," Chuck broke in. "His house on Saturday night is nothing but an orgy. He's even propositioned Gary and me." As Gary nodded in agreement I felt like an evil cloud heavy with foreboding had just settled over me. I wondered what effect this would have on the faith of these new, confused Christians.

"Does anyone else know about this—I mean around the base and at the coffeehouse?" I dug for clues.

"Everyone knows at the camp," Gary replied soberly. "Apparently this has been going on for several years. It's a big joke among all the guys now and it really hurts our witness for the Lord. Everyone thinks we come here just for that."

My heart went out to Chuck and Gary. I wondered how many others had stumbled because of this. How could this have gone on for so long? Where's discernment? Where's God?

After bedding them down in the church parsonage, I, too, went to bed but lay awake for a long time. I thought, Something has got to be done . . . but what? Tomorrow, I assured myself, drifting off to sleep, God will show me. . . .

The next day arrived all too quickly. I managed to preach the message I had prepared but I could scarcely think of anything else except how to deal with Jim. After the service I sat down in the fellowship hall where the G.I.'s had gathered for lunch. Jim seated himself on my right with his plate piled high with food. I felt a little sick watching him shovel it in. No wonder he's so overweight, I thought.

"Aren't you going to eat anything?" he asked me, looking puzzled.

"No, not today," I replied, trying not to show my pity.

Then as if the message was echoing inside me, I heard the words "Go read First Corinthians Chapter Five." Without knowing what the chapter was about, I hurried from the table to the pastor's study. I flung open my Bible and it fell right to the page. I was shocked as my eyes fastened to the subject heading above the chapter: "Dealing with Evil in the Church." Stunned, I eagerly read further to discover Paul's advice to the church at Corinth when the immorality of one of their members came to light. Upon rereading the chapter in the Living Bible, verse 11 seemed to jump off the page. ". . . you are not to keep company with anyone who claims to be a brother Christian but indulges in sexual sins. . . . Don't even eat lunch with such a person." Having just come from the lunch table, that hit pretty hard.

I quickly broke the news to Pat about Jim and how the Lord had spoken to me. She too, was sickened over it, but then things began to add up that she had been suspicious about. The following day we called him into my office. He seated himself in the lounge chair next to my desk.

"Jim," I said firmly, "we've received conclusive evidence that you're deeply involved in homosexual practices." A look of horror spread over his face. He squirmed, trying to stutter out a response when Pat backed me up.

"Don't lie anymore Jim, we know all about it." Guilt was written all over his face. Finally he broke and confessed that the reports were true.

"Listen, Jim," I said, "your activity is known widely over the island and you've given this church a black eye. Pat and I have decided to remove you from all ministry."

"You can't do that!" he protested hotly.

"Yes we can," Pat assured him. "Now that the G.I.'s know we are informed about your behavior, our action has to be firm."

"That's unfair!" he argued. "I certainly don't think Pastor Chesnut would ever do such a thing."

"I'm sorry, Jim," I countered. "I don't know how he would handle the matter. But for now, this church is my responsibility, and Pat and I both feel we have the Lord's leading."

I further advised him to burn all his bridges behind him and leave Okinawa as one would leave Sodom, without looking back. "Jim," I said, "as long as you stay here you will never overcome this problem. You have been too deeply involved, and too many people know about it. You need to go back to the States and ask God to help you get your life straightened out. That's your only hope for making things right with God and saving your marriage."

Though he resisted at first, he finally yielded to our counsel and began making preparations to return to the States. He joyfully concurred that God was helping him overcome his problem, and I was relieved that the ordeal was over. Little did I know this experience was a training ground for what lay ahead.

Not knowing of Jim's behavior, various church members accused me of shoving him out of the picture, thinking I was trying to take over the entire ministry. I tried to keep the matter as quiet as possible until the Chesnuts returned in August. Then it was painful to relate all that had transpired during their absence. But we felt that after having dealt firmly with the problem, the life of the church was revitalized. Even the building itself had a fresh coat of paint. Turning over the keys of the work gave us a good sense of a mission well done by the Lord's help.

As we drove with the Chesnuts from the airport back to the church, my mind was already racing ahead to our plans to try to get into Cambodia. We were hearing news reports that the United States had stopped all bombing of Vietcong sanctuaries in Cambodia, and that the country would fall to the Communists in a matter of weeks. A letter dated August 10th came from Tom Cornwall saying he and his wife had to leave Cambodia for Saigon. I wondered if this meant another delay in our plan, but DeAnn and I both felt strongly that we should make every effort to get into the country. We told the Chesnuts we planned to proceed with our original plan.

After visiting with the pastor and bringing him up-to-date on the status of things at the church, I went to the church office to get some papers out of my briefcase. To my horror, I discovered all the money I had been keeping in the briefcase had been stolen! We searched the church and the parsonage where we had been staying, but it was no use. Several days passed, but no clues turned up. That eight hundred dollars was our only means to get to Cambodia, and we earnestly prayed it would be returned.

As the days passed I became more and more frustrated by the delay. I complained before the Lord saying, "Lord, we are your servants and we have left all to follow you. Why is this happening? How are we going to fulfill our call if that money isn't returned?"

When I ran out of words and got quiet enough for the Lord to speak to me, it seemed He was saying, "Yes, you have left everything to follow me—everything but your money. Now it is gone, too. But I will show you who took the money and it will be returned to you. However it will no longer be your money; it will be mine."

I was so excited by this word from the Lord, I woke up DeAnn late at night to share it with her. We praised the Lord together, and then could hardly sleep because of excitement at the thought that the Lord was going to return His money to our keeping. Nothing happened for the next couple of days, but on the seventh day after the money had disappeared, a military man who was a member of the church heard of what had happened and said he would try to help us.

Several of the bills stolen were hundred-dollar notes, and Hank told us that whenever a soldier cashed anything larger than a fifty-dollar bill, he had to give his name and ID number. He called several military exchange posts and told them to check to see if any one-hundred-dollar notes had been cashed around August 19th (the day our money disappeared). In a matter of hours we had the names of two soldiers who had been at church on August 19th who had cashed one-hundred-dollar notes the next day. The case was as good as closed. We went directly to them.

I confronted the first one and said, "Why did you steal God's money?" He was shocked and tried to deny it.

"Look," I said brusquely, "you're not only lying to me, you're lying to God. Now you'd better confess, or you may end up sitting in a Japanese prison eating fish heads and rice for six months!"

He promptly confessed, and so did his accomplice. We were dismayed to learn they had spent almost every penny of the eight hundred on foolishness, but they agreed to start selling their possessions in order to return the money with interest within a week.

On the same day we found out who stole our money, I made reservations to go ahead and fly into Cambodia to "spy out the land." If the situation turned out to be stable enough, I would then send for DeAnn to join me. We knew the Cornwalls had left, and we knew the country was at war. More important, we knew we had no firm means of support. But the Lord had shown us Okinawa was a divinely placed stepping stone, and we were now under compulsion to continue our journey.

Some friends in Okinawa tried to dissuade us, and even offered positions for employment. The final confirmation that we were doing the right thing came the Sunday night before my departure. Just as DeAnn and I sat down in the pew for the evening service, a man I did not know stood up behind me, placed his hands on my shoulders, and spoke an utterance in tongues. Pastor Chesnut gave the interpretation as follows:

> Do not fear, for the decision you have made is my decision. I have gone before you and opened a door that no man can close. There will be those who will try to discourage you; there will be those who will try to close this door, but know this: the door that I open stays open and this door is open for you.

Any lingering apprehensions I may have had were drowned in tears of joy.

On September 3rd I flew from Okinawa to Hong Kong, where I had to stay overnight and visit the Cambodian Embassy to apply for a visa. I was so inexperienced at overseas travel that I scarcely understood what a visa was all about. I could barely keep track of my passport! But I quickly learned I had to have the endorsement of a country—granted through one of their embassies—before I could enter its borders. I also learned a traveler should carry photographs of himself at all times to submit every time he fills out an application for a visa. I spent a frustrating day running around Hong Kong getting pictures taken, and completed the application just before the embassy closed that afternoon. The Cambodian Embassy would grant me a visa good for only a seven-day visit to their country, and I realized later I was fortunate to get even that.

My last communication from Tom Cornwall stated that he and his wife were going to Saigon, so I decided to stop there before going on into Phnom Penh. I realized that by this time he could have gone on to the States, but I felt it was important to at least try to contact him before entering Cambodia.

I got off the plane in Saigon, claimed my baggage and went through all the checkpoints, then stood wondering, Where do I start to look for one man whom I barely know in a city of more than three million people? I knew it was like looking for a needle in a haystack, but I prayed the Lord would cause our paths to cross.

I must have looked very bewildered, because an American walked up to me and said, "Man, you look lost. Can I help you?"

He was driving into the city and offered to take me anywhere I needed to go. He was a Godsend. I told him I wasn't sure where I should go, and told him about the man I was hoping to find in Saigon. Looking rather dubious, he said, "Well, you could start at the United States Embassy. Sometimes they have information about American civilians residing in the country. It's really a shot in the dark, though."

"Fine," I said. "Drop me off at the embassy."

The main consular office at the embassy had no information on anyone named Cornwall. "You might inquire at the mail room down the hall," the clerk suggested.

Undaunted, I went to the counter in the mail room and inquired, "Could you tell me if a man named Tom Cornwall receives his mail here?"

"I'll check," the clerk responded.

She disappeared, then returned in a few moments with several letters addressed to Tom Cornwall and handed them to me.

"Excuse me, Miss," I said. "I don't want the mail; I want the man. Do you know where I can locate him?''

She shrugged her shoulders and replied, ''Mister, we can't keep up with every American who passes through here. We have no information on where he is. When we begin receiving mail for someone we hold it until they claim it. If no one comes to receive it, we either send it back or throw it away.''

Not willing to give up, I asked, ''Can you suggest another office where I could check on finding him?''

''I'm sorry,'' she answered, shaking her head. ''We would like to help you, but there's just no way.''

I turned from the counter and let out a sigh, ''Oh, Lord, now what?'' I was so distracted I hadn't handed the mail back to the clerk; Mr. Cornwall's letters were still in my hand. Then I looked up and froze in my tracks. There was Tom Cornwall standing right in front of me! I was so awestruck it took me several moments to regain my composure.

Before I could gather my wits to speak to him, he noticed his name on the letters in my hand. I could read the consternation on his face. I finally managed to stutter, ''T-T-Tom Cornwall! I'm Todd . . . Todd Burke . . . remember me?''

Now it was his turn to be awestruck when he realized who I was. We had spent only about one hour together six months earlier.

''Todd!'' he exclaimed. ''What are you doing here? And what are you doing with my mail? This is really amazing,'' he said. ''My wife and I were supposed to have left this morning for the States. For some reason the ship's departure was delayed until tomorrow, so I decided to make one last stop at the embassy to see if I had any mail here.''

''Well,'' I said, laughing, ''I guess you had more than just letters waiting for you!''

I got a room in the same guest house where the Cornwalls were staying, and he and wife began to share the experiences they had had in Cambodia. It was not encouraging news.

''Todd,'' he said, ''the door is closed to us in Cambodia right now. No one knows how long the present government can withstand the onslaughts of the Communist Khmer Rouge.''

49

My mind went back to that message a couple nights before when the Lord had assured me, "I have gone before you and opened a door that no man can close." But I just nodded and kept listening to Tom's report.

"Visas are impossible to obtain now," he continued. "Three times the Cambodian government told me to leave the country. One night someone planted a bomb outside the door of our building, but fortunately it didn't go off. After that, the United States Embassy asked me to sign a letter of 'nonresponsible action' releasing them from any responsibility if I continued to stay in Phnom Penh under the circumstances."

Louise spoke up and said, "The bombing around the city was really heavy, day and night. The city is full of refugees who have fled the outlying areas attacked by the Khmer Rouge, and the people are poverty-stricken. Trying to establish a school under those conditions is just impossible."

Tom shook his head sadly. "We really had no choice but to leave Cambodia, Todd. I'm just sorry our plan didn't work out."

"Well, this may sound strange to you," I finally responded, "but I'm going into Phnom Penh tomorrow."

"Todd, you can't do that!" they both exclaimed at the same time. "You're taking your life in your hands if you do!"

"I have a one-way ticket, a seven-day visa, a few hundred dollars in my pocket, and a word from the Lord," I told them. "The Lord has assured me I have an open door, and I must continue to move forward until it closes."

Once they saw I was determined to go to Cambodia, they tried to help me all they could. Tom gave me the address of the building where they had been staying, and told me several months' rent had been paid in advance. He explained about the Kuch Kong family who were staying in the building, and about some of the household goods they had left behind which we could use. I tried to convince them to return to Phnom Penh with me, but no amount of persuasion would alter their course.

The next day I helped them carry their luggage on board ship and we had dinner together. I waved goodbye on the open deck, then walked ashore. As the gangway was pulled up and the ship steamed slowly out of the harbor, a sense of loneliness crept over me. After watching the ship fade out of sight, I took a taxi back to the guest house and packed my bags to be ready for my early departure to Phnom Penh. Then I crawled into bed under the mosquito net. Before I went to sleep, the Holy Spirit brought to my memory the words of Jesus,

> I will never leave thee nor forsake thee (Heb. 13:5 KJV)
> . . . lo, I am with you alway, even unto the end of the world. (Matt. 28:20 KJV)

CHAPTER 5

Who Wears the Red Scarf?

Jesus' promise had been proven to DeAnn and me over and over again. He had demonstrated His power to the Cambodian people in miraculous ways. The group of believers coming to our building for study was being increased daily as more and more people accepted Jesus and renounced superstition and Buddhism.

My English classes soon became Bible classes—although I still taught in English with Thay interpreting. DeAnn taught the morning class, which had more emphasis on English. In the evening session I usually taught a Bible lesson, but the meeting was often more evangelistic in emphasis. Altogether, in the twenty meetings a week, we were ministering to about a thousand people. At Thay's suggestion we named the work Maranatha Church, for it seemed the Lord was truly preparing the people for His coming.

One evening just as the Bible class ended, I heard DeAnn call, "Todd! Dinner's ready!" I felt I had been rescued. Now I had a good excuse to escape the barrage of questions coming from several of my students and retreat to our quarters downstairs. DeAnn never knew when to schedule our meal together, because the questioning students always stayed beyond the close of our meeting. Having to cook a meal on a tiny kerosene burner was an additional frustration, but she exhibited infinite patience in spite of the inconveniences.

"How can I get in touch with Jesus?" Than Sina had questioned as he tossed his long straight hair out of his eyes. His inquiry caught me somewhat off guard. It was if he were asking for Jesus' telephone number or something. I smiled, musing over his attempt to use the English expression. Several others were standing around with pencil and pad in hand as if waiting for me to give some formula. Their innocent brown eyes searched my face for an answer.

"You can get in touch with Him by just asking Him to come into your life," I answered. "Jesus said, 'My sheep hear my voice; I know them and they follow me.' If you ask Him to be your shepherd, He'll keep in touch with you."

Sina looked satisfied. After answering several other questions I managed to excuse myself. I was determined to make it to the kitchen without any further interruptions. But out of the corner of my eye I saw Arith heading my way. My stomach growled. I was hungry and tired and didn't feel like talking to anybody else.

"Wait brother, please wait!" he cried out after me.

I heaved a sigh and turned to see what he wanted.

"Excuse me, brother," he said with a troubled look on his face. "Can you come to my home with me? My neighbor, she has evil spirit. She needs help. I'm sure you can help her."

Arith had been one of my first students, coming in off the street because of his interest in learning English. He had given me a hard time in class, asking stupid questions and cutting up in front of his friends. Until the crusade, he had made an open show of his skepticism. But seeing so many miracles and listening to the testimonies of the other students who had been transformed by the power of God, his whole attitude changed overnight. He expressed a desire to follow Jesus, then the majority of his friends followed suit and were baptized with him.

"How do you know your neighbor has an evil spirit?" I questioned him. Now I was the skeptical one.

"It's just like what we studied this night in the Bible! Just like it!" he exclaimed.

That evening, we had studied the ninth chapter of Mark which includes the story of the man who brought his demon-possessed son to Jesus. The demon would dash the boy to the ground, he would foam at the mouth, grind his teeth and stiffen out. The

53

disciples tried to handle the situation but were unsuccessful and afraid. In a disgusted manner, Jesus told the father to bring the boy to Him. The father cried, "If you can do anything, take pity on us and help us." Jesus replied, "If! All things are possible to him that believes."

When Jesus rebuked the unclean spirit, it cried out, throwing the boy into terrible convulsions, then departed. Everyone was amazed. His disciples later questioned him privately, "Why is it we could not cast out the demon?" He advised them prayer and fasting might help.

As I recalled this incident I wondered to myself, Could it really be as serious as that? But Arith's persistence assured me it was indeed serious.

I heard DeAnn calling again, "Todd, are you coming?"

"Be right down!" I yelled to her. I told Arith he could either wait for me or we could see the girl tomorrow since it was nearing curfew.

I took my time eating, hoping I'd find he had left so I could turn in early. But no, as soon as I opened the door he was there waiting.

"We go now?" he questioned with an encouraged look in his eyes.

With a sigh I replied, "All right, let's go."

I went to get Sam-Oeurn and found him in his quarters talking with Saran. They both agreed to go.

There were a few cyclos left on the street so we flagged a couple down. Sam-Oeurn and Arith bickered with the drivers and they agreed to pedal the four of us. They seemed to think they got a good deal but on the way over I was more concerned with comfort than cost. Arith sat on my lap and every time we hit a bump the impact of his bony body bruised my thighs. I kept asking myself, What am I doing here? I should be in bed!

The brakes of the cyclo screeched, sliding to a sudden halt.

"This is where she lives," Arith said, pointing to a dingy wooden shack sandwiched between two larger frame houses. "I live there," he said motioning to a cement building a few doors down. "Watch your step," he cautioned as I nearly stepped into an open sewer.

I looked up into the sunset and noticed the eerie smoke drifting from a nearby crematorium. The smell of charred flesh along with the stench from the open sewer nearly gagged me. I held my breath as I followed Arith through the small doorway leading to the girl's home.

As we waited in the porch-like enclosure my senses were alerted by the smell of incense floating through the curtain. I found this fragrance to be delightful compared to the odors outside, but I realized the family's intentions for burning the sweet-smelling sticks were not simply to eradicate the foul stench of sewage.

Arith was calling for somebody inside the next room when suddenly the curtain was yanked aside. After Arith's short conversation with what appeared to be the mother of the girl, we were invited to come in. I was shocked to find the room full of people, including a neighborhood witch doctor chanting in a monotone. He was wearing a robe covered with colorful geometric designs and had all sorts of objects hung around his neck. With incense in hand he was waving his arms, performing an incantation over the motionless form of a young woman about twenty years of age. She was lying on a pallet in a far corner of the room.

To my right, several were kneeling reverently before a stone image of Buddha. He was seen sitting in the lotus position on the coiled portion of a snake; the other portion of the snake went up behind him and fanned out into one large head and six smaller ones. From my studies at ORU, I remembered Buddhism is called a "philosophy of wisdom." Looking at the big head of the serpent, I thought, I wonder where Buddha got his wisdom. I think I'd rather abide under the shadow of the Almighty!

"What is that?" I whispered to Sam-Oeurn, pointing to what looked like a colorful dollhouse shaped as a pagoda and loaded with incense.

"Oh, that," he replied. "That's a spirit house. Nearly all Cambodian homes have them. The people believe an evil spirit dwells there."

The mother was talking to Arith in a quiet tone, her wrinkled

55

face looking tired and discouraged. Arith turned and began to explain to me what the mother had told him.

"She hasn't eaten or had anything to drink for four days," he spoke softly. "It started when another witch doctor cast a spell on her—"

Just then a scream pierced the air, bringing our conversation to a sudden halt. We rushed to the corner of the room. The young woman who had been lying deathly still a few moments earlier was now fighting to sit up. In one sudden motion she was jerked into a seated position. Her eyes caught mine and locked, seething with fire and hate. Totally unprepared for such an encounter, I began calling on the Lord out loud with all the strength I could muster. My eyes were still glued to hers when again she heaved violently, falling to the floor in a biting, screaming rage.

Her body went into convulsions, twisting into hideous contortions. Foamy saliva mixed with blood oozed from her mouth as her teeth sank into her lower lip. Several members of her family moved in to try to control her, but she lunged at them, forcing them back. The witch doctor had backed off, but the volume of his chanting had increased with her screaming. The noise had attracted more onlookers from the street. The mother clutched my arm in helpless desperation, appealing to me with terror-stricken eyes.

A mixture of fright and anger gripped me. I had never seen demon possession like this before. I was scared. Observing this incredible sight I thought, What can I do?

The young woman, whose name was Wandy, had now sunk her teeth into her own arm and was biting in a frenzy. She screamed, "He's biting me! He's beating me and choking me!"

I reached down, pulling her arm out of her mouth and held both arms tightly in my hands.

"Demon," I shouted, "I command you in Jesus' name to let loose of this girl!" Instantly she fell limp as a dishrag. I was surprised by the immediate result, but I somehow sensed that even though things were quiet, the demon hadn't left. Looking around at the witch doctor, the idols on the wall, the incense-filled spirit house and the confused faces, I thought, What good would it do even if I did secure deliverance, in this atmosphere?

Motioning to Sam-Oeurn, I had him help me lift her back upon the pallet. Then turning to the mother, whose face was beaming with hope, I assured her we would return tomorrow.

Stepping out into the night, Sam-Oeurn was quick to ask me, "Is this the kind that comes out only by prayer and fasting?" I frowned, remembering the big meal I had indulged in just before coming. I nodded and said, "Well, we'll see."

The next morning I arose early to meet with Sam-Oeurn, Saran, Arith and several others who had agreed to fast and pray for Wandy's deliverence. Nou Thay was moving some of his things into the building and we explained to him what had happened the night before.

Sitting down with Sam-Oeurn and Saran, I took them through the different cases in Scripture that paralleled with this incident. I then sent the two of them to talk with Wandy's parents. We didn't want Wandy's family to confuse us with other witch doctors, sorcerers, Brahman priests, monks or anybody else who might be called upon to perform an exorcism. In those cases the monk or priest would appeal to the evil spirit, trying to appease its wrath. On occasion they would even offer chicken or pig sacrifices or lacerate their own bodies, depending on the severity of the possession. I wanted the parents to know that we didn't appease evil spirits, but that we would order them to leave in the name of Him who has rendered them powerless and has already destroyed the works of the devil.

I warned Sam-Oeurn to be sure he had the leading of the Holy Spirit before he actively involved himself in a confrontation with the evil spirit. Even then, I told him not to do anything unless the parents were willing to cleanse their home of all the idols and witchcraft.

Late that afternoon Sam-Oeurn and Saran returned, drenched from a monsoon shower and cowed down with discouragement. As they poured out their fantastic story to Nou Thay and me, we could scarcely believe what we were hearing. For the first time I experienced what Jesus must have felt when His disciples returned to Him unable to cast out the evil spirit.

When Sam-Oeurn and Saran met with the parents they shared from the Scripture and explained the authority they had in Jesus. They assured them Wandy would be delivered if they would follow Jesus and forsake their witchcraft. Knowing the persecution that could follow such action, they hesitated at first. But finally in desperation, they decided to give Jesus a chance. They dismissed the witch doctor and proceeded to rid their house of all idols and witchcraft. Onlookers were attracted as the family burned some of the items in front of their home.

Afterwards the mother pleaded, "Now help my daughter; please help her." Sam-Oeurn remembered my advice but felt he could handle it. He and Saran were led into the room where we had gathered the night before. Others crowded in to watch. Wandy was motionless as a corpse. As they stood over the lifeless form, Sam-Oeurn and Saran looked at one another. "What do we do?" asked Saran, returning his eyes to Wandy. She still hadn't budged.

"I don't know," replied Sam-Oeurn. Then recalling how his brother had been delivered through prayer, he said, "Let's just begin by praying."

Their first words were suddenly interrupted by a shriek. "Stop that! Stop that!" screamed Wandy. Or wasn't it Wandy? Her eyes were still closed but her body was now coiled up like a snake and she appeared ready to strike. Her movements became convulsive. Every eye was captivated by the scene.

Laying hold of her arms, Sam-Oeurn shouted above her screams, "Demon, in the name of the Lord Jesus Christ I command you to leave!"

"Don't do that! Don't say that name!" came the voice once again.

Sam-Oeurn was astonished at the demon's reply. "Go, in Jesus' name!" he yelled.

"Quit saying that name! We're afraid!"

"In Jesus' name, in Jesus' name! I command you to leave in Jesus' name!" The revelation of the demons' fear of Jesus intensified Sam-Oeurn's confidence. Saran joined him in the command.

Pitifully the demons cried out for the last time, "Jesus has hold of us! He's driving us out of the country!"

With a scream Wandy fell back on the stained pillow, exhausted and motionless. Her mother was immediately by her side, wiping the perspiration and foamy saliva from her daughter's face.

The frozen atmosphere among the onlookers melted as they voiced their amazement. An undercurrent of suspicion flowed through the crowd.

"What is this? Who is Jesus?" questioned a half-naked young man. His inquiry was picked up quickly by those standing near him.

A woman spoke up, "Yeah, we've never heard of evil spirits afraid of a person, much less a name!"

A neighbor whispered to Wandy's mother, "Who are these fellows? Where did they come from?"

Sam-Oeurn's attention was drawn to the crowd as he overheard their questioning. He began addressing the assembly and everyone quieted down to listen.

"Jesus is Lord and Savior," he spoke loudly. "He's paid for our sins by offering His own life as a sacrifice. He's delivered us from the power of sin, Satan, and death. We who believe in Him do not have to fear evil spirits or live in the shadow of their dominion."

For several minutes he continued to purge their doubts about the Lordship of Jesus, contrasting the teachings of Christ with those of Buddha. No one made a move during his short message. This was the first time they had heard the gospel, and for them it was good news.

"How can we have this power?" one man spoke up. His question seemed to be echoed by everyone present.

Sensing their genuine interest, Sam-Oeurn responded, "If you will believe and accept Jesus as your Lord and Savior, turning from your witchcraft, then I will pray with you. I will ask Him to come into your life. He will then give you His power; you will not have to fear anymore."

"I do believe," a voice came from the corner.

"I, too," said another. "Please pray for us."

Sam-Oeurn's excitement soared. Raising his hands over the crowd he motioned for them to move in closer. Closing his eyes, he began to pray. A reverence seemed to grip every heart.

Suddenly the sacred moment was shattered by sinister laughing coming from where Wandy was lying. The holy moment was to become a nightmare.

"Ha!" a voice spit out in mock laughter at Sam-Oeurn. "Stop that! You will not do that in this place." Now it was as if he was being challenged by the evil spirit.

Sam-Oeurn shouted back with authority, "I command you in Jesus' name to leave!"

"Ha! You leave!" shrieked the demon. "This is my home!"

Bewildered, Sam-Oeurn mustered his courage again, "You must leave in Jesus' name!"

"Who are you?" the demon scoffed back. "I respect Jesus, but you're not His true follower! You leave!"

Sam-Oeurn felt as if someone had pulled the cork on his reservoir of faith. He looked at Saran but was met with the same consternation.

The demon lashed out again before they had a chance to counter. It even began speaking in English, which left them terror-stricken.

"I am the chief of the demons of Phnom Penh," the voice declared. "I wear the red scarf. No Cambodian has authority over me. You cannot cast me out. I command you to leave! Now leave!"

A heat of embarrassment rose in Sam-Oeurn's face as he imagined what the crowd was thinking. In a whisper Saran suggested, "Let's get out of here. Let's go get Brother Todd; he'll know what to do." Sam-Oeurn nodded with relief, made a brief excuse to Wandy's mother, then hurriedly followed Saran out the door.

As Thay and I listened to them recount what had happened we couldn't understand why they allowed the demon to get away with saying such things.

"But it even spoke in English and said 'I wear the red scarf,' " explained Sam-Oeurn defensively. "That girl doesn't even know English!"

"What does the 'red scarf' mean?" I asked.

Thay was quick in answering. "We Cambodians know very well what that means. The red scarf is a sign of authority. It commands respect. The military leaders on both sides of the war wear red scarves around their necks. It distinguishes them from the lower-ranking officials. The spirit said he was 'the chief of the demons of Phnom Penh.' That explains the red scarf."

"Wow," I said. "That means the causes behind this war could even be spiritual."

"Sure," said Thay. "Remember reading in the Book of Daniel where Daniel had been fasting and praying for twenty-one days? (See chapter 10.) Finally the angel Gabriel appeared to him. He told Daniel he had tried to come sooner but was detained, fighting with the prince over the kingdom of Persia. At last, the angel Michael relieved him so he could go to Daniel. At the same time war was raging among the celestial powers, there was war on earth. What was happening down here was just a shadow of what was taking place in the heavens."

Thay continued, "I believe that as the day of our Lord's return draws near, there's going to be increased spiritual warfare resulting in the 'wars and rumors of wars' Jesus foretold."

"I never thought of it like that," I said in wonderment.

Turning so Sam-Oeurn and Saran could hear me clearly I said, "The last thing the demonic forces want the Cambodians to know and believe is that you have authority over their power and influence in Jesus' name. The devil is a liar and the father of lies. His agents are no less than he. They'll speak in English, boast of their rank, challenge your position in Christ, and do anything else they can to make you doubt your salvation and authority as a believer."

Not having been with them for their first encounter I could be bold in my instruction. But really, this was my first encounter with demon power. This experience was breathing life into everything I

61

had heard and read concerning demon possession. We were all learning lessons we would never forget.

Our discussion was interrupted as Arith and some of his friends strode into the room. They had just come from Wandy's.

"They want to know if you're coming back," he said, referring to Wandy's parents.

"We're coming," Thay responded. "Please wait outside."

After we prayed together we headed back to Wandy's. No amount of restraint could keep half the people in the church from going too. DeAnn, with a mixture of fear and excitement said, "I wouldn't miss this for the world."

When we reached the house, people quickly gathered to see what would happen. Black clouds were building up in the sky, threatening another monsoon shower. Wandy's parents met us outside, then ushered us into the room where the girl lay. There was a marked difference in the atmosphere from when I had been there before. My eyes scanned the room searching for the spirit house, but it was gone. No witch doctor, idols, or witchcraft could be seen anywhere—a relieving sight!

Wandy was lying still on her pallet, but suddenly she lunged to the floor. I shivered, watching her body gnarl up with convulsions. Her teeth penetrated her arm. I wasted no time getting to her. Yanking her arm from her mouth, I picked her up and Thay helped me thrust her back upon the pallet. Her screaming ceased as we commanded the demon to be silent.

"You're a liar," I shouted in her face, addressing the evil spirit. "We are followers of the Lord Jesus Christ. We've been bought by the blood that has defeated you. "We've received the power of the Holy Spirit over all the works of Satan and his demons. That includes you! We command you in the name of Jesus to leave and not come back."

"I'll leave, I'll leave!" cried the evil spirit. "Bring back the witchcraft; then I'll go." As the demon spoke, Wandy's body stiffened out with the veins in her neck bulging. With every word the atmosphere seemed to become more contaminated. Now I understood why the Bible called them "unclean spirits."

"No!" I said. "We will not bring back the witchcraft! We will not worship you or try to please you in any way. Only in the name of Jesus will you go, and we command you to leave now!"

"I'm going, I'm going!" the voice whined pitifully. "Give me time; I've got some things to do."

One minute I was furious, wishing I could grab hold of the filthy thing and beat it to death; the next minute I found myself feeling sorry for the miserable creature.

"You have *no* time! You must leave now!" I spoke sharply.

With unusual strength Wandy's frail body struggled violently. It was as if the evil force possessing her was wrestling against an unseen power.

"Jesus has hold of me!" the voice wailed in defeat. "He's throwing me into the pit!" I felt as if we were reliving a gospel account. Then Wandy jerked terribly, letting out a bloodcurdling scream. Falling back onto her pillow, she lay peacefully. I looked up to see DeAnn's face break into a smile.

Thay nudged me. "Hey, it looks like she's free." Sam-Oeurn's face was beaming. As we continued to watch, her eyes fluttered open. Lifting her head, she was startled by all the faces staring down on her. Her mother rushed to her side.

"Who are these people?" Wandy questioned her.

Raising her to a seated position, the mother began to share what had happened and how we had helped her. Wandy looked embarrassed. Her mother handed her a plate of sliced oranges and she consumed them in a moment. Then she noticed the marks on her arms.

"What are these? What's happened to me?" she questioned as tears filled her eyes. The mother quickly wet a towel and began wiping the dried blood from her arms.

"Don't worry," reassured the mother. "Everything's going to be all right."

Thay suggested we leave the room so the family could be alone together. They had been through a lot during the past five days.

Once we were outside Arith and several of his friends gathered around. It had just stopped raining. Everything glistened as the rays of sun danced upon the beads of water.

"Oh, this is wonderful!" Arith exclaimed. "Before, I believed only sixty percent. Now I believe one hundred percent!"

I laughed, hugging his shoulder and said, "Yeah, me too."

Thay drew me aside from the group of students. "What shall we do with Wandy now?" he asked.

"What do you mean?"

He pulled a frayed handkerchief from his hip pocket and mopped the sweat from his brow. "Do you think we should leave her here tonight with her family? It seems to me we need to have someone stay with her for the next few days. She's very weak and needs to be strengthened in her spirit."

As he was talking I remembered what Jesus said about the unclean spirit when it goes out of a person (Matt. 12:43-45). I realized we needed to move some furniture of faith into her swept and cleaned house—her heart.

"Yes, Thay, I suppose that's necessary. She can stay at the church. That way Sam-Oeurn and the others can keep an eye on her."

As Thay and I were talking, Wandy and her parents came outside. I couldn't believe it was the same girl! She was strikingly beautiful. Her silky black hair had been brushed neatly over her shoulders, and she had bathed and changed clothes. Her mother seemed very proud of her. I suppose she had reason to; we learned later that Wandy was a dancer for the Royal Ballet.

Thay talked with her parents suggesting Wandy stay with us for the next few days. The circumstances were a little touchy since the family really didn't know us very well. However, they expressed complete confidence in our judgment, assuring us they were willing to do whatever we felt was necessary.

The next few days proved to be a struggle. Wandy was plagued with fear and depression, and appeared to be suicidal. We learned she had been in this state even before she became possessed. This was one of the things that made her vulnerable for the enemy's attack. We all prayed, fasted and worked with her, trying to encourage her and instill faith in Christ. Three days passed with little sign of improvement, and it was decided to send her home. We had done all we could do. Now we had to trust the Lord to complete what was started.

We didn't see Wandy for a week, and had about given up hope when one Sunday morning she came with her family and friends to the ten o'clock meeting at Maranatha Church. She was radiant with new life as she related a vision she had seen the day before. Several gathered around while she recounted her story.

"I saw myself walking along a beach in the moonlight," she began. "The tide was rushing in, splashing over my toes and ankles. I felt depressed and contemplated taking my life. I began walking into the ocean, the waves getting higher and higher. Suddenly I was swept out into the deep. I found myself fighting desperately to keep from drowning. It dawned on me that I didn't want to die; I wanted to live, but now it was too late. A burning fear gripped me.

" 'Jesus, help me!' I cried. 'I'm not ready to die.'

"Then a bright light came streaming toward me from the sky. I found myself enveloped in the warm rays. A figure appeared before me dressed in flowing white garments. His words seemed to pierce right through me.

" 'Will you take your life?' He said, 'Or will you give it to me?'

" 'You can have it! Take it, Lord! Save me,' I pleaded. The next thing I knew I was in His arms. He carried me to the most pleasant place I've ever seen. The serenity was overpowering. Peace and tranquility flooded my being. I never would have believed such a place existed. It was heaven. It's real; I've been there. And He told me that I will return.

"When the vision finished, I hardly realized it because the peace stayed with me. I know it will never leave me. He has given me His peace. Today, I've come to be baptized."

This beautiful young woman and her family became strong believers and faithfully attended the fellowship group that our workers started near their home. She soon returned to the Royal Ballet Troupe and became one of their star performers. Just before the country fell to the Khmer Rouge, we saw her in a parade celebration.

"Isn't that Wandy there—the one on this end?" DeAnn asked excitedly, pointing to a string of young girls wearing the *samput chok Kban*, a traditional Khmer costume. Wandy was standing directly in front of the presidential platform.

"Yes," I exclaimed, "she's standing next to President Lon Nol!"

We stood on our toes to get a better look over the throngs lining Monivong Boulevard. Just then Wandy spotted us in the crowd of thousands of spectators. Her eyes lit up and she flashed a radiant smile in our direction. "She is a real miracle of God's love," I said softly, not realizing we would never see Wandy again.

CHAPTER 6

New Life for Youvannette

"I have big problem," Sam-Oeurn began to explain as he shut the door of the room I had converted into an office. His face was solemn.

"What's wrong?" I said, motioning for him to sit down. I was busy recording the day's events in my diary.

"He didn't answer my question right away; he just sat there, looking at his feet. Sam-Oeurn had been living with us for three months. He ate with us and worked with us; I thought I knew him well.

Studying his expression I asked myself, What could be troubling him? His behavior the last few days had been peculiar, but I hadn't given it much thought. His silence made me impatient.

"Are you sick?" I said, hoping to initiate some response.

"No," he looked up.

"What is it, then?" I slapped at a mosquito munching my arm.

His eyes fell. "She wants to marry me."

His words were startling. "Marry you! Who wants to marry you?" I questioned eagerly.

"You know who she is," he said. "Youvannette! You baptized her."

Her face loomed clearly before me: a beautiful girl, petite and stately. She was from a wealthy, high-class family, a faithful student in Bible classes three times a day, always sitting in the front row. After the evening service she could always be found in Sam-Oeurn's prayer meeting. She was the last to leave every

67

night. Now everything was falling into place.

"That's a big problem," I said half-jokingly with my face breaking into a smile. "But what about you? Do you love her? Do you want to marry her?"

He blushed and nervously fingered the edge of his Bible. He was having a hard time finding words. After a moment of silence he finally spoke. "But she's from a wealthy family; I—I'm just a refugee with nothing. How can I marry her?"

Sam-Oeurn was in love. But he had a point. How could he support her? Where would they live? I began to think. I shuddered as I remembered the time I had visited Sam-Oeurn's family. When I saw the six of them sharing a single room with three other refugee families it made my skin crawl. Is that how the bride and bridegroom would live?

"What do you know about her?" I asked as my attitude began to sober. "Have you talked with her parents?"

"No, we're afraid to," he began. "We wanted to talk with you first. Her mother doesn't want her to believe Jesus. She would never agree to our marriage. In fact, her parents are trying to make her marry another man so that their family will not be shamed."

"Shamed? What has she done to shame them?" I asked, closing my diary and shoving it aside. My interest began to peak.

"In Cambodia it is disgraceful for a young girl to turn from the traditions of her family. She could be disowned for her belief in Jesus. They think that by marrying her to a wealthy fellow who's Buddhist they can persuade her to deny Jesus."

Thumbing through the pages of his Bible, he pulled out some folded sheets of paper and handed them across the desk to me. "This is her testimony," he said. "Excuse the poor English; I helped her translate it. After reading it, many have decided to follow Jesus. She has had much hardship, but the Lord has helped her."

It was getting late. I needed time to think about all this. Looking at my watch I said, "Let me read her testimony and we'll talk again in the morning."

As he closed the door it suddenly dawned upon me that the

question of their marriage was being placed in my hands. The decision was up to me. Now it was a problem—a big one! With what little money we had coming in, we barely had enough to support ourselves. Sam-Oeurn was already living off the crumbs from our table; there was no way I could support the pair of them. With hundreds of refugees flooding into Phnom Penh every day, jobs were impossible to find. But even if a job could be found, I couldn't afford to lose Sam-Oeurn from the work. He was too valuable.

I could feel myself becoming quite anxious over the matter. Then I heard a voice within say, "Don't worry; this is not your problem. I'll take care of it." With the words came a peace that surfaced into goose bumps all over me. I knew the Lord had spoken. The burden of the decision was in His hands now. I felt relieved.

Dripping with sweat, I decided to take the testimony upstairs with me where it would be cooler. Slipping quietly into our bedroom, I groped in the darkness for a match. DeAnn was already asleep. Lighting a kerosene lantern, I settled into a bamboo chair. The gentle breeze coming through the window was refreshing. I was relaxed and began reading Youvannette's testimony.

The New Life of Miss Eng Ly Youvannette— Cambodian Girl

I am Eng Ly Youvannette, Cambodian girl, have given my heart to the Lord Jesus Christ. In my name of a new Christian I would like to tell you how God saved me and made me repentant.

I am twenty-two years old, the fourth daughter in my family. I have enough knowledge and a good education, but in my life it was hard to live. I felt sad and broken-hearted every day. It's not because my family was poor, but because I was despised in their eyes. Every day I was scolded for having failed my examination in metric education. This made my heart troubled and upset. Sometimes I felt like I didn't have a part with my family. I was always worried and sorrowful. I could not live under this heavy load. My life, like a flower, was burned by the sun.

However, it is the custom in my country—they all worship

Buddha's image. So I thought that was the only way for me. Every night I bowed down to worship the stone image I bought at the market. I supposed it could give me peace and joy. I tried and tried to find peace, but finally became hopeless.

This is nonsense, I said to myself. My face looked sad continually; I looked like a foolish girl.

My friends felt sorry for me and tried to guide me to the way of joy. But as soon as they left, my sorrow returned. I wept and mourned in my room every night. I wanted to leave home, but I couldn't. Where would I go; what would I do? I didn't understand what was happening to me. My family was rich, but I had no peace in my heart.

This year after I again failed my examination, I decided to leave the college and find some job to do. I wanted to continue studying English and heard from a friend about an American who taught English without paying money. So I decided to study with him. The first day I was careful to hear the American's pronunciation. They taught about Jesus. That was strange. That is against my people's thought, I said to myself. But I wanted to know English.

When I heard all the students sing a song to praise Jesus I thought, These Cambodian people are foolish! They turn from their religion. I made fun of them in my heart. I didn't want to sing with them, but laughed instead. I thought, Jesus is the religion of the American people. However, I came to that church every day.

About a month later when I grew up in Jesus' words, I was surprised; they taught good, step by step. I kept in mind to make a comparison with Buddha's teachings. I began to realize that Jesus' words are much like Buddha's, but Jesus could prove himself by miracles. I hadn't yet seen it for myself though; just some friends told me that He did. Buddha said, "Whoever does good will be good; whoever does wrong will be evil." But Jesus said, "Whoever believes in me shall live forever." This reason made me want to study more.

Then one day my family ate bad food. Everyone got very sick. It was terrible; they were near death. No medicine would help. At that time I prayed. It was the first time I had ever prayed to Jesus. I said, "Oh, Lord Jesus! I have studied your words that you have the power to heal the sickness today. But I have never seen it before. Please prove your power today!" It was wonderful. They immediately got better and the next day they were well! It made me trust in Him so much.

This event amazed me. I began to clean my heart. I threw all the graven images out of my room because at that time I understood well how to worship God. I was baptized by American Rev. Todd Burke because I believed Jesus died and rose again, giving me a new life. All these things made me rejoice. I was so happy. My heart was filled with a gladness that I had never seen or received before.

So I became a courage girl, starting to preach the gospel to everyone. My family did not believe my words, however; instead they mocked and insulted me. But if no one go with me, still I will follow. I have a new job to do: read the Bible and pray in private room every day. I realized I had a great peace in my life. No matter what I did, my mind was on Jesus always.

Because I came to the church every day, I had many new friends in the Lord. One of them was Sam-Oeurn. He is the leader of the young people's prayer meeting. I asked him often about the Lord's words and went to pray with him every evening after class. I had a great doubt about his prayer because I couldn't understand his language. I thought to myself, I must keep my eyes on him and find the time to ask him about that.

I came early to class every day to meet with him and have him explain to me about that language. He helped me to understand well. He said that language is the reward of God. Anyone receiving it will be baptized with the Holy Spirit. So I asked the Lord to give me the Holy Spirit. One night I prayed in the private room and I asked Him with a great faith. It was wonderful! I began to shake and what I said in Cambodian didn't sound like Cambodian—it was a strange language that I spoke, but I kept my mind straight to God.

One evening when I returned home from church my family began to persecute me. "Do you really believe Jesus?" my mother

71

asked.

"Yes, mother!" I replied to her. "Jesus is the only real God in this world. He lives forever. He's the Savior and would forgive your sins today if you would confess and bow before Him."

My words infuriated her. She spoke out in a loud voice. "Foolish, you're really foolish!" she yelled at me. "You decide now; if you follow me, you can still be my daughter and live with me. But if you follow Jesus you must go away. I will cut you off from the family."

I couldn't say anything. I felt very sad.

"Answer me!" she shouted. "Are you going to follow Jesus?"

I had always obeyed my mother in everything. But at this time I told her that I had to follow Jesus.

She slapped me with a strong hand, knocking me to the floor. My face hurt. I quickly ran upstairs to my room and began to weep, praying for God to help me. I hid my Bible under the mattress.

"Where is Jesus' image that you worship!" she screamed, coming up the stairs. "Give it to me. I will burn it out and the words of Jesus too."

"I don't have an image of Jesus, mother, because He's not a thing. The real God Jesus is a Spirit. Whoever worships Him must worship by the Spirit and truth."

She cursed me. "If you follow Jesus you must go away and become a priest in Jesus!"

"We don't have a priest for Jesus, mother. Jesus is my priest. He died on the cross for our sins. I only believe and obey Him." I closed the door and began to pray. She kicked the door and screamed at me. She even tried to have my cousin climb up from the outside. I remembered what the Bible said, "Love your enemies, and pray for those that persecute you." I prayed and they went away, leaving me alone. Thank you, Lord!

The next morning my mother came to me with sweet words, "My daughter, don't believe Jesus. I take pity on you. I will sell this home and buy a new house for you. If you love me, obey my words. If you don't follow me, take the gun and shoot me. I want to die before you."

I felt sorry for mother as she said these words. I couldn't say anything, only wept. However, my decision to follow Jesus was final. Later on, when she went to the market, I hurried to the church to tell this story to Sam-Oeurn, Nou Thay, and Kuch Kong. I was surprised when they all prayed for me. I know they love me and have pity on me so much. This made me so happy. Thank you God, and thank you them.

Since that time, I have become a strong Christian. I am even very clever. The Lord has given me the wisdom to spread the gospel to all my relatives and friends. I am amazed at myself, because before I could not talk so much like this. Even if I am rebuked, I don't mind; I still follow Jesus.

One night as I was praying, a black thing came to me and grabbed my throat. I couldn't breathe. I shouted in a loud voice, "In the name of Jesus you must leave!" I said this three times and it went through my window. I quickly got up and went to my mother. "Did you see anything?" I asked her. "Yes, a big light right over there," she said excitedly, pointing near the door.

"Oh mother, that was the light of God coming to prepare the way for us!" She smiled, but didn't say anything. Maybe some day soon she will believe. There is only me to pray for her, and I will pray. It shall be done!

I now have triumphed over every difficulty. My mother hated me, persecuted me, cut me off from the family; even now she still does not believe, but she lets me go to church. By the power of God I won over the testing and the evil thing. Now my family does not curse me. I am free to go anywhere. This is the grace of the Lord preparing the way for me when I was very sad.

It has only been a month since I received the Holy Spirit. He remains in me and guides me in the right way. He has given me great faith so that I am not afraid of anything. I have received a new life. I am dead to sin but alive in Jesus. The Lord Jesus Christ is Savior and has all power and authority on earth and in heaven. He loves you and will give eternal life to whosoever will believe in His name.

Amen. Thank you, Jesus.

I was using my shirt sleeve for a handkerchief, wiping my eyes as I read through her testimony. I couldn't put it down until I had read it three times. Then I woke up DeAnn. "You have to read this. It's fantastic!" I said emphatically.

"Can't it wait until morning? What time is it?" she asked, still half asleep.

"No. Read it now. Please."

She struggled out of the waterbed. Sitting down near the kerosene lamp, she sighed impatiently, then began to read the pages I handed her. I watched the expression on her face light up with interest as she turned the first sheet. Before long she was wiping tears, as I had.

While DeAnn was engrossed in Youvannette's story, I crawled into bed. Thinking back, I said to myself, How could all of this have happened to her without our knowing anything about it? My mind turned to all the other students who attended so faithfully. The faces of Bopha, Somontha, Narithei, Lang, Sambo, and many others began to parade before me. Could they, too, have testimonies like this? I pondered.

Suddenly all my students changed from being just so many brown faces to being real people with personalities—people with problems and frustrations who could experience God's love and power and have their lives transformed. I, too, found myself falling in love. Maybe not quite like Sam-Oeurn, but with the same intensity. I curiously wanted to spend time with these young people and feel what they were feeling.

So many things had prevented us from really getting to know them. The language barrier was the main hindrance that had kept us from cultivating close relationships. I now felt challenged to step up our Cambodian studies. We knew enough of the language to haggle in the markets, but that wasn't sufficient.

I also thought of the physical difficulties that had weighed us down with worry. Like everyone else, we had problems that distracted our attention from the students. The diet affected us traumatically. Rice at every meal, flavored with a few vegetables, quickly lost its appeal. And the smells in the market were enough to make one want to fast for weeks at a time. Both of us lost weight.

Then for the first time in my life, I became plagued with constipation. I tried everything to get relief, but nothing worked. "Lord, I don't know if I like this missionary stuff," I said in despair. "Are you sure I'm cut out for this kind of work?"

Finally, after weeks of frustration, I picked up two books on healthful living that someone had given me. Each book had a chapter on colonic disorders. In both cases, for those having problems with constipation, they suggested staying away from starchy grains such as rice, and "eat more fruit, with the exception of bananas—stay away from bananas." I had been eating rice at almost every meal, and then eating several bananas at each meal to satisfy my craving for sweets!

"No wonder I'm constipated!" I gasped in amazement. Needless to say, I changed my diet in a hurry. But it still took a while to get things balanced out. Later we were told these were just symptoms of "culture shock."

I was reading the biography of Hudson Taylor and found it a source of strength during this rough period. Shortly after Hudson Taylor arrived in China his supporting organization collapsed, leaving him to trust God for every need. He coined the expression, "God's work, done God's way, will not lack God's supply." My question was, "What is God's way?" As we were scraping the bottom of our financial barrel, we tried several different avenues to become self-sufficient. But every effort proved fruitless.

One such attempt was a school project. Missionary friends in Japan had been successful in supporting their church through this method and they urged us to do the same. Nou Thay helped me and we worked hard together trying to set up a day school. It proved to be an embarrassing fiasco. I didn't have the money, supplies, or qualified personnel to make it a go.

"This is impossible," Thay said after we struggled for months. "Even if we had all that was needed, we'd barely break even."

Thay was right. The war situation along with the spiraling economy worked against us. The average Cambodian made only fifteen dollars a month. In Japan they charged three times that amount just for one month's tuition. And the school project actually seemed to sidetrack us from what we had been called to do—preach the gospel.

Later on a doctor friend came through and asked us to help him find orphans he could take to be adopted in the United States. Using my government contacts, we found three war orphans and arranged for their release. I had hoped this would also be the beginning of promising support for our ministry, but it never generated enough funds to break even. One bright thing, however, was the future of the orphans. They now had good homes, whereas they might otherwise have died. For this we were thankful.

Every day we checked our mail, hoping to find money to work with. But from the few letters that trickled in we received barely enough to survive. If it had been just the two of us, things wouldn't have been so bad. I had hired Sam-Oeurn; Kong's family looked to us for support; and Thay, who had a wife and four children, had joined us full time. On top of all this, I was now being confronted with Sam-Oeurn's marriage.

After DeAnn came to bed, we talked far into the night, making resolutions that would help draw us closer to our students. Somehow we both felt cleansed after reading Youvannette's story. It was as if the dark cloud of our failures and disappointments had lifted and the light of God's grace was filling our hearts. We were gaining a fresh perspective. DeAnn reached over and hugged me with a new excitement.

"There's that crazy rooster again," I grumbled climbing out of bed the next morning. "I'm going to ring its neck if it doesn't quit squawking!" Our neighbors were Chinese and they had actually turned their room into a barnyard. All day long you could hear the snorting and squealing of pigs, ducks quacking, chickens clucking, dogs barking. Their roof butted right up against our window. The stench was terrible. But it was Saturday, our day off—at least as far as the classes were concerned. We had been wanting to do something about the racket next door, but not today.

On Saturdays we went to the United States Embassy to pick up our mail and catch up on what was happening "back in civilization," as we called it. The embassy had a nice reading room that carried all the major newspapers. We not only found out what was happening back home in the United States, but we learned about the state of the fighting in Cambodia. The foreign newspapers informed us more about the war situation than we knew from actually being in the country. The constant pounding in the background from the artillery and rockets never told us who was winning. Occasionally we wanted to find out.

As we approached the embassy compound we could hear the powerful generators producing electricity—a scarce commodity during the war. Massive amounts of chain link fence covered the compound; it even covered the top of the four-story building. Walking up to one of the guards I asked, "I can understand this huge fence around the compound, but why all that fencing over the top of the building?"

"Oh, that stuff," he responded. "In case a rocket is headed for the embassy, that will set it off before it penetrates the structure." Pointing to my small briefcase he questioned me, "What do you have in there?" I handed it to him. He opened it to find my Bible and a couple of devotional books. I found the air-conditioned reading room a pleasant place to meditate in the Scripture, so I often brought such reading matter.

"What are you, a missionary?" the marine guard asked politely. His blue and tan uniform was pressed neatly; everything about him looked official.

"Yes, you could call us that. You're welcome to come to our meeting tomorrow morning at ten o'clock."

"Hey, I'd like to," he replied while frisking me, "but they make us work seven days a week around here. Maybe some other time."

Walking into the building, DeAnn motioned, "Go on in to the reading room; I'll check the mail and be right in."

I was seated comfortably reading a week-old *New York Times* when DeAnn burst through the door.

"Look at this!" she cried, before I had a chance to turn around. An avalanche of letters landed in my lap. Spreading them out onto the table I looked in amazement.

"W . . Wh . . Where did these come from?" I stuttered.

"I don't know," she laughed. "Let's see!"

"Hey, here's one from Jimmy," I shouted. Fortunately we were the only ones in the room or we might have been run out. "He's sent a check for a hundred dollars! Can you believe that?!!"

"What's this? It looks like a newspaper clipping," said DeAnn as she quickly unfolded it. We stared unbelievingly at the headline: "Cambodians Hear City Evangelist." Our eyes turned to an accompanying picture.

"Hey, that's a picture of the blind lady who was healed during the crusade," DeAnn exclaimed while smoothing out the ruffled edges. "She's counting your fingers."

"That fellow from Associated Press wrote this article," I said excitedly, pointing to the (AP) symbol. "He didn't do a bad job reporting."

We quickly opened another letter. "It's from Larry Romans in Tulsa," said DeAnn as she nervously slit the envelope. "He's sent two clippings!" She fingered them open and laid them before us. Chills went up my spine as I read the headline of the first one: "Sooner Tells Christian Message To Cambodia." The other read: "ORU Grad Preaches To 5,000 In Cambodia."

Larry's letter began, "I remember a few months ago when you guys were wondering what in the world you would do when you got there . . . are you still wondering???"

All the publicity was overwhelming. We continued opening letters for more than an hour. They came from all over the States, from people we didn't even know! "Evangelist Visits Buddhist Nation," the articles continued. Nearly every letter enclosed a check or money order. We counted over nine hundred dollars."

"Praise the Lord!" bubbled DeAnn. "It sure feels good now that people know we're here and are supporting us."

"Yeah," I agreed. "I've read how God spoke through a donkey and ministered through ravens, but I never would have believed He would use the major news agencies in our behalf. Look at that stack of clippings!"

We were quiet for several moments staring at the pile of letters we had just received. Both of us were thinking back to the day when we first felt the Lord speak to us about Cambodia. We remembered the disappointment we had over not being able to go immediately. We had watched others go instead, but then be forced to leave. Now more than two years later we were in Cambodia, and by the grace and providence of God it looked as if we were going to be able to stay.

I folded *The New York Times* and put it back on the rack. That news seemed insignificant. Quickly gathering everything together, we hurried back to our building. I couldn't wait to share the news.

As our cyclo neared home I could see Thay and Sam-Oeurn standing out on the second floor veranda. It looked as if Youvannette was with them. Then I remembered I had told Sam-Oeurn I would meet with him this morning. As they watched DeAnn and me climb out of the cyclo and pay the driver, I felt the question of their marriage settle upon me. I had almost forgotten about it in the heat of our excitement.

When we reached the top of the stairs we were greeted by their smiling faces. One look at Youvannette brought back all the sunshine I had felt while reading her testimony. She was the heroine of the story. I now had a deep appreciation for her, whereas before she had been just another student.

Seeing her standing next to Sam-Oeurn, I thought to myself, She would sure make him a fine wife. There's no conflict of interests here. They've both given their lives to Jesus and to the spreading of His word.

"Do you know about their desire to marry?" Thay questioned me.

"Yes," I replied while motioning for them to come into my office. "Sam-Oeurn told me last night. What do you think about it?"

"Oh, they told me about it several weeks ago. I was wanting to talk to you, but I felt I should wait until they told you themselves. But I've given it much prayer and thought. It's hard to live in our country now, but remember what the Bible says, 'Two are better than one. . . .' It won't be easy but they'll make it all right."

DeAnn and I began to unfold all the newspaper clippings and lay them out on my desk. "Look at this, Thay. These are articles cut out of newspapers in the United States. They tell all about the crusade we had at the stadium. You remember all those newsmen, don't you?"

"Look! There's my picture!"

Thay's eyes grew wide with amazement. Sam-Oeurn and Youvannette pressed closer, peering over our shoulders.

"And look at this," I smiled, shuffling a stack of letters. "We received over nine hundred dollars in the mail today! God used those newsmen to broadcast the news of our work, and people have responded by sending money to help us."

"Isn't that fantastic!" DeAnn cried. "The Lord knows just what we need!"

"Praise the Lord" Sam-Oeurn added.

Turning in my chair, I spoke to Sam-Oeurn and Youvannette. "You know, when you approached me last night about your marriage I thought it would be impossible. "Now . . ." I grinned, "I think we can help support you, that is if you still want to get married—"

Youvannette giggled her embarrassment, looking over at Sam-Oeurn. He kept his eyes glued to the floor for a moment, then looked at Youvannette smiling. "Yes," he declared. "We want."

Three weeks later I performed my first wedding ceremony.

CHAPTER 7

An Epistle from Saran

I was sitting at my desk, my shirt damp with perspiration, slapping occasionally at a mosquito. My accuracy was improving; I was now able to kill the pestering creatures in flight. It was June of 1974 and we were entering the hot season. As the days grew hotter, the siestas grew longer. I tried, but was never able to sleep through a whole siesta. So I used the time for reading, swimming, language study and translation work. Thay and I had begun putting together a five-lesson course for new believers entitled *Tuk Rueh* ("Living Water").

I was mulling over the rough drafts for the course when suddenly I was startled by an impatient pounding on my door. Looking at my watch I wondered, Who could that be? It's only two o'clock—still siesta.

"Come in! Come in!" I shouted, too lazy to get up.

Sophal entered. With an excited grin he handed me a letter. I looked at the envelope and tried to decipher the Cambodian letters. I was just learning to read the strange writing.

"S . . . Sa . . . Sara . . . Saran! It's from Saran!" I said, surprised. "Praise the Lord!"

Sophal couldn't speak English so I looked in the next room to see if Thay was around. He wasn't there. I wish Thay were here, I thought to myself. I need help with this Cambodian script. Then, as if my thoughts had been read, he and Sam-Oeurn walked in the door.

"It's fantastic," Thay exclaimed as his eyes scanned the page.

"Have you read it yet?"

"How can I unless you help me!" I answered, feeling like the Ethiopian eunuch. "It would take me all day to figure it out; just tell me what he says."

While I waited for Thay to finish reading the entire letter before translating it, my mind flashed back to the evening several weeks before when DeAnn and I had visited Saran and Phony in their home a few miles from our building. Saran had invited us to come.

After taking a cycle to that area of the city, we walked down a narrow dirt road with rows of wooden shacks on either side until we came to their tiny house. Murky sewers bordered the street, swarming with mosquito larvae. Phony, who was standing outside their house, quickly disappeared when she saw us approaching.

"Where did she go?" I asked Saran as we walked up to their door.

"She'll be back," he answered.

Moments later Phony returned with two chunks of ice she had bought from a local vendor, and she served us refreshing cold drinks. We felt awkward drinking the iced limeade while they had warm, unsweetened tea. But this was Cambodian hospitality and they bathed us in it.

Phony had made the best of their small, one-room dwelling. Colorful curtains hung at the barred windows, and pictures cut from old French magazines were neatly taped on the walls. She always looked pretty and well-groomed, and we never saw her without a smile.

We spent a delightful evening together looking through their picture albums and getting better acquainted. Saran told us of his work teaching in a government school, and we learned that Phony worked at an office job. She was expecting their first child.

Just after sundown, while the sky was still lit bright orange, we stood to leave. At that moment we heard shouting from outside. "Watch out!" a voice cried from the road. "Grab him! Don't let him go!"

Saran quickly darted out the door and I followed him, telling the women to stay indoors. Lying on the street was a skinny young man, kicking and rolling in the dust. Several men were trying to grab him and hold him down, but with unusual strength he was resisting them. The men trying to control him were fighting a losing battle.

"What's wrong with him?" I questioned Saran. "Is he mad?"

"Yes. He has demon," Saran said curtly.

Moving in closer, Saran instructed the men, "Step back!" With puzzled looks on their faces, they moved away. The fellow was now on his feet, frothing at the mouth and kicking the dust like a bull about to charge. Saran pointed his finger at him. "In Jesus' name I bind your power, demon; I command you to leave!" he spoke sternly.

The demon-possessed man lunged toward Saran. Then falling to the dust he lay silent. Every eye was fixed on Saran. For the next half hour I looked on while he explained what had happened and preached the gospel to the awestruck crowd.

"The demons know who Jesus is," he shouted to the people. "They're afraid of Him. They know He is Lord and Savior. If you will receive Him tonight you can have His power."

Saran's delivery of the gospel message carried an air of authority and a strong appeal. He told how he had once studied to be a witch doctor, but then heard the message of Jesus Christ and realized He was truly the Son of God with all power. "The night I received Jesus," he declared, "I ran home and loaded my arms with all the items I had used in sorcery. I took them out to the street and burned them where everyone could see. I wanted everyone to know that I was now following Jesus!"

His listeners were captivated as he shared how God had saved him.

After the crowd dispersed, DeAnn and I went home rejoicing over Saran's bold witness and the effect it had on his neighbors. He began holding a meeting in his neighborhood each evening after that, and many came to the Lord. It looked like the beginnings of a new church.

Then the news came. Less than two weeks after his meetings began, he received government orders to go to Andek-Hep, a small village two hundred miles north of Phnom Penh.

"Do you have to go?" I questioned him when he told me about it. "Can't you just refuse?"

"Before the war I could have refused," he explained, "but not now. People are drafted into government jobs like the army. The leaders can shuffle us around like soldiers; we cannot resist."

This seemed like a scheme from the enemy to thwart the work that had been started. We prayed, appealed to the government, and did all we could do to help him stay, but nothing worked. He left for Andek-hep, leaving Phony behind. Although she was pregnant, she couldn't afford to lose her office job.

More than a month had gone by, and I was eager to hear from Saran. This letter was the first word we had received from him. "What does he say, Thay?" I asked impatiently.

The letter began like an epistle: "Saran, a bondservant of the Lord Jesus Christ, to all the believers—"

He went on to say that upon his arrival in Andek-hep, he was briefed on his duties as a teacher in the primary school. There were only three hundred people in the whole village, so life was very slow. Having so much time on his hands he became bored, so he decided to spend his time visiting and getting to know everyone in the village. He tried to look for opportunities to share his faith in Jesus, but each time his witness was rejected. One time a man chased him out of his home, screaming at him so the whole village could hear.

As word got out that he followed Jesus instead of Buddha, some of the parents even refused to send their children to school. "I prayed for God to help me," he wrote, "because everything I did seemed wrong. Then one of my students got sick. Her parents tried medicine for many days, but her fever got worse. I visited her often. Finally one evening I asked them if I could pray for her."

"If you think it will help," they replied.

"So I prayed for her in Jesus' name. I saw no immediate change, but the next morning she awoke completely healed! Her parents brought me a gift and thanked me for what I had done. This was the first time anyone had received my words about the Lord. This

84

encouraged me and gave me more boldness! Thank you, Jesus!''

His letter continued, ''Then the news began to spread that I was a 'healer.' I kept insisting that Jesus was the healer—not me. People were coming to me and asking me to pray for everything. Once, a man led me to his home so I could pray for his pig. I hesitated at first, but then I thought, Why not? This might be just the thing that will bring him to Jesus. The man told me the pig was pregnant and would die unless it got help.

''As we neared the man's home, I could already hear the pig groaning. It was lying on its side, eyes rolled back, and heaving with every breath. I had never prayed for an animal before. Several people gathered around to watch. I knelt down putting my hand on the pig's back, and prayed. Nothing happened. I prayed again. I prayed a third time, but still nothing happened.

''I was about to give up when I remembered something out of my Bible reading that morning. I noticed how God was always addressed specifically—'The God of Abraham, Isaac and Jacob.' With so many gods in those days, I suppose they had to clarify which one to whom they were praying. This village worshiped many gods and idols, too. Maybe the Lord wants me to address Him specifically, I thought to myself. So I prayed once again. This time I prayed to 'Jesus, the God of Todd Burke.' Immediately the pig began to snort and grunt loudly. I watched its eyes roll back into place. It seemed to become alert. Then it heaved and started giving birth. In the next few minutes I watched seven piglets born into the world. It was a wonderful experience for me.

''I turned to the man,'' Saran continued, ''and he was crying as he watched his pig begin to clean its newborn. 'Who is Todd Burke?' he questioned me. I explained to him how Todd Burke had introduced me to Jesus.

''Then, pointing to one of the new piglets, he said to me, 'You tell Mr. Burke that one belongs to him. Tell him I now serve his God.' He wanted to give me a piglet, too. I tried to refuse it, but he insisted. So now I have a pig, and so does Brother Todd when he comes to visit me!''

We all laughed together, visualizing me coming home from a

visit there with a piglet under my arm. Then Thay shared the contents of the rest of the letter.

A few days after this incident Saran was on his way home from school late one afternoon. The village was beginning to accept Saran, but they still had considerable reservation about his faith. As he entered the yard of the government quarters where he lived, he found a man waiting for him. The man hurried to meet him and greeted Saran reverently as if he were a monk.

"Oh, sir," said the man, "I hear every day how your God answers your prayers. Please come and pray for my wife. She's sick. Her legs are paralyzed and she's been in bed for two years."

Saran agreed to follow the man to his home near the center of the village next to the market. He had a shop with the back half partitioned off as living quarters. As they approached the shop, Saran noticed a large number of people had already gathered out front. Apparently word had passed around that the shop owner had gone to get the "healer." They stared at Saran blankly.

"Wait here," the man instructed. "I'll bring her out front."

Moments later he returned, carrying his paralytic wife. When Saran looked at the emaciated body of the woman, he said he felt his faith rise up within him.

"Put her down there," said Saran, pointing to a wooden bench. Then turning to the crowd of about fifty that had gathered, he motioned for them to be quiet. For the next several moments he preached the gospel to them. He shared his testimony and how they, too, could have their sins forgiven and received new life in Jesus—eternal life.

"I'm going to ask the Lord Jesus to prove himself to you," he spoke to the crowd. "I'm going to ask Him to confirm what I've said to you by healing this woman." Somehow Saran knew God was going to heal her. He felt a rush of excitement go through him.

Pointing to the woman, he said to her, "In the name of the Lord Jesus Christ, stand up and walk!" Immediately, strength and feeling flowed into her legs. She began to move them for the first time in two years.

"Stand up and walk," commanded Saran once again.

86

She stood to her feet and took a few steps. "I can walk!" she shouted. "I can walk!" As her confidence grew, she moved faster. The crowd moved back. In a matter of minutes the whole village knew of the miracle. They began bringing to Saran everyone who was sick or lame.

Shoving them back, he motioned for the crowd to be quiet. "I'm not a healer!" he shouted. "I'm a believer. I believe in the power of the Lord Jesus to save and to heal. You can believe, also."

I could scarcely contain my excitement as Thay read the last paragraph of Saran's letter.

"As a result of this miracle," he wrote, "people are attending meetings every night. I'm using my classroom, but it's already too small. We need a larger room and more benches. I also need help in teaching all the new believers. There are too many. We have no Bibles other than the few I brought with me. Brother Todd, I beg for you to come to Andek-Hep and see what God has done. Please have Sam-Oeurn come with you. I'm looking forward to your soon coming."

Had it been possible, I would have left to go see him that moment. But we had to catch a flight out of Phnom Penh in order to get there, and that could take several days to arrange. Sam-Oeurn was also excited with the prospect of going, and he longed to see his good friend again.

"Do you want me to go check on tickets?" Sam-Oeurn asked eagerly.

"Yes, please do," I agreed, "if you think the ticket office has opened yet."

Most of the domestic flights in Cambodia were flown on government aircraft used primarily for carrying cargo. They carried a few passengers, but it usually took several days to make the arrangements. Because of the war, travel over land was too risky.

While he was gone, Thay and I went to try to buy some Cambodian Bibles from Son Sonne, who had a small office for the Bible society in his home. He was a dedicated Christian and helped us all he could, though at times he was restricted by those who were jealous of our presence.

"How many Bibles do you need?" he asked, pulling a few off the shelf. When we told him we needed at least three hundred, he looked at us as if he had just seen a ghost.

"Three hundred? What are you going to do with so many?"

As Thay began to relate the news we had just received from Andek-hep, a look of unbelief came upon Son Sonne's face.

"We need to send a hundred Bibles there immediately," Thay explained. "The other two hundred are needed for the Phnom Penh area."

"You'll just about wipe out my stock," Son Sonne replied. "Can't you wait until the new shipment arrives from Hong Kong? The other missionaries may give me trouble if they hear I've sold you that many."

"Do you work for them or for the Bible society?" Thay asked. "If they asked you for that many you wouldn't refuse." Thay understood the politics that had crept into the Christian camp, and he had no patience with such matters.

"That's all right," I interrupted. "Give us as many as you can and we'll wait for the shipment." I didn't want to do anything that would harm our relationship.

Son Sonne was silent for a moment. "I'll sell you the three hundred," he said hesitantly. "But don't pass the word around that I sold you that many."

When we arrived back at the building, Sam-Oeurn greeted us with a smile. "I've got the tickets," he said. "We leave tomorrow at two o'clock."

I hurried upstairs to tell DeAnn. I found her pecking on a little portable typewriter preparing a stencil for the monthly newsletter we sent to the people who supported our work.

"Guess what?" I said. "We just received word from Saran and it looks like I'll be flying up to see him tomorrow. Sam-Oeurn already has the tickets."

I shared with her about the letter, and then began boxing up Bibles and other materials to take along on the trip. I could sense DeAnn and Thay wanted to go too, but they needed to continue the

Bible classes and keep an eye on things while we were gone. This would be an opportunity to begin handing over more of the responsibility to Thay. Rather than my remaining as the principal Bible teacher, I was feeling a need to let Thay, Sina, Arith, and a few others assume leadership roles.

Worrisome questions had been running through my mind. Could the work survive if DeAnn and I had to leave or were evacuated? Do Thay and the others feel this is their work, too; do they feel they're just guests of a foreign missionary? A statement Hudson Taylor made in his book really impressed me: "Foreign missionaries are the scaffolding around a rising building; the sooner it can be dispensed with the better." It was time to begin dispensing!

The following morning I awoke as excited and as restless as a child on Christmas eve. I had never been out of Phnom Penh to see what the rest of Cambodia was really like. The morning seemed to pass slowly, but finally it was time to go. Sam-Oeurn flagged down a three-wheel taxi and we loaded the boxes of literature in back, leaving little room for us. As we neared the airport we could see black smoke ascending from the tarmac.

"Look," cried Sam-Oeurn. "A plane has been hit!"

About that time another barrage of rockets rained down on the airport. Our taxi quickly pulled to the side of the road. The driver was afraid to go any further.

"Could that have been our plane?" I asked Sam-Oeurn.

"I don't know," he replied. "I doubt ours has landed yet. That could be it there," he said, pointing to a plane circling over the city.

We watched the plane until it began approaching the runway in preparation for landing. Tipping our driver a few extra *riel*, we persuaded him to take us the rest of the way to the airport. People were still huddled behind walls and under anything that would protect them from the shrapnel.

"It is our plane," shouted Sam-Oeurn over the noise of the engines. We struggled with the boxes, running towards the aircraft.

"Hurry and get your stuff on board," urged the Chinese pilot. "We don't want to stay on the ground any longer than necessary."

We lugged the boxes up the loading ramp, then looked for a place to sit down and cool off. I was soaked with sweat. Then came the shock! "Where are the seats?" I asked Sam-Oeurn. The plane was filled with chickens and pigs. This isn't a passenger plane, I said to myself. It's a flying barn. But it was no time to be choosy.

I crouched between several one-hundred-pound sacks of rice and braced myself for takeoff. As the two engines began to roar, vibrating the aircraft down the runway, I began to pray. This wasn't a ride at the amusement park; it was the real thing.

When the nose of the plane lifted and the wheels left the ground, I let out a sigh of relief. We circled the city several times gaining altitude. I was told if we climbed over the countryside, there was danger of getting shot down.

"What's that?" I shouted as I felt something wet run under me. I looked over at Sam-Oeurn and he was laughing, pointing at the pigs. I grumbled, then broke into laughter, too. We're really flying the friendly skies of Cambodia I thought, shaking my head.

Two hours later we landed in Battambang, the second largest city in Cambodia. It was late in the afternoon, so the only transportation we could get to Andek-hep was a *remorque* ("a motorcycle-drawn cart"). Sam-Oeurn found a driver willing to make the thirty-mile trip, and we loaded our boxes into the two-wheel carriage. I didn't know it, but I was in for the most bone-shaking ride of my life.

Now I know what those cowboys in the rodeo go through, I said to myself as our driver raced down the rough, narrow road. Sam-Oeurn and I bounced around in the back, holding on to one another for support. We soon realized that the smoothest place to ride was as close to the cycle as we could get—where our rickshaw was fastened. The driver could maneuver his cycle away from the holes in the road, whereas the wheels of the carriage hit every bump and there were no shock absorbers.

When I wasn't trying to hold on for dear life, I was captivated by the breathtaking beauty of the landscape. It was nearing harvest time and as far as I could see, rice fields glowed brilliant green in the sunset. The landscape was peppered with palm trees, and an occasional mountain jutted out of the earth as if it had been divinely placed to break the monotony. It appeared to be a serene panorama; yet I knew the cities in the northern area had suffered the ravages of war.

"How much farther?" I asked the driver as we pulled over to let an ox-drawn cart loaded with hay go by. Without speaking, he communicated with his hands that we were about half way. I got out and stretched and soaked up some more of the view.

We finally arrived at Andek-hep just before dark. A roadside food stand was a convenient place to leave our boxes and luggage until we located Saran. The smell of freshly roasted coffee beans lured us into having a cup of coffee. As we sat there, people started standing around staring at me. I tried to ignore them, hoping they would go away, but before long a whole crowd had gathered.

"Why are they staring at me like that?" I asked Sam-Oeurn.

"It's not often these people see a foreigner," he explained.

"Let's get out of here," I urged, "and go find Saran." Just then I saw Saran's head bobbing through the crowd. He pressed his way through the people, hurried to our side and embraced both of us.

He turned to the crowd and said to them, "This is my friend, Todd Burke—you remember? He's the one I told you about who introduced me to Jesus." I watched their puzzled looks break into smiles and several started clapping, inspiring the whole gathering to applaud. I felt like a celebrity.

Saran reached into one of the boxes and pulled out a Bible, lifting it into the air.

"Look!" he shouted to the crowd. "He's brought the words of Jesus with him. Now everyone will be able to study God's words."

Saran seemed to have the respect of the people; I was amazed at how they responded to him. Motioning for others to grab the boxes and our luggage, he led us to the government quarters where he stayed. I was proud of this handsome young man, but at the same

91

time I couldn't help feeling a little anxious for him.

"Lord, keep him humble," I prayed as I walked behind him. "May he continue to lift up Jesus and glorify your name."

"I didn't expect you so soon," Saran turned and said to Sam-Oeurn and me as we walked into the compound. It was too dark to see anything. He fumbled with a lock on the door and finally got it opened. After lighting several candles he pointed to a cot in the corner. "You can sleep over there," he said. The cot had four poles sticking up at the corners supporting a mosquito net. I was so tired anything would have looked inviting.

He and Sam-Oeurn were engaged in a conversation, laughing and chattering back and forth, when my ears picked out the word "food."

"Yeah, let's eat!" I interjected in my rough Cambodian. "*Knyome kleein!*" ("I'm hungry.")

Saran quickly gathered some sticks and built a fire. Moments later he served us a rice soup called babaw, flavored with salty dried fish. At first I didn't think I would like it, but I found it to be quite satisfying. For dessert he handed us about a dozen peeled oranges.

"Eat all of them," he urged us. "Our village has an abundance of this fruit."

After our meal I turned in early. I lay on the cot and did my Bible readings by candlelight. When I finished, I found that without realizing it, I had burned a hole in the nylon mosquito net.

"Don't worry about that," Saran laughed. "Look at my net—many burns." He lifted his net, revealing a patchwork of repairs. He disappeared for a moment and returned with a needle and thread. "I'll show you how," he said, proceeding to fasten the gaping hole with expert stitching. I insisted on doing the repair myself since I was the one who'd been careless, but he considered it a privilege to do it for me.

The next morning I was up before dawn. I quietly made my way outside and went for a stroll. The rising sun began lighting the horizon as I paced through the small village. It was so still it reminded me of a ghost town. The buildings were roughly constructed of unpainted wood, and the wide, dusty road which ran through town was dotted with tumbleweeds here and there. As I neared the center of the village, I could smell the roasting of coffee beans again. I seated myself at one of the stands. The roof was made of palm leaves and supported by poles in the center and all around. A lady brought me a glass of coffee and a can of sweetened condensed milk.

As I sat there sipping my coffee, a parade of Buddhist monks walked by, dressed in bright orange (saffron) robes with pails in hand. They carried them from house to house begging for food. I watched them stop in front of a home and begin chanting piously until someone came out and put rice in their buckets. As I beheld this scene, a Scripture came to mind: "I have been young, and now am old; yet I have not seen the righteous forsaken, nor his seed begging bread" (Ps. 37:25, KJV).

They need to know the provision of their heavenly Father, I thought to myself. Begging and other forms of self-abasement don't please God. I recalled again the words of Hudson Taylor, "God's work, done God's way, will not lack God's supply."

"Oh, Lord," I prayed. "Help us to do your work your way and trust you for every need. Don't let us fall into the trap of depending upon the arm of flesh to support our ministry."

Hurrying back to the compound, I found Saran. "Where does the man live who owns that pig you prayed for?" I asked him.

"Come," he said. "I'll take you to meet him and also the woman who was healed."

I grabbed my Bible and we headed back through town. We stopped at a shop near the market first. I remembered from Saran's letter that this was where the woman lived who had been paralyzed. Saran opened the door and called inside. Finally her husband appeared. When he saw us, he rushed out of the shop, full of excitement.

"Wait here," he said. "Let me fetch my wife." He hurried across the street to the market and disappeared into the early morning crowd. Moments later they returned together. His wife, wearing a flowered sarong, walked toward me with thongs flapping. She smiled and handed me a basket of fruit. Except for the fact she was so lean, you wouldn't have known she had been sick or paralyzed.

"We are happy you have come to visit our home," she said, scooting a chair over for me to sit in. "The Lord Jesus has blessed us so much. I didn't believe I would ever walk again," she said, pointing to her legs and feet. "But Jesus has healed me. We thank Him for sending Saran to our village." As I listened, tears of joy filled my eyes. Her childlike expressions melted my heart; she was genuine.

Saran took her hands and we prayed with the family before parting. I looked up to see tears streaming down her face. She had received more than a touch in her body; she was spiritually healed too. I hoped to come back and spend more time with them later.

We walked to the edge of town before reaching the home of Koun, the owner of the pig Saran had prayed for. Children were playing out front in the well-worn lawn. Seeing me, they ran and hid under the house—which was where the pigs lived. Either I draw a crowd or I scare them away, I thought to myself. The novelty of being weird was wearing off in a hurry.

Koun saw us standing near the gate and quickly scrambled down the steps to greet us. With palms clasped in a prayerful way, he bowed as if we were royalty. This made me feel quite uncomfortable. Then he assisted me up the rickety steps and ushered us into his home.

"Did you come to get your pig?" Koun smiled, exposing his toothless gums. What few teeth he did have were black from chewing betel nut. I had anticipated his question.

"Would it be all right with you if we sold the pig?" I nervously responded, "and use the money to build a bench for the meeting hall?"

He frowned thoughtfully. Saran quickly explained how difficult it would be to take the pig back to Phnom Penh on the plane.

Koun smiled again, "That's a good idea—more people can come and hear about Jesus."

Just to hear him say that was worth the whole trip to Andek-hep.

94

Walking back towards the market, a sense of satisfaction welled up within me. We stopped to see a local carpenter and contracted for the building of eight ten-foot benches. He agreed to build three of them in exchange for our two pigs. Then Saran took me to see several buildings he had been considering as a place to hold his Bible classes. The present meeting place was dark and cramped, with just a few small benches. I agreed that a better place was needed. One house he showed me seemed ideal. It had a nice yard with several big trees and two large rooms—one indoors and one outdoors. They were well suited for meeting halls.

"How much is it?" I asked. The price he quoted equaled about twelve dollars a month. He was afraid the price would be too high.

"Is that all?" I said in amazement. "Let's take it!" As far as I was concerned, that was cheap! In Phnom Penh, a place like it would have rented for five times that amount—maybe more! Saran's face lit up with joy.

"Hurry!" he said. "We have to get back. A friend of mine is asking a girl to marry him today and we are a part of the ceremony."

"We're a part of it?" I asked, bewildered. "How can we be a part of it?"

"You'll see," he said, smiling. "It's hard to explain our custom."

But we didn't make it all the way back before we met the procession of men. There were about fifty of them, all carrying gifts for the bride's family. I was handed a tray of oranges with a ribbon tied around each one, and asked to be one of those heading up the procession. Saran was given a duck to carry, and Sam-Oeurn a stalk of bananas. The other gifts ranged from pigs and chickens to fine cloth, jewelry, and linens.

Now what do I do? I wondered. I followed Saran's friend until we came to the home of the girl he was wanting to marry. Standing outside, all the men began singing a traditional Cambodian song. I tried to act as if I knew what I was doing. The doors of the home opened and the parents of the girl stepped outside. They were dressed in formal attire.

"Where's the girl?" I asked Saran.

"She's not allowed to be seen until the wedding."

"When's the wedding?"

"It depends on the girl's parents. They have to receive the gifts first. If they receive them, that means they agree to have Aaun marry their daughter. But actually, they've decided on the marriage already." Saran explained, "This is just part of the ceremony."

Everyone began laying the gifts at the feet of the parents. Everything about the occasion was festive. Several others began carrying tables from inside the home and setting them out front. It looked like the makings of a feast. Before I knew it, I found myself seated at the head table with a huge pot of stew steaming in my face.

"Is Aaun a believer?" I asked Saran, who was seated next to me.

"Oh, yes!" he replied. "Aaun was one of the first to respond to the gospel. He came to my home every night with questions. Since then, we've become close friends."

Aaun motioned to Saran that he wanted to speak to him. When Saran returned, he whispered to me, "He wants me to introduce you and have you pray." Somehow I had expected this. I was told that I was the first foreigner ever to stay in their village.

After the prayer everyone was instructed to eat their fill. I was enjoying my chicken curry stew when my interest was attracted to a small mountain that overlooked Andek-hep. Pointing to it, Saran said, "That's where Andek-hep gets his name. From one side it looks like an abandoned turtle shell." I was intrigued.

After the feast everyone turned in for their afternoon siesta—that is, everyone but me. I decided to go mountain climbing. Grabbing my Bible, I began my ascent. It took over an hour for me to scale the turtle shell. Once I made it to the top, however, the view made it worth the hard climb. I found a clearing where I could sit down on a large rock and enjoy the divine exhibit of God's handiwork. I could see for miles. Only God could create such a scene, I said to myself.

On my right, two trees framed a vista with a road meandering out of sight toward a distant mountain. The hazy sky gave the countryside a blue tint, creating a picture one might find in a book of fairy tales for children. I sat there for a long time praising God and reading his word.

Arriving back in the village late in the afternoon, I met Sam-Oeurn and Saran near the market.

"We're sure glad you're back," Saran said with relief. "Several people saw you head for the mountain and came to us concerned for your life."

"I don't understand what you mean," I answered. "There was no danger."

"That's what we told them, but they insisted there was. They believe an evil spirit named Belial rules that mountain."

"Belial?" I said, surprised. "That's the name of a ruling demon in the Bible."

"There's a rumor that several people climbed the turtle shell but never returned. The people of this village are afraid to go up there. Some think you went to fight the demon."

"Fight the demon!" I exclaimed. "I didn't see anything but a beautiful view."

As we stood talking, a crowd began to gather around us. "What happened to him? Did he fight Belial?" several questioned. It was getting too noisy to talk. I didn't know what to think of their superstitions, but I realized I had an opportunity to preach to the people gathering. Motioning for everyone to be silent, I began to speak while Saran interpreted.

"I didn't fight Belial on the mountain," I began. "I don't have to. Jesus already fought and defeated him, along with every other demon, including Satan himself. I've received the Lord Jesus into my life. He lives in me," I said, patting my chest. "Now I don't fear Belial or any other demon."

At that point I turned it over to Saran. The pump had been primed, and he continued speaking and answering questions for the next hour. Backing out of sight, I watched him and Sam-Oeurn minister to the people. A sense of pride welled within me as I observed my spiritual offspring reproducing like this. They had grown so much in such a short time.

I thought back to our experience with Wandy. No longer were they frightened novices as they had been when praying for her. Now they were confident, invading the enemy's territory equipped with a reservoir of experience that gave them boldness before the crowds. Saran was aggressive and determined, whereas Sam-Oeurn was more passive and relaxed. I loved them both, and felt each one had a special place in the Lord's work.

The next morning Sam-Oeurn and I caught a flight back to Phnom Penh. I felt exuberant and confident about leaving the work in Saran's hands. The church was established and growing; the miracles had been confirmed. I had seen all I had expected to see—and more. At the time I didn't dream that the birth of this church would mean much suffering further down the road.

CHAPTER 8

Sheltered by His Hand

Our plane had circled Phnom Penh for more than thirty minutes. What's wrong? I thought to myself. Why don't we land? Sam-Oeurn's face was pale; he looked like he was getting sick. I found if I could keep looking out the window at the ground, it helped to control the nausea. Around and around we continued. Fortunately the plane was nearly empty. Thank God, there are no pigs, I said to myself. Finally I decided to make my way up to the cockpit.

"What's keeping us from landing?" I asked our American pilot, as I held on to the doorway. I thought maybe he was trying to accumulate flight hours in Cambodia so he could get a better job in the States. He couldn't hear me with the headphones covering his ears. I could hardly hear myself; the engine roar was deafening.

"Why don't we land?" I yelled, confident he would hear me this time. But there was still no response. I tapped him on the shoulder and he jerked around with an angry look on his face.

"I can't get clearance to land!" he yelled impatiently. "They're shelling the airport! We may have to return to Battambang."

"Return to Battambang? Do we have enough fuel?"

"I don't know," he said removing his headphones. "If not, we can stop in Kampong Chhnang, about halfway. But I'm still hoping we get clearance to land." He motioned for me to sit down on a canvas stool that folded out from the wall. I was glad he was letting me sit in the cabin with him. Squatting in the corner of the cargo section reminded me of Jonah in the whale. There was another seat for Sam-Oeurn, so I waved for him to come up front. I felt sorry for him as he struggled forward. As my dad would say, "He looked like he'd been dragged through a knothole."

I told Sam-Oeurn what the problem was and we joined hands and prayed. Moments later the pilot turned and said, "They've given us clearance to land; I'm gonna make a run for it."

He made a sharp nose dive towards the runway. It didn't look like he could pull out of it. Sam-Oeurn's brown face turned white as a sheet. I closed my eyes and buried my face in my lap.

Our trip up north had been so peaceful. There were no explosions; no thunder of war constantly in the background. I had almost forgotten that we were in a war-torn country. Now we were back in the heat of the fighting.

"Brace yourselves," the pilot shouted back at us. "I'm gonna try to make a short landing." The wheels screeched, hitting the runway. The engines roared in reverse, throwing to the floor everything that was loose. Somehow we managed to keep seated through it all. I let out a sigh of relief as the plane rumbled along, gradually slowing down. When we finally rolled to a stop, our pilot quickly opened the rear door and motioned for a ground attendant to bring a stairway. I was thankful we didn't have all those boxes to lug; we had only one bag to carry. As we hurried down the steps and ran to the terminal, we were surprised; the place looked deserted. But we could still see shells exploding in the distance.

"Where is everybody?" I asked our pilot once we were safe from rocket fire.

"How long have you been gone?" he questioned. "Haven't you heard? Almost all the French have left the country. The city has been under a heavy siege. Nearly all the airlines have discontinued their flights to Phnom Penh. An Air Vietnam jet full of passengers was shot down the other day."

"Was that the plane that burned near the runway?" I asked, pointing to the remains of the charred aircraft.

"No. That was just the beginning of the attack. Is that when you left?"

"Yes," I responded. "But I didn't think all of this could happen in so short a time. If the French are leaving, it's got to be bad.'' Since the war began, and as it crept closer and closer to Phnom Penh, other foreign residents periodically panicked and fled. But never the French. Never, that is, until now.

I began to worry about DeAnn. If something had happened to her, there was no way they could have notified me.

''Hurry,'' I called to Sam-Oeurn, while waving goodbye to our pilot friend. ''I want to get to the building as quickly as possible.'' I didn't want to choose between a *remorque* or a three-wheel taxi, figuring they would take too long. So I paid a man to drive us in his car. Even at that, the eight-mile trip seemed to take forever.

Everything was quiet around the building when we arrived. Sam-Oeurn's father was asleep in a chair near the doorway. I had hired him to guard the door during the daytime and he was on the job, even during siesta. The slam of the car door awakened him. When he saw us, his face lit up like a neon lamp. He hurried to grab my shoulder bag, then embraced both of us.

''It's good to have you home,'' he said smiling, exposing his remaining two teeth. ''Mrs. will be glad to see you. She has missed you very much!''

''Where is she?''

He pointed upstairs to her office. I left Sam-Oeurn with his father and scrambled up the steps to the room we had sectioned off for DeAnn. There she was, pecking away on her typewriter, catching up on correspondence. Her back was turned to me, and the noise of the typewriter kept her from hearing my footsteps. I stood quietly for several moments and gazed at the beautiful sight. ''Thank you, Lord,'' I said under my breath. ''What a wonderful gift you have given me.'' Relief flooded over me when I realized she was safe. It was an emotional moment for me. ''Lord, help me to give her the love she needs, and may I never take her for granted,'' I prayed silently.

Sensing someone was in the room, she jumped in her chair, and turned toward the door. When she saw it was me the startled look on her face broke into an excited smile. She leaped from her chair into my arms.

"You're back! You're back!" she cried. "Thank God, you're back! I've been so worried." She kissed my dirty, unshaven face as tears filled her eyes. "Oh, you're so hot and sweaty. Take off those stinky clothes and let's get you cleaned up. So much has happened that I must tell you."

"You mean about the French exodus? I heard about that already."

"Yes, but did you know that the other missionaries have left the country? They left yesterday."

"They've gone, too?" I exclaimed.

She nodded, "Yes, and the U.S. Consul stopped by this morning to see you. He asked me to have you come down to the embassy as soon as you return. They're trying to get everyone to leave. I told him we probably wouldn't go unless there was an evacuation. He said, in that case, he wants us to attend a briefing on evacuating procedures so we'll be prepared for an emergency."

We were interrupted by someone rushing in the door and I turned to see Thay's handsome face beaming. He wasted no time giving me a big hug. We had become very close friends, and I had really missed Thay.

"How's the prophet of Nehru Boulevard?" I said half-jokingly. "Are the Bible classes doing all right?"

He responded with a confident smile. "We've never had so many coming to hear the gospel. The uncertainty of the war situation has people seeking peace from the only one who can give it."

"What about the war situation? Tell me what's happening."

"It's never been quite this bad," he explained. "But it's likely to get much worse before it's all over."

"What do you mean?" I asked, feeling disturbed.

"During the rainy season the war slows down considerably. The rivers overflow and the countryside turns to mud, making it impossible to mobilize troops. What we are experiencing now is called the "dry season offensive." The Communists have two more months to try to take Phnom Penh before the rainy season begins. If they don't succeed, they'll have to wait and try again

102

next year. They don't want to wait; they're trying to take it now.''

Thay's words carried a sobering effect. We knew that someday we would probably have to leave Cambodia, maybe for good, but we never really entertained the thought seriously. Like death, it was one of those things too distant to think about. The war had become as commonplace as the sunrise, but the Khmer Rouge had not bothered with the capital city of Phnom Penh at the outset. They would send a barrage of rockets into the city occasionally just to keep the people terrified and conscious of their presence, but their main activity was in the rural areas. They would overrun the smaller towns and villages, burn them to the ground and kill the disabled. This forced those who were able to flee into Phnom Penh, making it the main city of refuge. Before the war began in 1970, Phnom Penh's population had been 600,000. Now it was approaching 3 million as the Khmer Rouge tightened their stranglehold on the country.

As the population increased the food supplies dwindled and starving people became a common sight. This sowed seeds of unrest and anarchy and could only lead to the collapse of the capital with its government. After cutting all the roads to the city, the Khmer Rouge began giving their attention to the only two lifelines left—the Mekong River and Pochentong Airport. They filled the river with mines, so the airport became more and more the city's only hope for survival. By this time almost thirty airline companies were operating in Phnom Penh, but with all of them flying full time they still couldn't keep the city supplied. It became obvious that it was no longer "if" but "when" the country would fall.

The constant pounding that echoed from the battle zones seemed to take on new meaning. It was now a personal threat, and for the first time I felt a chill of fear when i realized it was quite possible we could lose our lives.

"What do your people feel about the war?" I asked Thay. "Do they really know what the fighting is all about?"

"No," he answered. "Very few, if any, know what's happening. This is especially true among the Khmer Rouge. Most

103

of them are country boys who can't read or write. They're just given a gun and trained to fight. What the people do understand is that life once was easy; now, they can scarcely live."

Thay was right. Before the war spilled over into Cambodia, it had been considered a paradise and Phnom Penh had been a tourist's haven. The city had offered the most comfortable, leisurely life anywhere. But at the same time, there was little place for the gospel in the hearts of the people. When they would hear of the war in Vietnam and Laos, they would boast, "Buddha has protected us." But now they were dancing to a different tune—to the music of bombs and rockets, to the sounds of war and the death cries of loved ones. Their once proud boast was being reduced to the despairing utterance, "Nothing can help us now—not even Buddha."

"Cambodia is being shaken to its foundations," Thay continued soberly. "Everything is crumbling. But in the midst of all the destruction, God is laying His cornerstone and building a kingdom which cannot be shaken. I don't like war; but if that's what it takes to awaken my people to the gospel of Jesus Christ, then I welcome it."

"You guys can talk later," interrupted DeAnn. "Todd has to get cleaned up so we can go down to the embassy. I promised the consul he would come as soon as he returned."

DeAnn and I went downstairs and headed for the nearby house we had recently rented. The constant noise and activity around the building had made it necessary for us to find a quiet place to which we could retreat. But that wasn't the only reason we moved from the building. Located in our home was also the beginnings of an orphanage. I revved up our Yamaha motorcycle and DeAnn perched on the back fender.

"How are the babies doing?" I asked.

"Pretty well," DeAnn answered. "Timothy is doing so much better now."

"He's home!" I heard Kong's voice come from inside their living quarters when I turned into the yard. San came running out holding Timothy Paul. He was now three months old and the first orphan we had taken into our home. His father had been killed in the war and his mother abandoned him when he was five days old. Some Christians found him in a school and brought him to us, begging us to take him in. We had never cared for babies before, but it didn't take long to get initiated. Day and night we worked with him, trying to restore his health. He had developed pneumonia, and one night his breathing got so difficult we thought he was dying. We prayed and anointed him with Vicks. The next morning we awoke to find him completely healed. We praised the Lord!

"How was your trip?" Kong asked as he walked out to greet us.

"It was great! I'll let Sam-Oeurn tell you about it. I have to hurry and get cleaned up to go to the embassy."

"Are you thirsty?" he asked, pointing to the top of one of the coconut trees in our yard. He hit a soft spot. The consul would have to wait. Nothing was better than the milk from one of those big ripe coconuts. I smiled and nodded eagerly. One of Kong's boys shimmied up the tall tree, holding a large knife in his mouth. Whacking a few coconuts loose, he dropped them down to Kong. While Kong worked on opening the top of one of the coconuts, I looked around at the other trees in our yard. We were not only blessed with coconut trees, we also had mangos, papayas, bananas, and a delicious fruit called lamut.

Kong handed me the coconut he had opened, and smiled as I drank the cool, sweet milk.

"Hurry," DeAnn yelled out the window. "The embassy will be closed in an hour. You still have to get cleaned up."

During the hot season there wasn't enough pressure in the daytime to supply water to our house. So at night we filled several clay cisterns and would take baths by dipping a pan into the water, then pouring it over ourselves. After taking a dip bath, I put on some clean clothes and we caught a cyclo to the embassy. Dozens of helicopters whirred constantly overhead carrying the wounded from the battlefields and sending out more replacements. When we turned down the street that ran parallel with the Tonle Sap and Mekong rivers, three T-28 fighter bombers flew overhead, dumping a load of bombs on the other side of the river. Every time one hit we could actually see the ground jump. Seconds later, the sound of the blast would reach our ears.

"Look!" I cried to DeAnn. "The Khmer Rouge are just on the other side. We've never been this close to the fighting." I felt my skin tighten as more aircraft flew over. Then our cyclo driver pulled to the side of the road and stopped while a caravan of army trucks went by. There were about twenty trucks, each filled with soldiers, most of whom were in their teens. Some were as young as ten years old. It looked like they were headed for the narrow bridge spanning the wide river. The main bridge the Japanese built after World War II had been blown up, leaving huge stumps of twisted iron sticking out of the water.

Shortly after that caravan passed, another one came along. This one was loaded with tons of ammunition. All sizes of wooden crates housed rockets and heavy field artillery. One part of me craved to go along and watch; the other part wanted to hurry and get to the embassy and learn about the evacuation procedures.

As we entered the highly protected area of the embassy compound, we felt overshadowed with a sense of security. Before, I had considered all the protective measures they had taken to fortify the compound extreme and unnecessary. But now I greatly appreciated their efforts. The screened canopy over the building, along with the marine guard and the towering fence, sheltered us from the war that grew more threatening every moment. The ground shook as the explosions around the city intensified.

Upon reaching the consul's section, we were quickly escorted into his office. He was sitting behind his desk with several stacks of Cambodian passports in front of him. Looking up with a frustrated expression, he motioned for us to be seated.

"How are you, Mr. McCarthy?" I said, hoping to break the icy atmosphere. He gave no immediate response. Then he flopped back in his chair and tossed his pen onto the pile of passports.

"Do you really want to know?" he snarled, letting out a string of curse words. "To be frank with you, I want out of this mess. All I do around here is issue visas and solve people's problems. It's not

106

worth it!''

''What about you?'' he continued, still disgruntled. ''Your wife told me you had flown up to Battambang. I was beginning to wonder if you would make it back. What were you doing up there?''

I briefly told him about Saran's ministry among the people of Andek-hep. As I shared about the miracles and other experiences, his blank stare grew colder and colder. He was totally disinterested.

''That's very interesting,'' he interrupted, while nervously shuffling some papers on his desk. ''What I wanted to see you about is this. The ambassador has asked me to encourage all Americans to leave while the leaving's good. Your wife told me you probably wouldn't go unless there was an evacuation. Is that right?''

''Yes,'' I nodded, feeling quite uncomfortable.

''Well, we can't make you go; but in case there is an evacuation you should know the procedures. They're having a briefing in about an hour. If at all possible, you should stay for it.''

After the briefing that evening, we were instructed to visit the optional gathering locations and become familiar with them. We were told to review the different code words and to keep tuned to an FM radio station broadcasting out of Saigon. If we heard the words ''Battery Charger'' that meant there was an evacuation alert and we were to listen for further orders. If the words ''Dry Cell'' came over the radio, we were to go quickly to one of the assembly areas. Helicopters would then transport us out of the country, probably to Thailand. We would be allowed to take only one briefcase with us.

That night DeAnn and I stood on the small balcony of our house and watched the fireworks of the war. All around the outskirts of Phnom Penh dozens of flares lit the skyline. The planes moved in, firing missiles. They looked like shooting stars. Occasionally a red flare would be sent up from an area of intense fighting. That would be an emergency SOS. Someone needed help.

Can they hold off the Communists from taking the city until the rainy season sets in? we wondered to ourselves. If there is an evacuation, what will we do with our babies? Will we be able to get them out of the country with us? All kinds of questions flooded our minds.

Families in the United States and Canada were trying to adopt our orphans, but were encountering all sorts of difficulties with their adoption proceedings. Also, as a result of a new law, the Cambodian government was now refusing to let orphans leave the country. Only time would answer our questions.

The next morning we awoke just before dawn. "Listen!" DeAnn said. All I could hear was our orphans downstairs crying for their milk.

"Listen to what?" I asked. "All I can hear is the babies."

"No. Not that. The bombing; it sounds like it's stopped." I held my breath and listened closely. She was right. Except for a few faint rumblings, things had quieted down considerably. We had no way of knowing this stillness was going to be the calm before the storm.

It was Saturday, so we were free to answer letters that had stacked up while I was gone. We worked all morning and into the afternoon. I was in the middle of dictating the last letter when suddenly a series of explosions shook our house.

"What's that?" DeAnn cried fearfully, gripping the arms of the chair. The window panes of our room rattled, threatening to break. The blasts sounded like crackling peals of thunder not far away. As the barrage of artillery shells pelted the ground, I wondered if we were included in the target area. Up until this time, our part of town had been out of range for artillery and rockets.

We stared blankly at each other, scarcely believing this was actually happening. Several more rounds shook our house before the shelling stopped. There had been more than twenty explosions. I saw Kong dart past the window of our balcony. Moments later he returned and pounded on our window.

"Brother! Brother!" he yelled excitedly from outside. "Come quickly!" We hurried out the door and raced down the side of the balcony.

"Look!" he said, pointing to the south. Huge clouds of black smoke already darkened the blue sky. I could see flames leaping into the air not more than a few hundred yards away. Fortunately for us, a strong wind was blowing from the north—very unusual for the hot season. The wind was carrying the devouring blaze through acres of highly flammable dwellings. The forest of wooden shacks exploded into wildfire as the flames raced through the villages.

"Grab the camera," I called to DeAnn. We hopped on a cycle and hurried to the nearby market where the first shells had landed. The street was full of terror-stricken people trying to escape the flames. They were fleeing with what few possessions they could gather; some were pulling carts, others had bundles slung over their shoulders.

Hysteria swept over the crowd like a raging disease; it was uncontrollable. People were oblivious to one another. Their primary concern was survival for themselves and their fortunes, no matter how meager. A car, filled to capacity with household goods, slowly emerged from a smoke-filled alley. With the cost of fuel being so exorbitant, the family was having to push the vehicle from the advancing flames, barely able to squeeze through the masses of people.

The street by the market was strewn with bodies, each in its private pool of blood. One young girl wailed over the loss of her mother, who lay face down in the gutter, her neck broken and her face shredded beyond recognition by shrapnel. Paper money from the market whipped along the sidewalks—none dared take time to retrieve it. I stood staring at two women who had been hit by flying pieces of white-hot shrapnel. The metal had mercilessly torn into their smooth brown skin, exposing now a network of useless veins, muscles and tendons. It looked more like the bionic stuffing of a robot than the flesh of a human arm. Blood poured from their gaping wounds.

A small boy with tears streaming down his face cradled his mother's head in his arms. She still showed signs of life. I wanted to help her. What can I do? I thought to myself. Within a few minutes, DeAnn and I were the only ones left in the market area, except for the dead and wounded. Everyone else had fled. Standing at the foot of a stairway, I was horrified to see more than twenty people who lay mangled on what was left of the stairs. When the first shell landed, they all raced up the stairway to take cover. The next shell landed on the stairway, blowing parts of bodies fifty feet away.

"Come here!" DeAnn yelled. "Two fellows are crying for help!" I quickly made my way over to where she was standing, stepping over the body of a cyclo driver who had been blown off his bike. He had a huge puncture in the side of his chest. He was dead.

"They're over there," she pointed to two young men about twenty years of age. They were lying next to the curb with hands clasped and lifted in the air, pleading for help. One looked like he had a severe leg injury. The expressions on their faces were heartbreaking.

"What can we do?" I cried. I ran out into the main street and tried to get help. But no one would stop. Everyone was panic-stricken. I tried to stop several taxis that sped by, but they wouldn't even slow down.

"Why doesn't anyone help?" I grumbled under my breath. Finally I chased down a three-wheel taxi and muscled the driver to the side of the road. He tried to drive away so I took his keys and had DeAnn watch him. Then I hurried to the curb and picked up the young man with the leg wound. He had a large gash just below the knee. When I raised him in my arms the injured portion of his leg fell dangling by a strip of skin and muscle. The bone was splintered terribly. I put him back down and tried to hold on to his leg. Blood was spurting all over me. I finally managed to get him into the back of the taxi.

DeAnn helped the other fellow who wasn't hurt so badly. His buttocks had been ripped open, but he held the lacerated portion tightly to keep it from bleeding.

I gave the driver his keys. "Hurry!" I spoke firmly. "Take them to the hospital. Go quickly!" But he didn't budge. He just sat there holding out his hand.

"He wants money," DeAnn yelled from the other side of the

110

taxi.

"Money?" I exclaimed in disbelief and disgust. I shouted in Cambodian for him to go, but he still didn't move. Impatiently reaching into my pocket, I grabbed a wad of *riel* and slapped the bills into his hand.

"Now go!" I said, gritting my teeth. I stood baffled, shaking my head, as I watched the taxi roll out of sight.

"How could he be so hard-hearted?" I mumbled as my insides quivered. The look on DeAnn's face expressed the same bewilderment. By this time reporters had arrived on the scene. They were running around taking pictures of the victims and getting interviews from families who had fled the flames. We saw one of the reporters who had covered our crusade and hurried across the street to greet him.

"Man, did you get hit?" he asked, noticing the blood on my pants.

"No. We've been helping some of the wounded."

We followed him down a dirt alley towards the fire. It had already leveled nearly a square mile of homes and was still raging out of control. We could hear screams and death cries as we neared the devouring flames. A delirious man was fighting to break the grips of several who were trying to hold him back from running into the flames. He screamed and kicked as if someone were torturing him.

While tending to duties at the market that morning, his home had been shelled and was quickly eaten up by the relentless blaze. Now it was a smoldering ruin. He had lost his wife and three children. Exhausted with grief, he fell to the ground in a heap, sobbing uncontrollably.

"Father! Father!" a voice strained above the tumult. "We're all right!" A young boy about thirteen squirmed his way through the crowd, falling in the dust beside his father. Shouts of joy, tears, and explanations followed in the next few seconds. Then three other figures emerged from the smoke. The father scrambled to his feet to embrace his wife, daughter and tiny infant.

The wife and children had been visiting a friend when the shells

111

bombarded their own home. They had escaped the danger of flying shrapnel by huddling into a makeshift bunker at their friend's house. When the flames finally threatened their security, they were forced to vacate even the home of their friend, and had since been searching for their father. For the first time during the holocaust our eyes streamed with tears.

"What a story!" our reporter friend commented as we interpreted to him the conversations we'd overheard among the family members.

We looked at the smoke-filled sky; the sun looked cruel, a blood-red orb shining through the black vapor. The happiness of this one family seemed minute compared with the agony of hundreds whose loved ones had been blasted into eternity.

"I wish all the casualties could have such a happy ending," DeAnn added in a somber tone.

"Come," I motioned. "We've seen enough; let's go home."

We weaved our way through the masses of humanity who were carrying the only possessions they had left in the world. Where did they have to go? What would they do? Would they become more statistics in the spiraling number of refugees? Later we learned the catastrophe had left ten thousand homeless. The hungry flames had incinerated more than two hundred civilians, to say nothing of the dead and wounded from the shelling itself. This was by far Phnom Penh's worst disaster of the entire war. Reporters spoke of it as the Gotterdammerung. It was a victory for the Khmer Rouge.

When we pulled into our driveway, Thay, Sam-Oeurn, and several others raced out to meet us.

"Thank God, you're all right," Thay said emotionally. "We thought your house was included in the shelling. What's that?" he asked, pointing to my clothes. "You've got blood all over you. What happened?"

As we walked the cycle up the driveway, I began recounting the incident. But when I told about the taxi driver, a burning sense of indignation swept over me once again. I found myself choked with anger.

"Many Cambodians are like that," Thay explained.

"Buddhism has instilled in them a lack of concern for death. They believe the victims earned their fate because of sin or bad Karma that they accumulated in their past lives. They will be reincarnated into another form of life, they think. They're taught to suppress emotion and desire."

"Yes, but I don't see how anyone could be so callous and insensitive. That fellow would have let those boys bleed to death without batting an eye." As those critical words flowed from my lips, I felt a deep conviction rise within me. An inner voice caught me unexpected:

> Is the body of so much more value than the soul? You condemn the taxi driver and others; they would have left those boys for dead. But what about the millions who are left to perish eternally? What of Christ's command: "Go ye into all the world, and preach the gospel to every creature."? (Mark 16:15, KJV)

Those words continued to ring in my ears the rest of the evening. The light of this revelation exposed my own nakedness—my own callous indifference to the dying souls of men. Oh sure, I was preaching the gospel—probably more than many others were. But not from an urgency, not from a consuming burden that a soul might slip into eternity without hearing the message of Christ. It's hard to define what my motivation actually was; but whatever it was, I knew then that I was seriously lacking. I hadn't come to Cambodia to fulfill our Lord's command among the Khmer people. The Great Commission was the least of my concerns. I was more concerned about *me* than them. I wanted God's will for *my life*.

I saw myself as selfish as that taxi driver—maybe more so, in light of the eternal implications. I thought of my Christian friends back in the States and the body of Christ as a whole. While we were busily though profitably occupied, more than half the world was dying without God and without hope—never tasting of Calvary's love. While we were busy trying to find the more perfect way, Jesus, who is the way, was left unknown to the greater masses of the world. Did we believe that He and He alone is "the way, the

113

truth, and the life," and that "no one comes to the Father" except through Him?

Suddenly the judgment seat of Christ loomed clearly before me. At the same time I felt a God-inspired determination well up within me. It seemed I was cleansed and given a fresh perspective. The war threat and every other concern rolled off my shoulders, and I received the yoke of Jesus and the Great Commission. This proved to be a great turning point in our ministry.

Early the next morning I was surprised to find Thay waiting to see me as I walked down the stairs of our house. With him was Oum Panaan—a tall, slender man in his forties who had known the Lord for about a month. A friend of his, a major in the army, had encouraged him to come to one of our meetings. Afterwards, Oum Panaan came forward to give his life to Jesus. He and Thay both greeted me with smiling faces.

"Good morning," I said. "What are you doing here so early?"

"Panaan wants you to go with us to his home," Thay responded. "His house is located in the neighborhood that burned to the ground yesterday."

My eyes quickly glanced at Panaan's still-smiling face. "I'm sorry to hear that. How's your family? Are they all right?"

He nodded, but before he could say anything Thay interjected, "Oh, they're fine! That's why he wants us to go with him. He said God miraculously preserved his home and family. I want to see for myself." The gleam in Panaan's eyes confirmed what Thay had said.

"All right, but first let me call DeAnn. I'm sure she'll want to go too."

As we made our way to the scene of the holocaust, I could tell by Panaan's rapid strides that he was eager to show us something. My curiosity grew more intense. When we passed the market area I stopped and relived the horror of the day before. Now, the market was busy as if nothing had happened. No one seemed afraid or concerned that yesterday's events might be repeated. Life must go on, I said to myself.

"Come along," Thay motioned. We walked into the

neighborhood where thousands of homes had been leveled by the raging fire. A well-beaten path took us to the northern end of the demolished area. I couldn't believe what lay before me. As far as the eye could see it looked like a smoldering wasteland. Heaps of smoking rubble were everywhere. Crumpled tin roofing lay twisted on top of the collapsed dwellings. The area was dotted with the charred stumps of palm and coconut trees. Hundreds of people were rummaging in the ashen debris searching for their possessions and loved ones.

I stood still for a moment, cringing inside as I viewed a sobbing man dig the remains of his wife and children out of the ashes. I couldn't bear to watch; we quickly moved on. We worked our way towards the middle of the ravaged area. Our shoes were covered with black soot. Then we stopped.

"There's my home," Panaan pointed to a wooden two-level structure on stilts a few hundred yards ahead of us.

I was astonished! All the matchbox dwellings that once bordered Panaan's home were now reduced to powdery ash heaps. But his house stood untouched in the midst of all the rubble, as if it had been divinely protected.

"God covered us with His great hands," he explained as we neared his home. "When the shells began to land around us, we raced inside to take shelter. Between each explosion we could hear screaming and the crackling of what sounded like fire. Finally the shelling stopped, but we were scared to go outside for fear more artillery was on its way. We waited a long time before venturing out to see what had happened. But then we found we were really in trouble. Hoarded fuel supplies had erupted into flames during the shelling, and we were engulfed in a sea of fire. I raced around and around our house, trying to find a way of escape, but it was too late. Homes were already collapsing as the fire in its fury stormed on."

Panaan's eyes misted with tears as he continued. "The heat and smoke were unbearable, forcing us back inside. I knew it was all over for us. We had no chance to survive. We hunched up tightly together in a trench I had dug under our house. My children were

115

screaming with fright. My wife gripped my hand, asking me to pray. It was then that I remembered the story in the Bible of those three men in the furnace. God protected them, I thought to myself. 'Oh Father,' I prayed, 'in Jesus' name please preserve our lives. Save us Lord!' ''

Thay and I gazed at the destruction all around us while we listened to this amazing story.

''I don't know how long we lay crunched up in that hole,'' he said, shaking his head. ''It seemed like a long time. I tried to encourage the children by singing choruses. It helped a little. Then suddenly we heard voices and people walking around outside. I climbed out of the hole and could hardly believe my eyes. Black smoking ruins lay everywhere. People were already digging frantically in the wreckage. Ours was the only home left standing as far as the eye could see. My heart was filled with joy and sadness as my family joined me. We had been ridiculed for our faith in Jesus. But now, different ones walked up to us, pointing at our house. ''Why is yours left standing?' they questioned. I explained how I prayed to God, and that it was His mercy through Jesus that had saved our lives and our home.''

Panaan stayed at his house as we made our way back through the wreckage. As we turned around to see Panaan and his family waving goodbye, I stood still for a moment, pondering this incredible monument to God's grace. When I saw his home sitting like Noah's ark in the midst of all the destruction, an inner peace assured me that our future was in God's hands. From that day on, I never feared for my life again.

CHAPTER 9

Kong's Gift of Power

Three weeks had passed since the bombing. The dark sky was just beginning to give way to the sun's dawning light. I had been wide awake for probably an hour and as I lay in bed, my thoughts were interspersed with prayers of concern for the work. It was growing and beginning to weigh heavily upon my heart. I had never carried so much responsibility. We had been baptizing as many as twenty or more each week, but there was no way I could give proper attention to so many. I had tried, but soon came to realize I was spread too thin in ineffective activity. More and more I was having to withdraw from the front lines and channel my energies into cultivating leadership. I had no books to read or methods to follow. I was having to learn to rest in Jesus, depend upon the leading of the Holy Spirit, and stay saturated with the word of God. In order to cultivate leadership, I was having to fertilize my own spiritual life and create a disciplined life style that could serve as an example.

Through prayer and meditation in the Scriptures, I had been inspired to design a Bible-reading plan. It arose from a personal need to have a daily tie to the Scriptures. With several meetings a day, I ran out of "canned" messages in a hurry. I was forced to live in the word, and as Paul would say, "be a living epistle."

My Bible readings increased from once to three times daily, covering a total of nine chapters throughout the Bible. This plan enabled me to cover the New Testament more than four times a year, and the Old Testament more than twice. By meditating on specific Scriptures three times each day, my mind was more alert and open to hear God speak through His word. Each reading offered variety and many times the Holy Spirit would breathe revelation into the various chapters, weaving them into a beautiful theme. More than ever before, the word of God was coming alive. After finishing one reading, I could scarcely wait for my next one to find what God would say. Before long, everyone was following the plan, even the new believers. Thay called it his "breakfast, lunch and dinner" for his spirit. To me, it was simply my DBR (Daily Bible Reading). Ultimately, the reading plan proved to be one of the primary instruments the Lord used to channel the revival into the word of God, giving it positive direction.

We also began holding a prayer meeting every morning from seven to eight o'clock. At first, just a few attended, but before long, the elders from the different works we had established around the city began coming. Some rode their bicycles ten miles every day. We met in a room on the top floor of our building. There were no chairs, just thin grass mats on the floor. As we entered the room, each of us removed our sandals and sat reverently, praying alone. For over thirty minutes, every thought and word was directed to God. Together we prayed and sang in the Spirit until unity reigned among us, then a time of spontaneous sharing would follow. Some would testify how God had spoken to them through their morning Bible readings. We would part, refreshed and ready to meet the day.

Before long every one of our key workers, men and women alike, were faithful to the morning prayer meeting—everyone, that is, except Kong. He had withdrawn almost completely from the ministry.

Kong's family had seemed really happy since moving from the building into the house with us. Now they had more space than just a single room, and they seemed to enjoy their work. They took care of the yard, cleaned the house, and helped with the orphans. But Kong had come from a very conservative evangelical background. When it came to healings, deliverances, and people being baptized with the Holy Spirit, he was skeptical. "These experiences are not for us today," he had been taught. "They were only for the early church to get things started, but today we don't need them. We have the Bible—that's enough. If these things happen now, it's probably of the devil." Kong couldn't deny the miracles that had taken place, so he searched for an explanation. He had even been warned by other Christians that we used spiritism. My talks with him had not altered his indifference.

On rare occasions Kong would come around the building, but he seemed to resent Thay, Sam-Oeurn, and the other workers who strongly emphasized the power of God. We tried to encourage him by giving him translation work to do, hoping he would feel a part of the ministry. But his attitude remained cold. We asked his wife, San, if she would begin holding a women's meeting once a week. She reluctantly agreed, feeling unqualified.

As I lay in bed that morning I was questioning to myself, Were we right to have asked her to do this? Maybe we're trying too hard to make them feel accepted. Should we just let them go? But what would they do? "Oh, Lord," I prayed, "give us wisdom and guide us. I'm weary of the hassle."

My thoughts were interrupted by the chirping of birds nested in the coconut tree outside our window. Glancing at my watch, it read a quarter past five. I eased quietly out of bed so I wouldn't wake DeAnn and sat in a cushioned bamboo chair to begin my morning Bible reading. I had read only a few verses, when suddenly I was startled by a loud racket downstairs.

"What's that?" DeAnn jumped, awakened by the noise. "It sounds like someone yelling, but who could it be at this hour of the morning?" I questioned.

Seconds later, there was a loud rap on our door. I scrambled out of my chair to see who it was.

"Oh, brother!" Kong panted breathlessly, pointing downstairs. "It's my wife! Come quickly!"

I took a moment to grab a towel and wrap it around my loins, sarong style. My mind raced, trying to guess what could be wrong, as I slid into my thongs and flip-flopped hurriedly after Kong. I supposed his wife was near death or something, judging by his haste and anxiety. I could hear DeAnn's footsteps on the stairway behind us.

"What's going on?" she demanded.

"I don't know—guess we'll find out in a few minutes."

When we reached the doorway to their quarters, Kong stepped aside and motioned for me to enter. DeAnn peered over my shoulder to see San kneeling at a chair beside their bed. Her tiny frame trembled as her voice resounded in an unknown tongue. San had always been so shy and quiet, it was hard to believe that strong voice was hers. With her hands raised and face beaming, it reminded me of what Sam-Oeurn looked like when he was baptized with the Holy Spirit.

"Wow!" DeAnn whispered. "Praise God!"

I looked over my shoulder at her and we laughed together. "Hallelujah!"

Kong stared at his wife in amazement. My mind shifted gears when I saw his face and realized he was probably doubtful about her experience.

"Oh, Brother Todd," he began, when he saw I was looking at him, "I must tell you something." We stepped quietly into the hallway. His brown face wrinkled thoughtfully and he batted his eyes, fighting back tears that sought release.

"I have to confess and repent," he said. Then he nervously gripped my arm. "I have thought and said evil things about you and the others. I did not believe these experiences were from God. But now I know they must be. Since you asked my wife to begin holding meetings for the women, she has been reading her Bible and praying for God to help her. This morning she was up early peeling fruit when suddenly she dropped what she was doing and hurried to our room with a burdened look on her face. I asked her what was wrong, but she said nothing; she just knelt and prayed. All of a sudden she began to shake and speak in that strange language. I know she didn't believe in this experience either but now look at her! God has given her His Spirit so she can do His work."

He wiped tears from his eyes as he made his confession. I

120

realized God was doing more than baptizing San with the Holy Spirit; He was answering our prayers by resolving a matter that had developed into a major concern. He was changing Kong's heart.

"Please pray for me," he added, "so that I, too, will receive this gift. I want to be used by God."

I was deeply touched by the appeal of this humbled man who was more than twice my age. I explained to him that he should cleanse his heart completely and ask forgiveness from Thay, Sam-Oeurn and the other believers whom he had offended.

"If you will do this," I suggested, "then I believe God will baptize you with the Holy Spirit and use you in a mighty way."

It didn't take long for him to establish his change of heart with the rest of the elders. In the prayer meeting that same morning Kong shared with everyone about San's experience, and how it had convinced him of God's power.

"I want you all to forgive me," he begged earnestly. "I want to do God's will and receive everything He has for me." After hearing his testimony, several others confessed a lack of power in their lives and expressed a hunger for more of God's Spirit. Kong had not only restored fellowship, but was already being used to challenge the other leaders.

Convinced of his need to be baptized with the Holy Spirit, Kong prayed diligently and searched the Scriptures about the subject. One afternoon he stopped me as I was leaving my office.

"Brother Todd," he said with a peaceful smile on his face, "do you have a moment? I would like to talk with you."

"Sure," I responded. "Come on in." He sat down in a chair with my desk between us.

"Todd, ever since San received the gift of the Holy Spirit, she hasn't been the same. She's happy and bold, and often prays in that strange language. Can you explain to me about this? I'm confused. It's like I don't even know her!"

"I'm not surprised," I said, reassuring him, "especially in her case. She really received a full dose." I opened my Bible and scooted my chair around to where he was sitting. "You remember how the disciples acted before they were baptized with the Holy

Spirit? When Jesus was around, they were full of faith and power; when they were separated from Him, however, they were abysmal failures. Do you know why it was like this?''

"No," he answered, shrugging his shoulders.

"They failed when Jesus was not around," I explained, "because they depended upon His physical presence to give them power. Peter told Jesus, 'I'll never leave you nor forsake you.' But when they took his Lord away, he was fearful and powerless. He cursed his Savior and even denied Him three times. After the day of Pentecost, however, he was no longer a coward. He stood, full of the Holy Spirit, and ministered with power and boldness before the multitudes. He was a changed man.''

I could tell by the glimmer in Kong's eyes that my words were sinking in. Picking up my Bible, I flipped the pages to the Gospel of John and continued.

"You see, Kong, Jesus warned His disciples that one day He was going to leave them and they could not go with Him. When they heard these words, sorrow filled their hearts. 'It is to your advantage that I go away,' He explained, 'for if I do not go away, the Helper (the Holy Spirit) shall not come to you; but if I go, I will send Him to you.' But when He was crucified they all got discouraged and gave up. They left their Master in His tomb and returned to their old fishing jobs.''

Kong nodded thoughtfully, absorbing everything I said.

"Thank God, it didn't end there!" I exclaimed, turning to Acts, chapter 1. "Jesus arose and appeared to as many as five hundred over a period of forty days. Just before he ascended to the Father, He gave them His last command: 'Stay in Jerusalem and wait for the promise of the Father'—the baptism of the Holy Spirit. It wasn't that they weren't saved; they were saved, but they were weak and fearful; they needed boldness. 'You shall receive power,' He told them, 'when the Holy Spirit has come upon you; and you shall be My witnesses. . . .' This is not a command to go witness, as many believe," I explained. "It is a promise that you will receive power. In Acts 19, the Apostle Paul met some disciples who were trying to witness about Jesus. His first question to them was, 'Have you received the Holy Spirit since you believed?' ''

I closed my Bible and looked at Kong. "I believe the Lord is asking you and every believer that same question. After Pentecost, when the disciples were endued with power, they turned the world upside down. The same thing can happen in Cambodia!"

Kong's serious expression broke into an excited smile. "That would be wonderful!" he bubbled with enthusiasm. "How can I have this experience?"

I quickly opened my Bible again to Luke 11:9-13. Pointing to the passage, I asked Kong to read it.

His eyes were fastened to the page for several moments. "But I've done that; I've asked the Lord. I've prayed, fasted, repented of my sins; what else can I do?"

"It's a gift," I answered. "You can't earn it. You simply receive it. There's no special way either. The Book of Acts records many people being baptized with the Holy Spirit. Some had hands laid upon them (8:14-24; 19:1-6). Others received while praying (2:1-4) or listening to the preaching of the gospel (10:44-48)."

He looked puzzled. I quickly jotted down a list of Scriptures for him to read.

"Here, Kong. Study these passages tonight. Don't worry," I assured him patting his shoulder, "the Bible says, 'Blessed are they that hunger and thirst after righteousness: for they shall be filled.' When you're ready, God will fill you to overflowing."

Folding the paper, he placed the list of Scriptures between the worn pages of his Bible. "Thank you, brother," he said, now encouraged. "I must go now." With that, he smiled and we walked together to the door. As I watched him descend the staggered stairway, I wondered whether I should have prayed for him to receive right then. But I had felt checked; it just didn't seem to be the right time. As it turned out, I was glad we waited.

The next morning DeAnn and I were up before the sun. Silencing the alarm, we rolled out of bed, donned our gym clothes, and scurried down the stairs to jog a mile before breakfast. San was already up boiling water to mix with the babies' powdered milk formula. When she saw us, she lit up with excitement. I rummaged through our cupboard, only half listening to the Cambodian words that spilled from her lips. Then I heard her clearly say her husband's name and something about the Holy Spirit.

"What was that you said?" I interrupted her. "Please speak slowly!"

"Kong," she laughed, pointing toward their room, her eyes lit with excitement. "Last night he was filled with the Holy Spirit. He woke up speaking in tongues."

Then I heard a voice coming from their room. Glancing down the hallway, I saw a light appear. Kong emerged from the dark corridor with a kereosene lamp in hand. His broad grin exposed a mouthful of shining teeth.

"Praise the Lord, Brother Todd! Did San tell you what happened?"

"Yes, but just briefly. Tell us more about it."

"Last night she and I went over those Scriptures you gave me," he began, still smiling. "They helped me to understand well. Afterwards, we prayed that I might be filled with the Holy Spirit. We prayed for a long time, but nothing happened. I thought maybe I wasn't ready or something. Finally, I grew discouraged and went to bed. I slept, but San continued to pray. The next thing I knew I was awakened by a torrent of words in a language I didn't know."

I looked at San's beaming face as she listened to her husband. He continued, "Then I found, to my amazement, it was me who was speaking! I felt I was saying things to God I couldn't find words to express before. A warm feeling rushed through me. Several moments passed before I realized what had actually happened; the Lord Jesus had baptized me with His Spirit."

Kong was radiant with new life as he told of his fresh experience. But I think DeAnn and I were more excited than he was, as we hugged Kong and San and then hugged each other. God had now given us a nucleus of leaders that were empowered by His Holy Spirit. We were amazed at how He had dealt with each one of them sovereignly. Actually, we preferred it this way. We didn't want them becoming too attached or dependent upon us. We never knew when we might have to leave their country.

Now that Kong and his wife were equipped with the power of the Holy Spirit, they wasted no time putting their divine energies into operation. But their new experiences were contested by a small group of Christians who had been strongly influenced by the same missionaries who were giving me opposition. Kong was even called to a meeting where they challenged his views and advised him not to associate with our workers. But no amount of human argument could persuade him against God's power. He gave a powerful witness of his own experience of receiving the Holy Spirit. They couldn't believe it was the same man they had known before. He appealed to them with authority and boldness, leaving them dumbfounded. "What I knew before in theory," he declared, "I know now as reality."

From that time on, Kong's life was a walking testimony. Everywhere he went, he witnessed to his faith, leaving the seeds of the gospel. He cultivated faithfulness among the elders, rarely missing a service or prayer meeting.

His new zeal caused us some problems, however, not in the area of ministry, but in the neglect of the family's practical duties around the house and with the orphans. At first, DeAnn and I tried to take up the slack but soon found there was more work than we had time or strength for. We were afraid to say anything, thinking it might discourage them or hinder their spiritual growth. Instead, we hoped the Lord would minister the needed reprimand.

One day they returned from an evangelism outing and found us hard at work scrubbing the floors, exterminating cockroaches, burning stacks of trash, and doctoring boils that had spread to all the babies because of unsanitary conditions. They seemed to feel since they had received the Holy Spirit, such mundane tasks were unimportant. But their thinking quickly changed. They were ashamed to see us laboring over their chores, and they tried to slip in the house unobtrusively to avoid possible confrontation. The next day they were diligently tending to their duties with renewed vigor.

Without our saying a word, Kong felt thoroughly chastened. But a few days later I did offer him some encouragement. He was sitting on the porch under the shade of a coconut tree, poking wicks in a kerosene cook stove. His hands were black with carbon soot. The expression on his face read, "What am I doing here? I should be out preaching the gospel!" His eyes were fixed on his work as I walked up the driveway.

"Hi, Kong!" I greeted him. Sitting down beside him, I picked up a rod and began swabbing the holes for the new wicks in another stove. He didn't say anything, so I took the initiative once again.

"I was thinking about something really interesting today: Do you remember the story of Stephen in the Book of Acts?"

He continued working but nodded his head to let me know he was listening.

"Because he was a man full of faith and of the Holy Spirit, he was chosen along with six others to serve food to the widows, waiting on their tables. That doesn't sound like a very spiritual job, does it?"

He looked up and smiled. "Yes, I know. I'm sorry we ignored our duties. We were wrong. The Lord spoke to me and said, 'If you're careless in little, how can I give you more work to be faithful with?' We will try to do our best from now on."

"But that doesn't mean you can't preach the gospel," I quickly added. "If you read on in that same chapter, you find that after Stephen finished his duties, he went out preaching the gospel, performing signs and wonders among the people. The religious leaders tried to argue with him, but they couldn't cope with his wisdom and the Spirit with which he spoke. Finally, they had to stone him to shut him up."

I gently slapped Kong on the back, "I believe you can be used in the same way." Then jokingly added, "But I'll pray the Lord will protect you from flying stones."

We laughed together and finished loading the stoves with new wicks. Though the tension was eased between us, I still sensed a note of despondency in him, since his aspirations for the ministry were frustrated by work. My encouragement seemed no more than wishful thinking. But little did either of us realize how prophetic

126

my words were going to be.

It was a Sunday, several days later. Our auditorium was packed; more people were standing outside on the balcony. This was usually our largest meeting of the week. The room could only hold about three hundred people, and that was if we packed them in like sardines. We had tried to find a larger facility, but none were available at a price we could afford. Instead, we had to increase the number of services.

It was Cambodian custom for the women to sit on one side and the men on the other. This was strange to me at first, but I got used to it. "That's the way they did it in New Testament days," Thay explained.

The meetings would begin with spontaneous singing, interspersed with testimonies. We were always sensitive to see what direction the Holy Spirit was leading the service. There were occasions when Thay and I would have to lay aside the messages we had prepared because they didn't always flow with the leading of the Holy Spirit. If we went ahead and preached them, it would be like swimming against the current; not only would it tire us, but our listeners would grow weary. But usually we found that the messages we had planned beautifully harmonized with the spirit of the meeting.

On this particular morning, I had planned to minister on Ezra and the rebuilding of the temple in troublesome times. I was going to parallel this story with the way God was enabling us to establish His kingdom in a country being torn by war.

Thay stood to minister first. Without knowing what I was planning to talk about, he centered his message on Nehemiah and the rebuilding of the wall. My ears tingled as I listened to his words. God was truly ordering our meeting.

"Opposition was so great," he exhorted, "that Nehemiah's men had to work on the wall with one hand while keeping a weapon ready in the other. We are in a spiritual warfare and the word of God is the sword of the Spirit. No matter what we do, we must always be prepared for an attack from the enemy of our souls."

Our teachings fit like a hand in a glove. Just as the Bible records

127

how Nehemiah prepared the way for Ezra, so Thay's message had prepared the way for mine. After the service, Thay and I looked at one another and grinned confidently, knowing the Holy Spirit had been at work behind the scenes. Every day a handful of new converts came to accept the Lord.

After praying with those who had come forward for salvation or special needs, I hurried to my office to change clothes. We were having a baptism of twenty-six new believers on the roof of our building.

As I started up the stairs a young man named Narein stopped me. He was a new believer who had been baptized the week before. "Sir! Please, can I talk with you for a moment?"

"Sure." He followed me to my office. "What can I do for you?" I asked, closing the door behind us.

"Oh, I've been so happy since Jesus entered my life," Narein said exuberantly. "It seems no matter what I do, my mind is on Him always; I have so much peace. But it is still very hard for my family. My father cannot find work and it's so difficult for us to live. Every day, my parents burn incense to the spirits and pray to Buddha's image. I try to tell them about Jesus and ask them to come with me to class, but they refuse to come and I don't know enough to explain so they understand clearly. I need someone to come to my home with me, someone who can share Jesus with them."

Immediately my mind flashed to Kong.

"Wait here," I said, motioning for him to sit down. "I'll be right back." I raced up the stairs and found Kong, still seated in the auditorium talking with several young ladies.

"Excuse me, Kong, can you come down to my office for a minute?" He quickly ended his conversation and followed me to the stairs. On the way down I explained Narein's situation.

"How would you like to go with him to his home and share Jesus with his family?"

Kong's eyes brightened at the opportunity. "Yes, I'll go. Where is he?"

"He's waiting in my office," I answered. "You can go with

128

him right now if you're free." Kong was encouraged by the challenge, and the two left promptly. I ran upstairs to join the others who were waiting.

"Are you ready to begin?" I asked Sam-Oeurn, who was giving instruction on the significance of baptism.

"Almost finished, brother" he nodded. "The tank is not quite full yet."

Our building was equipped with a large square cistern that was ideal for this purpose. The tank sat next to the prayer room and had an overhanging canopy that served as a shield from the hot sun. Except for the small enclosed area, the rest of the roof was spacious with concrete railing around the sides. Potted bushes and flowering trees lined the railing, providing a fragrant, gardenlike atmosphere, set four stories in the sky. One could see for miles in any direction, since there were few buildings as tall as ours. There was one building to the north of us, however, where it seemed half the neighborhood gathered to gaze at our ceremony. They pointed in our direction and laughed among themselves. We must have seemed crazy to them, giving people baths once a week with their clothes on!

The weekly baptismal was always a festive occasion, full of praise and rejoicing. All the faithful believers crowded around to watch as one by one the new converts identified themselves with our Lord's death and resurrection. Immediately after being raised from the water, they partook of the Lord's supper, while the others welcomed them into God's kingdom with clapping and singing. Watching each new believer take his first steps in Christ was thrilling. Every week I relived that fresh excitement I had experienced when Jesus became Lord of my life.

Following the baptismal, DeAnn and I returned to our house. Sundays were usually set aside as our day of fasting, so we either went for a swim at a nearby sports club to cool off, or just rested and caught up on some reading. On this particular Sunday, we decided to relax around the house and read. I was absorbed in *Perelandra*, a fiction book by C.S. Lewis, until late in the afternoon. Then I heard the latch on our gate clang as someone entered.

"Who's there?" I asked DeAnn, who was sitting near the window.

"It's Kong. He's back from Narein's."

"Let's get down and find out what happened." We hurried downstairs and greeted him as he walked his bike up the drive.

"Hey, Kong, how did it go?" I called to him. He lowered the kickstand and locked his bike to a concrete support.

"Oh, it went well," he said smiling. "They've asked me to come back next week. They're inviting their friends and relatives."

"Wow! That's great. Tell us what happened."

"When we arrived at Narein's home, I was surprised," Kong reported. "The house was huge, with two floors and a spacious porch and balcony. He told me his father had once been a wealthy man, owning fruit groves, salt mines, and many other things. But now all his land is in the areas occupied by the Communists. He had not had work for several years."

"How do they live?" I interrupted.

"Mostly by selling their valuable possessions," Kong explained. "Narein led me up the polished wooden steps, across the balcony, and inside their living area. He told me they had sold all their nice furniture; only a ragged sofa and a few wooden chairs were left to sit on. The rest of the house looked empty, except for the room where they kept their spirit house. It was filled with images of Buddha and other idols. Divination charts and Buddhist pictures lined the walls. He told me his parents were very religious. They feared evil spirits and offered food and incense to the idols in the spirit house before every meal."

"Did you get to meet with them?" I probed.

"Yes. Narein called for his parents and the other members of his family. He introduced me as one of his Bible teachers and said I had come to explain to them about Jesus. I was surprised by how well they received me. They even fixed me a cold drink. Then we all sat down and for the next two hours I shared with them the gospel. I gave them my testimony and they listened closely as I told them about my life before I found Jesus—how I searched for truth in Buddhism, lived in the fear of evil spirits, and wasted all my money on alcohol and gambling.''

As I listened I could scarcely imagine Kong having been an alcoholic. He exuded enthusiasm as he related the experience.

"Then I explained how I found the life I had been seeking in Jesus, and how He had not only forgiven my sins, but set me free from the power of evil spirits. I told them I don't worship idols or evil spirits any more; I worship the only true God and have received His salvation through Jesus. I felt the presence of the Holy Spirit as I talked with them. When I finished, they asked many questions and begged me to come back. If I agreed to return, they said, they would invite their friends and relatives to come and listen. So we decided on next Sunday afternoon."

"Praise the Lord!" exclaimed DeAnn. "That's wonderful! We'll fast and pray that God anoints you with power." I added my "amen" to her statement as we walked in the house together.

The following Sunday finally came and after our morning service, Kong returned to Narein to his home. Narein was bubbling with excitement. When they arrived at his house, instead of going upstairs as they had done before, they entered a large room on the ground floor that had once been used as the garage. Everyone stood and greeted Kong respectfully, as they would any religious teacher. Narein kept the children quiet outside, while his father, Chappeay, introduced Kong to the group. Nineteen of his friends and relatives had come to hear Kong speak. Everyone settled down quickly; there was a reverent silence except for the rythmical swaying of the ladies' palm leaf fans.

First, Kong simply told them what Jesus had done in his life. The idea of God being so personally interested in this man seemed to intrigue the people. At times they quietly chuckled as Kong related how God answered his prayers. Their amusement wasn't meant to mock, however, because their interest quickened as Kong's message deepened. From his personal testimony, the Holy Spirit introduced Jesus in a relaxed but firm manner.

"Jesus is the only man who had His coming foretold long before

131

He was born," Kong said to his listeners. "He's the only man who was born of a virgin and lived a sinless life; He's the only man who claimed to be God in the flesh."

Stating the credentials of Jesus Christ carried a certain authority and power. "He healed the sick, raised the dead, and cast out demons—proving that what He said was truth. He's the only man who offered His life as a sacrifice for sin, and then was raised from the dead to live forever. You can find the bones of Buddha and every other religious leader, but you'll never find the bones of Jesus; He has risen! He is Lord and He is Savior."

Narein had broken away from the children outside, leaving them to play by themselves. He silently stood in the shadow of the doorway, praying as he searched each face for a hint of acceptance of this good news.

"There is no other name under heaven," Kong continued, "that can give you salvation. At the name of Jesus, demons tremble. He has all authority over the works of Satan and His demons, and He gives His authority to those who trust and believe in His name. I don't fear evil spirits; I curse them in Jesus' name. Only Jesus can forgive your sins and give you power over the enemies of your soul."

"What must we do to have Jesus?" Chappeay asked, his face portraying the genuine cry of his heart. Others of the group nodded with serious interest.

"First," he replied, "you accept the salvation He has accomplished for you, believing He died for your sins. Then turn from your sin and witchcraft, and ask Him to be your Lord and Savior."

The atmosphere of inquiry was building Kong's enthusiasm. Their eagerness convinced him they were earnest in their response.

Kong asked if they would each kneel beside their chairs while he prayed with them. Without wasting a moment, everyone slipped quietly from their chairs to the floor. Being well versed in piety, they reverently folded their hands and bowed their heads while Kong prayed for each one individually. Narein crossed the room, joining Kong in praying God would open hearts to the spiritual

132

truths they had heard.

Suddenly, their senses were alerted by the smell of smoke. Chappeay looked up, sniffing the air, then jumped to his feet.

"What's that?" he cried. By this time his wife had been aroused by the threatening vapor.

"Something's burning!" she spoke out in fright.

"Up there," a friend pointed towards the ceiling. Smoke was seeping through the cracks between the boards of the floor above them. Narein dashed out the door with Chappeay right behind him. As they raced up the steps they could see smoke coming from the small room where they kept their witchcraft. They opened the door and stepped back until the smoke cleared enough to see what was on fire.

"Look!" cried Narein. There in the middle of the room, the spirit house was enveloped in flames. Chappeay rushed to the window, unlatched the shutters and flung them open. Then, picking up the stand to which the spirit house was attached, he heaved it and its contents out the window. Narein stuck his head outside in time to see the burning frame hit the dust. They stood still for a moment and watched the flames devour the remains of the idols and witchcraft. Then looking around the room, they marveled—nothing else had caught fire, though everything was highly flammable. Thoroughly persuaded that this fire had come from God, Chappeay hurried downstairs. Everyone gazed in astonishment at the blazing heap while he explained what happened.

"Is everything else all right?" Chappeay's wife interrupted him.

"Yes!" he said nervously. "The spirit house was all that was on fire. I believe God is confirming what *kruu* ("teacher") Kong said to us."

As Kong listened to Chappeay's words, he knew this was no freak accident—it was a direct act of God. He began to tremble as the Holy Spirit came upon him.

"Jesus is telling you," he thundered boldly, "that there is no harmony between His way and the devices of Satan. You cannot worship God and evil spirits at the same time. You must cleanse your hearts and your homes of all idols and witchcraft. They have to go if you want Jesus to be Lord of your lives.''

After Kong spoke, several hurried to their nearby homes and came running back, carrying spirit houses and armloads of idols and witchcraft. They even cut off their charms and devil strings, dumping everything into the flames.

Others looking on were encouraged to do the same. The small flaming heap soon became a bonfire.

That evening, Kong excitedly related to us all that had happened. I could hardly believe my ears. As I sat in my favorite cushioned chair, listening and marveling over the wonderful events, my eyes fell to my Bible open on the table beside me. I smiled, remembering the passage I had just read before Kong's arrival. Elijah had challenged the prophets of Baal, saying, ''The God who answers by fire, He is God'' (1 Kings 18:24).

CHAPTER 10

Sam-Oeurn Gains New Strength

Greater than a spirit house being consumed by fire was the miracle of lives that had been changed by the power of God. Every day Kong returned to Narein's house to hold a Bible study with the new believers. They continued to spread the news of the event until there wasn't enough room to hold the crowd. In a morning prayer meeting, Kong shared with us his concern about the matter and all the elders prayed with him that God would provide a larger meeting place.

That evening he stopped Thay and me as we were leaving the building.

"Something wonderful has happened!" he said, gasping for breath. Beads of perspiration dotted his brow. He had feverishly pumped his bicycle the full five miles from his meeting at Narein's house in order to catch us before going home. "A man has given us a building to be used as a meeting place for the church. His name is Maran. He was there the day God sent fire down upon the spirit house, and he has come every day since then."

"That's fantastic!" Thay exclaimed. "Where is the building located?"

Come, I will show you," Kong answered excitedly. "It's near Narein's home, on the corner. We've already decided what we'll call it—Solomon Church."

"Solomon Church?" I questioned. "Why that?"

"We read how fire came down from heaven when Solomon dedicated the temple in the Old Testament (2 Chron. 7); so we decided on that name because God did the same thing for this church.''

When we arrived at the site, I was amazed. The building was much nicer than I had expected. It was surrounded by a plush garden area with several palm trees, providing much shade. The structure itself was of plastered brick with a tin roof. By removing one wall, the room could seat more than a hundred people. The only problem was the open sewer that ran parallel to the main window. The smell was putrid, to say nothing of the droves of mosquitoes that bred and swarmed in the green slime. But it didn't seem to mar Kong's impression of the grounds at all. He was too busy thanking God for the provision to worry about such a minor problem.

The next morning we hired a carpenter named Horn to build benches and make the necessary alterations in the structure. Though in his fifties, he didn't look over thirty years old; his body was trim and muscular. During lunch break one afternoon, he read Sam-Oeurn's testimony posted on a bulletin board near the entry way to the church. Work had to wait, as Horn felt the need to find Sam-Oeurn and talk to him. They spent the rest of the siesta time talking about the Lord and before it was over, he had pledged his life to follow Jesus. Sam-Oeurn prayed with him, and he was never the same again.

The change in Horn's life was so immediate that the next morning he brought his three daughters, Sokly, Sokka, and Sokani, to attend the children's Bible class Youvannette had started at Maranatha Church. That afternoon when his wife came to pick up their daughters, she stopped to talk with us. She didn't know what to think about Horn's recent strange behavior.

"What has happened to him?" she questioned in a delighted tone. "He's so different; he's quit smoking and drinking, and doesn't waste our money on gambling anymore."

I listened as Sam-Oeurn explained to her about the new life in Jesus.

"I want to follow Jesus, too," she responded.

The following Sunday both Horn and his wife were baptized

136

new creatures in Christ.

Within a short time Sam-Oeurn and several others had to begin helping Youvannette with her children's classes. At first she started with just a handful meeting only once a day. But when the government schools began closing down for lack of funds, more and more children began to come. Those already attending started bringing their friends, until she had to begin another class in the afternoon. Soon she had four classes a day with as many as three hundred children divided up into age groups ranging from seven to fourteen. Her classes were limited to a Bible lesson, testimonies from the children, and lots of singing. Some of her younger students even learned to read and write just from their eagerness to study the Bible. The older ones formed groups and went around the neighborhood witnessing and passing out tracts. I had never seen such a serious bunch of kids.

One Sunday morning after the service, a man came forward for prayer. Thay noticed a wad of devil strings around his neck and waist. As usual, we explained that it was necessary for him to remove them before we could pray for him but he refused. Instead, he opened his mouth wide and pointed to a nasty scar on the side of his tongue.

"See this?" he boasted. "I did that!" He described how he had sliced his tongue open and sewed an idol into the middle of it. "It controls everything I say," he said, his face wrinkled with a devilish grin.

Now, I've seen everything, I thought to myself.

We didn't know what to do with him. He obviously intended to make a scene, so we asked him to go sit down. But rather than returning to his seat, he quickly rushed out the door. I figured that would be the last we'd see of him.

A while later, as we went downstairs to leave the building, we suddenly stopped in our tracks. There he was, cornered by three of Youvannette's twelve-year-old students. They had him boxed in between the building and a barbed wire fence. With open Bibles, they fired Scriptures at him one by one, revealing the error of his way. A look of astonishment, almost fear, spread over his face, as these young boys left him defenseless. We went on home, doubting they could dislodge the confidence he had in his fetishes. However, late that afternoon we returned to find he had not only given his heart to Jesus and cut off his devil strings, but after prayer he couldn't even feel the idol that he had sewn into his tongue. We were amazed and humbled. He was baptized in water, and every day he joined the young people as they went about spreading the gospel.

Sam-Oeurn's ministry along with Youvannette's classes became the heartbeat of Maranatha Church. Thay and I had backed off, placing the bulk of the responsibility into their hands. Sam-Oeurn's preaching was powerful, with people being saved and healed in nearly every meeting. But the evening prayer meeting was where he had the greatest impact. After the service, new converts and young believers met with him for instruction and prayer. He and Youvanette had an intimate contact with these believers—much more so than DeAnn and I could have had. We thought both of them were quite fulfilled in their work. But we were in for a rude awakening.

Late one evening DeAnn and I had stayed around after the service, waiting for the drizzle to stop so we could ride home without getting so wet. The rainy season was just beginning. Though the fighting was still heavy, it looked as if the government forces had resisted the seige of the Khmer Rouge, at least for another year. The Communists would have to wait until the next dry season before they could launch another offensive against the capital.

The door of my office was left open to allow the cool breeze to enter the room. I looked up and was startled to see Sam-Oeurn and Youvannette standing in the doorway. The solemn expressions on their faces let me know something was wrong.

"Don't just stand there," I said, surprised. "Come on in and sit down." They came in and sat down in the chairs in front of my desk, keeping their eyes glued to the floor. I was almost afraid to ask why they looked so troubled. I continued writing in my diary, hoping they would break the silence, but they just sat there staring at their feet. Finally, my curiosity got the best of me.

"Why do you guys look so sad?" I asked, closing my diary. "Tell me what's bothering you."

Youvannette looked up at Sam-Oeurn as tears welled in his eyes. Then his weeping turned into heavy sobs and his shoulders shook silently for several moments. Eventually, he calmed down enough to talk.

"Brother Todd," he said, still sniffling. "I don't know what to do!"

"Do about what?" I questioned eagerly.

"Thol and the others—they're jealous of me. Some of the ladies are jealous of Youvanette, too. You know how it is; when they first come to know Jesus, they're happy and hungry for God's words. They love to come to hear us teach and never miss a prayer meeting. But when they grow older in their Christian walk, some of them become envious and begin causing problems. They either stay around and breed strife, or fall away. Many of them have left and we've never seen them again. It makes us feel that we've failed. We're praying the Lord will send us away somewhere."

"Now listen," I spoke firmly, interrupting him. "You can't just run away from difficulty. All of us go through periods of depression where we feel like everything we touch is a failure. There are many times I've felt betrayed by others, and I know times where I, too, have failed. But that's no reason to quit. We have to forget what lies behind us, as Paul said, and keep looking ahead."

"That's just it," he said, pausing thoughtfully. "I don't know what to look forward to. I'm afraid my failures will be repeated."

"What you call failure may not be failure at all," I said, trying to encourage him. "Through man's eyes, the cross looked like a defeat; but through God's eyes it was a victory. Remember the parable of the sower? Most of the seed he scattered was wasted, landing on the rocks, in the road, and among the thorns. The seeds sprouted, but for various reasons, many of them died away. Only one-fourth of the seed landed on the good soil where it remained and bore fruit. Anything more than that, we should consider a bonus."

My words seemed to cheer them up a bit. Both of them lifted their heads and looked at me. I could tell they were hoping I would have more to say that would boost their spirits. I thought for a moment.

"I think I understand," DeAnn broke in. "The different ones who are envious of your position probably just want to minister like you do. Perhaps you should organize them into evangelizing teams and send them into the surrounding villages; that might help ease the tension. What do you think?" She looked at me for approval.

Sam-Oeurn and Youvannette exchanged glances, then both started talking excitedly at once. "That's what we were thinking, but we weren't sure if it was such a good idea." They laughed, embarrassed, then Youvanette let Sam-Oeurn continue.

"We could do like you, Brother Todd, just teach them to be preachers and teachers, then let them take over the groups. Maybe God will use us this way and move us out gradually."

They seemed thrilled at being able to see light at the end of their gloomy tunnel. We prayed together that God would encourage them and direct their steps.

They immediately set to work on organizing teams and practicing music. The next weekend they were out putting their plans into operation. They ministered in refugee camps, market areas, on the streets, or in neighborhoods near the homes of fellow believers. Their strategy was to draw a crowd through singing, then deliver a message with others testifying. Many listeners were compelled to turn from their fetishes and give their lives to the Lord Jesus Christ. On occasion they met strong opposition, but there were always a few who received their message openly and with gladness.

The success of these evangelism missions rekindled their joy and extinguished the flame of jealousy, almost. Three weeks later, it surfaced again into another problem.

One evening after dinner, we rode over to the building to pick up some kerosene. DeAnn snuggled up close to me on the motorbike since we were sharing a large poncho that was protecting us from the rain. It kept everything dry except our legs and feet. When we pulled into the drive we were surprised to find the garage door open and the lights on.

"Who's left this door open?" I grumbled to DeAnn, as we dismounted the bike. Since Sam-Oeurn and Youvannette lived in the building, we had given them strict orders to lock up everything after the evening prayer meeting.

As we pulled the bike out of the rain we startled Sam-Oeurn, who was tying a suitcase onto the back of Youvanette's cycle. She was standing next to him, holding extra rope.

"Hi!" we greeted them. "What are you guys doing?"

Youvannette was quiet and didn't look up. Sam-Oeurn fiddled with the ropes and barely turned around to acknowledge our presence. Obviously something was wrong. I flipped the kickstand down, worked my way out of the poncho and hung it up on a nail to dry.

"Are you going somewhere?" I asked, looking at their new blue suitcase fastened tightly on the back. They had received it as a gift at their wedding only a few months ago.

"I'm sorry, brother," Sam-Oeurn started, "but God has spoken to us, and we must leave tonight."

"Leave?" I countered. "What do you mean?" Youvannette clung tightly to his arm as if she were afraid of something. Then she broke. Hearing her weeping triggered Sam-Oeurn's emotions, but he fought to hold back the tears and control his quivering voice.

"It's not because of you," he began. "You have helped us so much. Youvannette and I love you and don't want to hurt you in any way. But we've decided that this is what we must do."

"I don't understand," I said calmly, trying not to appear too shocked.

"Every day we feel pressure from different ones," he explained. "Because of the war everyone is needy. We preach the gospel to them and encourage them to look to the Lord and trust Him to meet their needs. But when they find out we are working with you, they become resentful of us. Several have come to me

141

about the matter. 'It's easy for you to trust God,' they say. 'We, too, could be strong Christians if we had an American providing a place for us to stay and giving us salary.' And then they spread the bitter feeling to others, or just leave and never come back. We've tried to explain to them, but no one seems to understand, so we feel this is what God wants us to do.''

''Why is it so urgent that you leave tonight?'' I asked incredulously. ''It's pouring down rain! Can't you at least wait until morning when the rain stops?''

''No,'' he answered, quite determined. ''For many days we have been seeking the Lord as to what we should do. This afternoon He spoke to us from Ezekiel 12. He told us to prepare baggage and leave in the evening after dark. So that is what we are doing.''

''But where will you go?'' I asked, as I opened my Bible to read the passage.

''We don't know,'' he said quietly, avoiding my eyes.

In a way, I admired their sincerity and willingness to step out on faith—even in the pouring rain—trusting the Lord to make a way for them. But at the same time I couldn't help feeling they were being a bit too presumptuous. Then I thought about Abraham, heading out to a land he didn't know.

I looked down at my watch. ''But it's only thirty minutes before curfew,'' I reasoned. ''You'll be driving around in the rain and not know where you're going.''

''The Lord will show us where to go,'' he said, as they both nodded confidently.

''All right, if the Lord told you to go, you must go. But if He doesn't give you a place to stay in the next thirty minutes, you get back here. Otherwise you may spend the night in jail or even get shot.'' They gave no response. Sam-Oeurn reached over and gripped my shoulder, then helped Youvannette get on the cycle.

''Here,'' I said. ''Take our poncho—you'll get soaked.'' He shook his head, refusing like a martyr. With somber faces they drove out into the rain. A sense of bewilderment came over me as I watched them roll out of sight.

"Where do you think they'll go?" DeAnn asked, taking the poncho and hanging it back on the rusty nail.

"I can't imagine," I replied, shaking my head. I didn't feel much like messing with kerosene, so we decided to go upstairs to my office and wait to see if they would return.

All this had happened so unexpectedly. The thought of losing Sam-Oeurn made my insides ache. I had felt things were working out for them, when actually, their problems had continued stacking up like dark clouds before a storm. I couldn't help feeling condemned—like I had missed the Lord somewhere.

"God," I groaned quietly in an agonized voice. "What have I done? Sam-Oeurn's left—and it's all my fault."

I settled into the chair behind my desk and opened my Bible to my evening reading. Skimming the chapter, I searched for a word of encouragement. Then my eyes fastened on the last few familiar verses. They were underlined boldly.

> Though youths grow weary and tired, and vigorous young men stumble badly, yet those who wait for the LORD will gain new strength. . . . (Isa. 40:30-31)

As I read the passage, my mind flashed back to the day my pastor had given that Scripture to us. I remembered how strongly we had felt called to Cambodia, but at the same time, the question of support loomed heavily over us. The word to us was "wait." Then it dawned on me that Sam-Oeurn and Youvannette were much in that same predicament. They were sure God was going to send them out, but the problem of support haunted them. I wanted them to be weaned from having to depend on me as much as they did; but once again, it seemed the Lord was saying, "Wait, be patient, and I'll make the way."

DeAnn had left me alone in the office and was standing out on the veranda overlooking the drive, as if she were expecting them to return any minute. Her faith was rewarded as they pulled up just a few minutes before curfew.

"Honey, they're back!" she cried excitedly, bursting through

143

the door. I breathed a prayer of thanks, closed my Bible, and hurried behind her down the stairs to the garage. The rain had leveled off to a soft drizzle, but Sam-Oeurn and Youvannette had been out during the relentless downpour. They rolled their bike in, looking like two drowned rats.

"We couldn't find a place," Sam-Oeurn said, hanging his head in defeat.

I lightly slapped him on the back, gripped his shoulder, and suggested they come on up for a talk. DeAnn hurried back upstairs to get a couple of towels and put water on the stove for hot tea. I helped them with their bag, while they sloshed up the stairs. Youvannette was shivering by the time she reached my office and welcomed the big thirsty towel. She blotted her hair and promptly wrapped herself up tightly. Sam-Oeurn hung his wet jacket over the banister before coming in.

"Don't be discouraged," I said, trying to lift them from their despondency.

"But Brother Todd," Sam-Oeurn reasoned, "we were sure we were doing what God told us to do." He sat in a chair and listened as I began talking.

"God sometimes has us do strange things," I said reassuringly, "if for nothing else, just to test our obedience. Look at Abraham; God told him to go sacrifice his only son, Isaac. But just as Abraham was about to thrust the knife into Isaac's body, God stopped him. He had proven his obedience. Even though you may feel foolish, I believe through this experience you, too, have proven your obedience."

Sam-Oeurn sat quietly for a moment, pondering my words. "But that still leaves the problem of having to depend on you for our support. I don't know what to do about that," he said in earnest.

"While you were gone," I interjected, "I sought the Lord for an answer." I opened to the passage. "Here, you can read it in my Bible." Youvannette got up from her chair and read it over his shoulder. They nodded as if they understood, while I continued.

144

"You see, Sam-Oeurn, what you feel God is telling you may not necessarily be to move at this time. He may only be preparing your heart to receive a move that will come later. What I had felt in my heart was confirmed in this reading, as I asked God to give us an answer for your situation. I think His word to you is "wait.""

I briefly related the story to them of our anxiety to become missionaries, and how the Lord had given us this same Scripture. As they listened, I could feel their encouragement swell. Their expressions bore signs of hope, and our conversation soon shifted into lighthearted fellowship once again. The hot tea had warmed their bodies, while the Spirit had revived their hearts.

Youvannette remarked to Sam-Oeurn with a teasing smile, "That's the last time I'm riding around in the rain with you!"

"Come on," I said, pointing to the door. "You need sleep! Get on up those stairs," I commanded laughingly.

DeAnn and I ended up spending the night there, too, since it was far too late to be out on the streets. But just knowing Sam-Oeurn and Youvannette were safely sleeping above us compensated for the discomfort of having to sleep on a hard mat on the floor without a pillow.

We heard nothing more about the prospect of their moving away. One might describe Sam-Oeurn's struggles as the "birthpangs of an apostle." The waiting period soon ended, and doors of opportunity began to open for them.

On Saturday morning, a week later, the other teams had already departed for their designated areas. Sam-Oeurn's group was the last to leave. They had made plans to visit a new area in the vicinity of the airport, so it was convenient to hop a local taxi for transportation. They had to walk a couple of miles from the main road to reach this certain village where they knew no one had heard of salvation in Jesus.

Spotting a large vacant lot, they proceeded to ask the nearby homeowner for its use. The old gentleman was relaxing in the breezy doorway of his home.

"Excuse me, sir," Sam-Oeurn spoke quietly. "We were

noticing your fine grounds, and were wondering if you would allow us the privilege to hold a short meeting here this morning.''

They exchanged dialogue for a couple minutes and finally the man agreed. He watched them open their guitar cases and boxes of literature and briefly catnapped as they continued preparations.

Half-clad, dusty children popped out, as if from nowhere, to see what this interesting group of people were up to. Seeing the children curious about the activity, Youvannette cheerfully invited them to tell others to come. Within minutes every child within the village radius had assembled. In the meantime, Sam-Oeurn rigged up a portable battery-operated speaker with a bull horn, while a couple of the other fellows tuned their instruments and practiced a few choruses. The women organized the literature, separating the Bible portions from the tracts.

Everything was ready. They began with singing and testifying, using this means to stir interest and draw a crowd. A few of the older children ran home, returning with their parents or older brothers and sisters. The growing crowd silently watched in wonder as this peculiar group proclaimed a promising message about a Savior who died for their sins.

"Sing another one,'' a man requested eagerly when they started to put down the instruments. The team's enthusiasm was contagious. Sam-Oeurn encouraged them to clap along with the music and the people gladly joined in. After a few more songs, the fellows put away their instruments while Sam-Oeurn opened his Bible to the Gospel of Mark. He adjusted the small plastic microphone and clipped it to his shirt.

"I want to tell you a story about a blind man named Bartimaeus,'' he began. The Cambodians are story lovers, so this attracted their interest. One by one they shuffled closer, some even taking a seat or squatting in the shade of the wooden house on the grounds.

When Sam-Oeurn reached the part of the story where Jesus touched Bartimaeus, resulting in his miraculous healing, he was suddenly interrupted.

"Hey!'' an elderly woman yelled, as she stumbled and felt her way towards the front of the crowd. Judging from her blank stare, Sam-Oeurn gathered she was blind.

"Which one of you is Jesus?" she asked, pointing a bony finger in Sam-Oeurn's direction. "Will He do for me as He did for that man? Will He touch my eyes and make me see again?"

Sam-Oeurn tried to gather his thoughts, not having been prepared to receive such pointed questions. "Well . . . uh . . ." he stammered. "Jesus isn't here . . . I mean . . . uh, He isn't here physically. Well . . . He's here, but even if you had your eyesight, you couldn't see Him. His Spirit is living in us . . . we are His servants. If you would like, we will pray with you that by His power you will be healed."

The little old lady tightened the waist of her sarong as Sam-Oeurn spoke. "Oh, yes," she said without hesitation, nodding her head. She didn't appear to be the least disappointed at the fact that Jesus wasn't actually there in person. She seemed to have complete confidence that His servants could help her to reach Him.

Sam-Oeurn looked over his shoulder and motioned for Sina and Arith to join him in prayer. If she could be healed, he thought to himself, this might make believers out of everyone standing here.

He had in mind to lay his hands upon her and then make a strong appeal to Jesus in her behalf. He reached down, barely touching her, when suddenly, she jerked back with a startled look on her face. Then she began to shout, "I can see! I can see!" Turning to those near her she blurted, "Look! My eyes! I can see!"

Probably the one least prepared for this was Sam-Oeurn. He didn't even get a chance to pray for her. He stared in bewilderment at the little lady, who apparently had been completely healed. She made her way through the crowd, touching everyone, and ecstatically remarking about the colors she could see. The crowd was slowly realizing that their fifty-two-year-old blind neighbor, Chankry, was truly healed. They joined her excitement until it almost became a riot.

Down the street, a young woman dressed in a military uniform neared the elated assembly. Stopping to ask a group of children about the noise, they told her that her mother, who had been blind for fifteen years, had been healed by some man.

"Mother! Mother!" she cried, running hurriedly the rest of the way to join the boisterous crowd.

"Kim Ly!" Her mother called, recognizing her daughter's voice. "I can see! I can see you!"

With quick, sure steps, Chankry made her way through the crowd to meet her daughter. They embraced while tears flowed freely.

"Tell me what's happened to you," Kim Ly lovingly demanded, as she held her mother at arm's length, examining her alert, tear-filled eyes. "Can you really see me, mother?"

"Yes, oh, yes!" Chankry assured her, shaking with emotion. "The God, Jesus, has made my eyes like those of a child again."

"How did this happen?" her daughter asked in astonishment, looking around at the crowd.

Chankry pointed through the mass of people to where Sam-Oeurn was talking with others about the Lord.

"Come," she said, pulling her daughter's arm gently, "you must meet this man."

Throughout the crowd, members of the evangelism team were counseling, witnessing, praying and teaching those who gathered around to listen. They passed out tracts, and to those who showed real interest, they gave a gospel portion in the Cambodian language.

Chankry and her oldest daughter, Kim Ly, surrendered their lives to follow Jesus that afternoon, along with countless others who witnessed the miracle in her life. Sam-Oeurn stressed the importance of abandoning their witchcraft, fetishes and idol worship. After lengthy teaching, almost everyone responded to his appeal. Wads of devil strings, spirit houses and fetishes were burned before their eyes.

The news of Chankry's healing spread through the village like wildfire. It wasn't long before the number of inquirers was uncontrollable. Even the military police were called in to see what the ruckus was all about. Some of the villagers had complained about the burning of religious items and wanted action taken against Sam-Oeurn and his team. But when the police learned what had actually happened, they were afraid to do anything. The crowd defended Sam-Oeurn saying he didn't make them burn their idols. "We did it willingly!" they testified. One of the policemen even ended up giving his heart to Jesus when he saw it was Chankry who had been healed of blindness. He had known her for many years.

The meeting broke up late that afternoon. A mob of new believers walked the team to the main road where they could catch a taxi-bus back to the church.

"Please come again tomorrow," they begged, as the team loaded their equipment in the rack on top of the taxi. "We want to learn more about the words of the Lord Jesus." The homeowner who had lent them his property for the meeting was so touched he invited them to come every day if possible to meet on his grounds. He even made his house available as a meeting place, and they named the new congregation Emmanuel Church.

Early the next morning, Bopha, one of the ladies in the team, drove her cycle back to the village in order to accompany Chankry and her daughter to the Sunday service at Maranatha Church. Chankry testified before the whole congregation, leaving them electrified with excitement. She was amazed that there were so many of her people following the Lord Jesus Christ.

Later that week, Son Sonne from the Bible society met with Thay to discuss his concern over news he had heard about the evangelism teams.

"If you are not careful," he cautioned, "you will make it very rough for us to live as Christians. The government will put restrictions on us."

"I don't understand what you mean," Thay responded innocently.

"Haven't you heard the reports over the radio? One of those teams you send out is really causing problems in a village near the airport."

"No," Thay asserted. "I haven't heard any reports. What do they say?"

149

Son Sonne opened his briefcase, drawing out a mimeographed sheet of paper, and handed it across the table for Thay to read. "This is a copy of the news broadcast that was on the radio yesterday."

Thay read the copy that was certified by the government's Buddhist radio station:

> A serious thing has taken place in a village near the Pochentong Airport. We have reports that Christian proselytizers have visited the village, persuading the people to turn from their worship of Buddha and follow the teachings of Jesus. This is a deplorable act of religious aggression perpetrated by rebels seeking to undermine the traditions of our country. However, this is not going unnoticed; the religious authorities are already sending out monks to correct the problem. Special teaching sessions are scheduled. . . .

"This is unbelievable!" Thay exclaimed. "Did you actually hear this on the radio?"

"Yes," Son Sonne nodded seriously. "It doesn't sound very good, does it?"

"Well, that depends on how you look at it," Thay explained. "We can't spread the gospel effectively without expecting a little persecution in return. Anyway, let me tell you what happened in that village."

Thay proceeded to share the event of Chankry's healing, and as he did so, Son Sonne's face whitened with astonishment. Knowing now that all the publicity was a direct result of a miracle from God, he had no defense against the evangelism team's effort.

After he left, though, we became concerned whether this new thrust by the Buddhist monks to correct the "problem," as they called it, would hinder the move of the Holy Spirit among the believers. Our fears were soon relieved, however, for that afternoon Sam-Oeurn returned from the village bearing good news.

"Oh, brother!" he called from the driveway. Thay and I were standing on the veranda and we both stepped to the banister to see what he wanted.

"Good, you're here!" he said. "I have something to tell both of you." Parking his bike, he bounded up the stairs and into my office.

"Early this morning Sina came to see me," Sam-Oeurn began. "He was concerned about a report he had heard over the radio last night."

"Yes, we know," Thay interjected. "We've just learned about it from Son Sonne. We were just wondering how this was going to affect the new believers. Have you heard from anyone out there?"

Nodding his head, Sam-Oeurn explained, "We were afraid of that, too, so we hurried out to the village to see what was happening. When we arrived at Chankry's home, we found that many of the new believers had met for prayer and Bible reading. They, too, had heard of the news and laughed about it as if it were a joke. We thought it might leave them discouraged, but instead they were challenged and more united than before."

"Praise the Lord!" Thay responded with joy.

"So," Sam-Oeurn concluded, "we have nothing to worry about." He raised both hands in a gesture of praise to the Lord.

"Hallelujah!" I joined. "That's wonderful!"

"And that's not all," Sam-Oeurn's voice rose with excitement. "Chankry has made a large sign and nailed it to the front of their house. It reads:

All the members of this household have given their hearts and minds to the Lord Jesus Christ. May He help us to show His power to save and to heal!

No amount of persuasion will cause them to turn from Jesus now! I know that for sure. Their faith is not founded on man's wisdom, but on God's power."

CHAPTER 11

Trouble up North

I received a letter in June 1974 from a Scandinavian missionary, Oddvar Johanson, in Bangkok, Thailand. He had heard about our work and offered to assist in any way, especially in the printing of literature. We considered this an answer to prayer. The Bible course we had designed, entitled *Tuk Rueh,* was ready for printing, but we had lacked the means to finish the project. With all the new ministries being established around the city and up north, we needed the Bible course now more than ever. Saran had written several times, requesting literature for new believers, but up until now I had only been able to send him promises. Now it looked as if the Lord was making good those promises.

I immediately made plans to fly to Bangkok, and eagerly looked forward to my first trip outside Cambodia. While in Thailand, I could also get flight information for sending our orphans to the States and Canada. We were far from ready to make any final arrangements—in fact, we wondered if we would ever get them released for adoption at all. But I did need flight information in order to make plans.

Thay and I worked with various government officials and ministries almost every day, hoping to secure the release of our five orphans. But we were refused at every turn. Necessary documents from the United States had been delayed. Approval of the Canadian family had been granted, then denied all in the same week. We were beginning to feel like Balaam, hitting a brick wall every time we tried to make a move.

When we first took the orphans into our home, we figured it would only be a month or two before we would have them relocated with their new families. But now seven months had passed and we still had made no progress in finalizing the proceedings. While the spiritual side of the ministry seemed to have God's approval and blessing, our humanitarian endeavors kept us worn out and frustrated. We were wondering if God was trying to tell us something.

After spending several days trying to get reservations to go to Bangkok, I was finally able to catch an embassy flight out of the country, which cost me nothing. Now that we were entering the rainy season, the airport was much safer. When we arrived at the terminal, no one was huddled for protection from the rockets and artillery as we had seen before, though the sounds of war could still be heard in the distance. The monsoon showers had forced the Khmer Rouge to withdraw back into the rain forests.

After hugging DeAnn and waving goodbye to all my Cambodian brothers and sisters who had accompanied me to the airport, I boarded the twin-engine aircraft. In a matter of minutes the plane was airborne and headed towards Thailand.

Strapped into a canvas seat, I stuffed pieces of tissue paper in my ears to filter out the terrible roar from the engines. It was worse than those cargo planes I had traveled on a few months ago. Then I glanced out my window and noticed what looked like pillars of smoke ascending from small villages that dotted the countryside.

"Do you know what they're doing down there?" I asked a U.S. Air Force advisor who was seated next to me. He closed his military newspaper, then leaned over.

"What did you say?" he yelled above the roar.

I dug the tissue out of my ear. "Is that smoke down there? What's going on?"

He leaned over, peering out the window. "Yeah, that's smoke. Those are villages that have just been overrun by the Communists. You're lucky you can't see any more than that. Innocent people are being butchered and barbecued alive down there."

I was silent for a moment while I looked out the window again at

153

the war-torn countryside. I shuddered as scenes from the bombing near our home flashed before me. Then my mind began painting gory pictures of what it was probably like in those besieged villages.

"Can't something be done to help them?" I timidly interceded.

"What would you suggest?" he countered. "Our hands are tied. We're only allowed to help the Cambodian government partially, and that's worse than no help at all—it only serves to prolong this painful war. We should either help them win this war once and for all—or just get out."

His face got red and angry. I seemed to have touched a sore spot. Fortunately, I knew nothing about how to fight a war, so our conversation ended on that note. But what he had said triggered a stream of thought for me. In my language it could be put this way—lukewarm commitment is worse than no commitment at all. No wonder Jesus said lukewarmness made Him vomit. He would rather have us hot or cold—totally for Him, or totally against Him.

Then my attention turned back to the smoking villages. I wondered how many of them had received the gospel witness, or if our teams had visited any of these remote areas. Occasionally the government forces were able to open a road to a town or city that had been cut off from the capital by the Communists. When this would happen, we would take advantage of the opportunity by sending a team there to minister for as long as conditions would allow. They would stay several days or a week, depending on the stability of the area.

There was always the risk of the road being cut while they were gone, leaving our workers stranded. This had happened two weeks earlier when a team went to an area south of Phnom Penh called Takeo. They had been gone only one day when we learned the Khmer Rouge had overcome the government troops and cut the road once again. Everyone gathered for unceasing prayer until word came three days later that the road had been reopened, enabling the team to return safely. My eyes remained glued to the smoldering villages, hoping some of the victims had heard the gospel at least once.

It was easy to tell when our plane had crossed into Thailand. There was such a marked difference in the development of the land. Parallel canals crisscrossed the countryside, forming squares of cultivated land with perfectly even rows.

Once we landed in Bangkok, it was as if I had returned to civilization. Quickly checking through customs and immigration, I was soon on the curb, haggling with taxi drivers. I had grown accustomed to the slow pace of Khmer taxis and cyclos, so I was in for a shock as we drove from the airport compound. We sped down a modern divided highway in bumper-to-bumper traffic at seventy miles per hour. It felt as if we were flying! My fright was compounded by the awkward feeling of driving on the left side of the road. I found myself gripping the armrest, bracing for the sudden crash I anticipated at any moment. It was with great relief that I finally unloaded my luggage outside a hotel an hour later.

A few minutes after making a phone call, Oddvar and another Scandinavian missionary were in the lobby to meet me. They wasted no time grabbing my bags and scurrying out the door. They laughed together as they stashed my bags into the back of their car.

"Come," they said. "You don't want to stay here; this is a brothel!"

"A brothel?" I said naively. "What's that?" They looked at one another as if to say, 'Boy, how did he ever find his way around to this part of the world?'

"A brothel," Oddvar explained as we got into the car, "is a house of prostitution. Since that's where most foreigners begin their tour of Thailand, your taxi driver probably figured that's where you wanted to go. He also draws a commission if you stay there."

On the way to Oddvar's house we stopped by their mission headquarters and they showed me around. I was impressed, to say the least. As they led me through their air-conditioned offices, complete printing house, newly constructed Bible school and church auditorium, I was amazed. I even found myself becoming envious of such facilities. Then they gathered several other missionaries, including some from the United States and Canada, and began asking me questions about the work in Cambodia. I shared briefly about how God had sent us there, about the miracles that had happened, and the hundreds who were coming to know Jesus as their Savior. They could scarcely believe what they were hearing. Now *they* were feeling envious!

"Why aren't we seeing this happen in Thailand?" Oddvar questioned the others.

"Yeah," another one added. "For years we've been praying for revival. Why doesn't it come?"

As I listened to them talk among themselves, I remembered a story in the gospels that I had read on the plane. One day, two of Jesus' disciples came to Him with a request. "Master," they said, "grant that we may sit in your glory, one on your right, and one on your left."

"You do not know what you are asking for," Jesus answered them. "Are you able to drink the cup that I drink, or to be baptized with the baptism with which I am baptized?" (Mark 10:38).

As I listened to the missionaries question among themselves, I sensed the Holy Spirit inspiring an answer. "What do you think?" Oddvar asked as the others quieted down.

I first shared this account from the gospels. Then I replied, "It is true that Cambodia is seeing many miracles and is experiencing a wonderful move of God. But along with that glory, the people have had to drink a bitter cup, and undergo a painful baptism. When you pray for a spiritual revival in Thailand, you just might be praying for more than you know. Nothing will awaken a people to the real issue of life more readily than the hardships of war. However, that doesn't mean you should begin praying for war—God has other means of sending revival. But no matter how it comes, there will be a cup and a baptism—there will be a price to be paid."

They nodded solemnly as if I had captured in words what they had known and felt already.

The next few days I ministered to different groups and worked in the layout section of the print shop. We finally got the *Tuk Rueh* Bible course on the press and I was very happy with the way it was turning out. It was much nicer than I had expected.

156

Late one evening I returned to my room, and after I had cleaned up and crawled into bed, I opened my Bible to my evening readings. I was reading in 1 Timothy 3 about the qualifications of a Christian leader. As I was meditating on this chapter, I started to think about our different workers in Cambodia. One by one I began to pray for them, when suddenly I was startled by an unusual awareness of the presence of God. Then the voice of the Holy Spirit spoke within me.

"There's something wrong up north—the work is threatened. Saran has defiled his integrity and morality, and has ceased to follow me."

Those words kept rolling over and over in my mind until they were branded upon my spirit. I waited and prayed for more explanation, but none came. I couldn't conceive what might have happened. Finally, I tried to dismiss it as my imagination. "You're tired," I said to myself. "Just get some rest. You can't do anything about it now." But the more I tried to forget about it, the harder it was to shake off the idea that something was terribly wrong.

My concern about Saran continued to gnaw on me all the next day, but my attention was occupied with many other things. I spent all morning and most of the afternoon buying things to take back to Phnom Penh. I couldn't believe the shopping centers; it was like being back home in the States. After purchasing clothes, medicines, foods, and other equipment for our babies, I went to check on flights to the U.S. and Canada. Fortunately, there were many discount flights, so if we could just get the orphans released, we would be ready to make final arrangements.

It wasn't until I was boarding my flight the following morning that I realized how much I had missed Cambodia. At first, the fast, modern pace of Bangkok was enjoyable; but after several days, it became nerve-racking. Most of all, I missed the spiritual fellowship and hunger for God among my brothers and sisters in Phnom Penh—something I found little of in Thailand, though one could find just about anything else. Then, of course, there was the mounting concern over Saran that continued to haunt me. I had to find out what was wrong.

157

It was fortunate I was able to use the embassy plane; I must have had ten boxes to load on board. Had I flown commercially, there was no way I could have paid the cost of shipping all that material to Phnom Penh. The four boxes full of Bible courses weighed over three hundred pounds alone, and that was only one third of what was printed. We decided to ship the rest of the courses in at a later date. Little did I realize that God had an unexpected future for those courses left in Thailand.

As our plane flew over the northwestern sector of Cambodia, my eyes followed a faint meandering road, hoping I could spot the village of Andek-hep where Saran was located. My heart churned with anxiety, not just over him, but wondering if his village was one of those that had gone up in smoke. With our plane flying in and out of the clouds, I found my search too frustrating. I decided to relax and wait until I arrived in Phnom Penh to begin my inquiries.

It was midday when the plane touched down at the Pochentong Airport. The skies were clear, though there were still puddles from an earlier monsoon shower. Shimmering waves of humid heat rose from the black asphalt as the hot sun beat down upon the runway. An embassy van quickly pulled up alongside the plane while several ground attendants flung open the tail doors and hurriedly unloaded the luggage into the back of the van. I was thankful to have a ride to our building, since Thay would not have been able to manage both me and all the boxes too.

How I love Cambodia! I thought to myself as I rode along in the van. I enjoyed watching the bustle of cyclists, *remorques* and pedestrians on their way to market. "This is home for us now, Lord," I said under my breath. "I hope we never have to leave it."

When the van stopped in front of the building, several students helped unload boxes and carried them to the second floor. I went to find DeAnn and Thay. DeAnn fixed tall lime drinks for the three of us while I slit open a box to show them the Bible course.

"This is wonderful!" Thay exclaimed. "These couldn't have come at a better time. Remember Yanny? His whole company has come to the Lord and we've had to send workers to his camp every day.''

"Yanny?" I said in amazement. "You mean that fellow who said the Lord told him to join the army?"

"Yes," Thay nodded. "God has really used him."

I remembered Yanny well. When everyone else was trying to dodge the draft, he had come to us explaining how God had spoken to him three times to join the army. Not only that, the Lord had told him to enlist as a private, when his education would have given him the rank of an officer. As a private, he would have more opportunities to witness of his faith in Christ. We didn't know what to think about it at the time; it did seem rather strange, but we prayed for him and sent him out, anyway. Now over a month had passed, and apparently God was honoring his obedience.

"How did this happen?" I questioned.

"Well," Thay began, "when Yanny first arrived at the training camp he found it to be much different from what he had expected. All the fellows laughed and mocked him when word got out that he followed Jesus. After several weeks of this he got discouraged and began to think he'd made a mistake. Then one day it was his turn to be chief over the company during the practice drills. They were marching back from their exercises, when suddenly, a soldier collapsed to the ground as they passed under a bodhi tree."

"Wait a minute!" I interrupted. "Wasn't it under a bodhi tree that Buddha was supposed to have received his enlightenment?"

"Yes, it's considered sacred in our country," Thay explained. "You'll usually find images of Buddha and spirit houses at the base of the trees; people go there to worship spirits and offer incense and sacrifices."

"So what happened to the soldier?" I asked. "Did this have something to do with him falling to the ground?"

"Well," Thay went on, "since Yanny was the company chief that day, he was called to the scene. His first impression was that the fellow had just had a heat stroke. But after using several methods to revive him, nothing seemed to help. Then, to his amazement, the collapsed man began to squirm crying out, 'demon! demon!' Four or five soldiers tried to hold him still, but a

159

terrific strength came over him and he flung them to one side with little effort. He was now standing on his feet and raging like a madman. When he lunged towards the others, Yanny put his hands out to shove him back. But the moment his hands touched him, the soldier fell to the ground again and lay whimpering.''

"Was it a demon?" I asked eagerly.

"Yanny wasn't sure at first," Thay continued, "but from what he had read in the Bible and heard from his Christian friends, it looked like it—especially since the soldier fell to the ground when he touched him. When Yanny had discerned it to be an evil spirit, he spoke directly to the demon, saying, 'Why have you entered this man?'

" 'Because he's mine,' a voice cried out of the man. 'It's my right to enter into him.'

" 'It's not your right,' Yanny challenged the voice. 'You must leave him now!'

" 'No,' the demon protested. 'Anyway, I haven't been offered anything yet; why should I leave so easily?' Yanny then remembered what Sam-Oeurn had told him about his experiences.

" 'So you don't want to leave,' Yanny replied. 'Do you know the power of the Lord Jesus Christ?'

" 'Oh yes!' the voice trembled, 'I do!'

"The whole company had gathered round closely to watch. Their faces were covered with astonishment, almost fear. Yanny turned and spoke to them loudly: 'Do you believe Jesus can help this man?'

" 'Yes!' they responded, probably out of fear more than anything else. Yanny then asked them to pray with him for the man's deliverance. After several minutes, Yanny opened his eyes to find the soldier sitting up, asking those about him what had happened.''

"Praise the Lord!" I said excitely. "That's fantastic!"

"Yeah," Thay added, "and now nearly the whole company has come to the Lord. Workers from Messiah Church have been going out there daily with tracts and gospel portions. We haven't had enough to go around and Yanny says the soldiers fight to get what they can. They need teaching, and this Bible course is perfect for that. God knows what we need and when we need it!''

"Here you are, honey." DeAnn handed me a cool drink and I downed it instantly. While Thay sipped slowly on his drink, my thoughts shifted to Saran.

"Hey, Thay, have we received any word from Saran?" I asked.

He followed me to the doorway, then looked up after swallowing the last gulp. "No—it's been a long time since we heard from him."

"Yes, I know," I commented, hesitant to voice my suspicions. "While I was in Thailand the Lord seemed to speak to me about him and I've hardly been able to think about anything else."

"Like what?" Thay questioned cautiously. His countenance darkened.

I refilled my glass with lime drink before answering him. "Well, I'm not sure, but it seems there's something wrong up north."

"What is it?" he pried. "I, too, have an idea something is wrong, but I'm afraid to repeat it. I may be wrong."

"Go ahead and tell me," I urged, crunching on a piece of ice. "Maybe it will confirm my leading."

His eyes dropped for a moment. He was nervous and quite reluctant to open up.

"I don't know if it's true," he began, "but the other morning when I was doing my Bible readings, I came to 1 Samuel, chapter 2—you know, where it talks about the sons of Eli the priest. They stole the sacrifices and lay with the women. It said their sin was very great before the Lord because it dishonored His name. Then, as I read how God rebuked Eli for their behavior, I suddenly felt impressed that we have the same problem with Saran and that we must deal with him immediately."

I gazed at him, astonished. "This can't be true—not Saran!" My thoughts protested to myself. But it was too clear to ignore.

"This may be hard to believe," I said to Thay, "but God showed me the same thing—Saran has forsaken Him in two areas—his integrity and his morality." A look of consternation

161

came over Thay's face as I related the details. "Thay, you don't think—?"

"You mean stealing and adultery? No, surely it's not all that bad," replied. "But someone needs to go see him to find out for sure. Maybe it's just a warning from the Lord. Saran could need guidance and help in these areas, and perhaps the Lord is giving us advance warning."

"You know, you're probably right," I added. "Phony is still here in Phnom Penh. Maybe the Lord wants us to help her move up north so she can be with her husband. They've been apart for more than five months. DeAnn and I could make a short trip to Andek-hep to talk with Saran and make arrangements for her to join him."

"How soon do you think you could go?" he asked.

"I guess as soon as we can get booked."

Two days later, DeAnn and I boarded a plane to Battambang. For her sake, I made sure we got an aircraft with seats—a rare commodity since the greatest need was to transport cargo. Landing in Battambang late in the afternoon, we hired a *remorque* and made the rough ride to Saran's village, arriving shortly before dusk. We both found the cool country air to be refreshing.

As we walked past the small market area on the way to Saran's quarters, I noticed there wasn't as much activity as I had seen before. But I didn't think anything about it at the time. When we finally reached the government compound, everything was locked up tight. I knocked on Saran's door, but there was no answer.

"Come on," I motioned to DeAnn. "Maybe he's living at the building we rented for the church. As we hurried back across the village, I began to notice how deserted everything looked. The sun was about to sink below the horizon.

"Where is everybody?" I said aloud. "They couldn't be in bed yet." There were a few stragglers out on the dusty street but I was afraid to ask any questions. When we arrived at the church building, we were surprised to discover that it, too, was barred shut. I walked around to the side of the building and peeked through a crack in a shutter.

162

"This place has been vacated!" I exclaimed to DeAnn. "Even the benches are gone! Where's Saran?"

I rushed out to the road to stop a man who was pulling a wooden cart. My heart burned with curiosity. "Sir, please wait a minute," I waved to him. He stopped until I reached his side. "Do you know what has happened to Saran?" I asked him, pointing to the church building.

"He's gone," the man answered in a somber tone. "Several weeks ago the Khmer Rouge overran our village in the middle of the night. Fortunately, government troops were nearby, otherwise the whole village would have been destroyed."

"But where are all the people?" I asked.

"Nearly everyone has fled to Battambang," he replied. "They're too afraid to stay around here for fear it will happen again. The government closed the school and I heard they moved your friend to Pailin." He pointed towards the sunset.

I looked back at the building. "What happened to all the benches?" I questioned him.

"I saw him helping some soldiers load them onto an army truck," he answered. "I suppose he paid to have them transported to Pailin."

Shaken by the news, DeAnn and I walked slowly out to the main road, discussing what to do next. We decided to try to get a ride back to Battambang and spend the night there. We were relieved to find our driver still sitting at the roadside where we had left him. He was headed back to Battambang anyway, so he was glad to have some paying passengers.

After arriving in Battambang, we roamed the streets for two hours, trying to find a hotel with a vacancy. All the inns were full of wealthy landowners who had escaped from the besieged countryside. We wondered if we would ever find a place to sleep. Finally we located a dingy, mosquito-ridden room where we spent the night. It had a terrible, musty stench.

"What a horrible experience this has been," I said with a deep sigh as I flopped down on the dirty, frayed sheets.

"Well, praise the Lord," DeAnn countered. "Surely He's had

some purpose in this trip; if nothing else, just so we would know what's happened to Saran.''

"You're right," I agreed. "But I can't understand why he hasn't written us and told us what's happened. It's been over a month since he left Andek-hep.''

I saw when checking a map downstairs in the lobby that Pailin was a mountain town located about eight miles from the border of Thailand, and it was a long, rough journey to get there. I didn't feel we should try to make the trip without Thay or Sam-Oeurn along, so the following morning, after a restless night's sleep, we decided to return to Phnom Penh. At the airport we saw an American who helped service the Cambodian Air Force planes, and he allowed us to fly with him to the capital in a six-seater gunner aircraft.

"We aren't going to get shot down in this thing, are we?" I asked smiling.

"Oh, you never can tell," he answered nonchalantly. "It's been known to happen. Don't worry, though; I wouldn't be flying if there was any danger!''

It turned out to be the most enjoyable flight I had experienced yet. We made several stops along the way and the scenery was spectacular. On arriving in Phnom Penh, we were given a ride to our building in an army jeep. Thay and several others rushed down the stairs to greet us.

"I didn't expect you back so soon!" he said, amazed and smiling. "How's Saran?" Thay's anxiety was evident.

"I don't know," I answered. "We didn't get to see him. He moved to Pailin over a month ago.''

"What?" Thay exclaimed with surprise. "Is something wrong?" As I explained what had happened, a saddened look came over his face.

"But I don't understand why he hasn't written," I added. "We should have heard from him by now!''

A few days later we made contact with a company that had a coffee plantation in Pailin whose small plane made trips up north three times weekly. They agreed that as soon as space was available, they would allow us to fly with them. We had just decided to go to Pailin when finally a letter came from Saran; it was three weeks old.

"What does he say?" I begged Thay, as he was absorbed in reading the pages. Then he laid it down.

"Not much more than what you've told us already," he explained. "He's now teaching in Pailin and has rented a building to begin holding meetings. He says several people have been healed and many have come to the Lord already. He wants to know if you'll help him pay rent on the building."

"Does he say anthing about having Phony come to join him?" I asked.

"No, and that's what concerns me. He seems to have forgotten her," Thay answered, looking troubled.

"Well, maybe we should wire him and have him come to see us. Does he give an address where we can reach him?"

"Yes," Thay replied. "That's a good idea. But we'll also have to wire him the money for the trip."

We sent the wire and waited. More than a week passed and we still had received no word as to whether he was coming or not. One day he showed up at the building without warning.

"Todd," DeAnn burst into my office early one afternoon. "Saran's here! He's coming up the stairs now."

"Praise the Lord!" I exclaimed. "Tell Thay he's come." I met Saran with a hug at the top of the stairs. Thay was next, then Sam-Oeurn and several others crowded in close to greet him. Then I invited him to have lunch with DeAnn and me.

As we sat around DeAnn's desk eating rice with *Chaa* ("a stir-fried vegetable-meat dish"), Saran described the Khmer Rouge attack and all that had happened in Andek-hep. He went on to explain his move to Pailin and what had taken place since. Some of the believers in Andek-hep had moved to Pailin and the rest fled to Battambang or even further north.

There was silence until we all finished eating. Then we moved across the room and relaxed in bamboo chairs while DeAnn served tea.

"Saran," Thay began, "the Lord has had you on our hearts

for some time now. "Don't you think you've been away from Phony long enough—or is there some problem?"

Saran squirmed nervously in his chair with his eyes shifting back and forth between Thay and me. "No," he replied. "There's no problem."

"Then why don't you have Phony join you?" I asked. "We feel you've been separated too long."

"Yes, I would like for her to be with me," he explained. "but she's almost seven months pregnant, and the trip would be too rough for her. She would also have to give up her job."

"Thay and I have checked into it," I responded, "and we've found a way we can fly you there directly in less than two hours. As for her job, we will help you until after she has the baby and can find more work."

He nodded in agreement, but I could sense his reluctance. Thay also felt he was holding something back.

"Saran, are you sure there's nothing wrong?" he questioned. "You aren't hiding anything from us, are you?"

"No," he answered. "I have nothing to hide; everything's fine—I'll go talk with Phony now." He sipped the last mouthful of warm tea, then rose and confidently strode out the door and down the stairs.

Thay and I sat silently, holding cups of tea now growing cold. We knew instinctively that everything was not fine, but we had no hard evidence to support that feeling.

"Let's just continue to pray for the Lord's guidance," I said wearily as Thay rose to leave.

CHAPTER 12

The Dove Descends

During the next few days we made final arrangements for Saran and Phony to fly to Pailin. We helped them pack up what few possessions they owned and promised to bring them up on a cargo plane in a couple of weeks, since they were allowed only one suitcase on the small aircraft. We felt a sense of satisfaction as we watched them board their flight.

But there was still an air of mystery about Saran's behavior. Little did Thay and I suspect that our forthcoming trip to Pailin would unveil, to our horror, the seriousness of Saran's situation.

Pailin, a city of about five thousand people, is located in the midst of a lush mountainous area and the main occupation of the townspeople is mining precious stones. We flew as far as Battambang, then had to travel by car caravan to Pailin. The narrow dirt road from Battambang to Pailin was in the war zone and unsafe for civilian travel. Government forces provided military protection for long caravans of cars and vans carrying passengers and supplies to and from Pailin. A huge truckload of armed soldiers led the caravan. When they spotted areas in the road that appeared to be mined, the soldiers would fire a weapon to detonate the mines so the caravan could pass safely. Another truckload of soldiers brought up the rear of the caravan.

The dirt streets of Pailin, deeply rutted from much use, were muddy from the recent rain. Now the sun was beating down and the car we were in was like a steam bath. The caravan of cars unloaded everyone at the central market and I promptly found a roadside stand and bought a tall glass of freshly squeezed orange juice while Thay hired a *remorque*. We then loaded Phony's boxes and our luggage into the back, climbed in, and made our way down the rough road to the edge of town.

I dug in my pocket for a map Saran had sketched for us and showed the driver where to go. Somehow, the news of our arrival had already reached Saran and Phony and they were standing in front of the house as we pulled up. Saran eagerly assisted Thay in unloading the boxes while I paid the driver. Phony hurried to prepare cold drinks and we sat down in front of the house to relax after the long, hot ride.

We had been there only about ten minutes, chatting and listening to Saran tell about meetings he had been having, when we were suddenly interrupted by unexpected visitors. On the road, not more than twenty yards from us, a small scooter, carrying a couple, slid to a halt. The woman, who had been riding on back sidesaddle, took to her feet even before the vehicle stopped. Running up the dirt drive and cursing, she yelled and screamed at Saran in Khmer. Thay and I jumped to our feet.

"What's going on?" I nudged Thay.

"Shh . . ." he motioned with his hand. "Listen." We backed out of the way as she approached Saran.

"Saran!" she snorted, pointing accusingly in his face. "Christian! Ha! You're a liar and a thief!"

Saran glanced over at Thay, shrugging his shoulders. He shook his head and said, "Don't listen to her." Then, trying to appear confident, he remarked, "She has demon."

I began to listen more closely.

"You lived with me!" she continued, narrowing her fiery eyes. "You slept with me; you told me you had no wife! You promised to marry me—ha!" She threw her long black hair behind her, revealing the angry flush that inched up her neck and cheeks. She was a pretty Khmer woman, with an unusually fair complexion.

"Who's this pregnant woman that's living with you now?" she pointed menacingly in Phony's direction and snarled. "Are you going to tell me you married her last week?"

Thay was silent, absorbing everything that was being said. I, unfortunately, could catch only a few key phrases in the Khmer language and was trying to piece together the whole conversation. From the words I was able to decipher, I was becoming acutely suspicious of Saran's part in the whole matter. He looked nervous. Phony had withdrawn into the house, probably embarrassed by the scene, since the girl was shouting and arguing with Saran now.

"And where's my precious stone you stole from me, you thief!" she snapped.

I caught that. Saran? Stole her precious stone? What could this mean?

They continued to argue, their voices rising sharply. Saran completely denied her accusations, until finally he refused to speak to her any longer and told her to leave. With that, he turned and motioned for us to go inside their unpainted, wooden house. But I couldn't move. I stood dumbfounded, watching the raging woman until she finally recoiled and returned to the motorscooter. She mounted behind the man driving, who apparently seemed pleased with what had just transpired. His smirky grin seemed to suggest he had arranged the incident. My thoughts spun with confusion as I watched the trail of dust from the scooter disappear in the breeze. Grabbing Thay and pulling him aside, I began to probe for the details of this unbelieveable scene.

"It's just as the Lord had showed us," he said softly with a sickened expression on his face. "But wait, let me have a chance to talk with Saran. I want to hear it from him first." I waited outside while Thay went indoors.

"Don't lie to me, Saran," I overheard Thay say in a threatening tone, once he managed to speak with him alone. "Before God we want to know the truth about this." After several minutes, Saran began to open up and confess. I waited for what seemed like forever until finally the two of them appeared in the doorway.

"Come," Thay said soberly, "let's go have something to eat."

Eat, I thought to myself. How could anyone think of eating at a time like this! Then I realized he was wanting to get the three of us away from Phony so we could talk openly. She had suffered enough hurt over the incident.

As we walked towards the market, Thay unveiled what had happened. "When Saran first arrived here," he began, "there was no place for him to stay or to store the benches he brought from Andek-hep. It was then he met this woman Elly. She offered him her home and this eventually led to an affair. He had even promised to marry her." In horror I turned to Saran.

"But what about Phony?" I asked. My face was dripping with sweat. "And what about God?" He kept silent, showing no sign of remorse.

"The worst thing," Thay continued, "is that many people already know about it. In fact, Saran was chased off Elly's premises by another man who considers her to be his mistress. That was him we saw a while ago. He even shot at Saran with a gun once when Saran tried to see Elly."

I didn't want to hear anymore. I felt as if someone had hit me with a brick. I mopped my face on my shirt sleeve and shook my head, wondering how we were going to handle this. When we reached a roadside stand we sat down and ordered a bowl of *kuey tiev* ("Chinese noodle soup"). We ate quietly; then I looked up at Saran and began to question him.

"What do you plan to do now?" I asked.

"I don't know what you mean," he responded with a puzzled look. His tone of innocence was startling.

"Saran, you've sinned before God and man," I said sternly. "You've wrecked your reputation, your ministry, and probably your marriage."

Jumping immediately to defend himself he said, "If what I've done is so wrong, why does God continue to do miracles when I pray for people?"

I could hardly believe my ears. I looked at Thay in amazement as Saran proceeded to explain further.

"Just the other evening I prayed for a lady with a goiter and the next morning she was healed. The goiter completely disappeared—"

"Listen Saran," I interrupted firmly, "the Bible assures us that if we preach the gospel and pray in Jesus' name, we can expect results. But even the Apostle Paul said, 'I buffet my body and make it my slave, lest possibly, after I have preached to others, I myself should be disqualified' (1 Cor. 9:27). Ananias and Sapphira both dropped dead for a lesser sin than you've committed. When the Spirit of God is moving you have to walk a fine line. God spoke to us about your sin long before we knew anything about what had actually happened.''

"It's like this," Thay added. "Before your life is cleansed by the blood of Jesus, you're like a sheet that's black with sin. But when you become a Christian, God forgives your sin and your life is cleansed, you're like a white sheet. But now you must be careful. If you allow a black spot to appear on your white sheet, though the spot may be small in comparison, it attracts all the attention—especially from those who look for it. For this reason the life of an overseer must be above reproach.''

Our words seemed to roll off him like water off a duck's back. There was no hint of repentance in his attitude. In fact, he didn't even seem like the same Saran we had once known. I didn't like the changes I was seeing in him. Thay and I both felt the Lord wanted us to deal with the matter and not to treat it lightly. My experience in Okinawa had taught me that. But what to do?

My spirit was so clouded with mixed emotions that all I could think of was to cut off any and all of Saran's support. We explained to him why this was necessary and that we would also have to send someone to take over the work since his reputation had become so marred. The black spot was also on us since he was related to our ministry. To continue supporting him would be the same as condoning his behavior before all who knew what had happened. In fact, we decided to leave town as soon as possible before we were firmly identified with him. We didn't realize it at the time, but we had only scratched the surface of what God was requiring of us. We were in for the lesson of our lives.

Later on, Thay talked alone with Phony and she sadly expressed her desire to return to Phnom Penh to live with her elderly grandmother. Since we had been the instigators of her move to

Pailin we naturally felt responsible for her and promised to help in any way we could. Thay guaranteed her return flight and offered to take her boxes back with us that evening.

We quickly gathered our things and caught the taxi caravan back to Battambang to spend the night. Early the next morning we boarded the first flight to Phnom Penh. We found seats on one-hundred-pound sacks of rice as our plane carried us over the Communist-occupied countryside. All we could think of or talk about was the problem of Saran. We both agreed Kong would be the best candidate to replace Saran's position of leadership. He was not only accustomed to the rough life style of the country, but he had even lived in Pailin for a short time.

"His pastor's heart," Thay added, "along with being familiar with the area will help overcome some of the difficulties stemming from Saran's problem."

As soon as we arrived in the capital we gathered all the leaders from our surrounding ministries and explained the problem about Saran; then we had prayer together that the Lord would guide us in handling the matter.

The following morning Kong and his wife San came to the building to talk with me and Thay. Because they were dressed in their best clothes, I wondered if this was some special occasion. They had even arranged for someone to watch the orphans for them so they could come together and formally present their request.

"Brother Todd," Kong said after they seated themselves, "San and I have been praying and we want you to know we are willing to move to Pailin if you're looking for someone to take over the church."

I glanced over at Thay just in time to see a smile break on his face.

"But what should we do with Solomon Church?" I asked Kong.

"As you know," he responded, "Dana and Narein have been working close with me. I feel they're ready for leadership. Sam-Oeurn can oversee their ministry and since they all meet with you for prayer every morning you can help guide them."

In a matter of days our leaders chose Dana to assume the

pastorate of Solomon Church and appointed Kong and his family to take over the work in Pailin. I gave Kong enough support to pay the advance rent on a building for the church, and a place for them to live. A week later DeAnn and I vacated the house where we had been living with Kong's family. We rarely had running water, and this, along with the problems of rats and thieves, made the place impractical. We moved our things back into a one-room apartment in the building and located the orphans in the room next to ours.

With Kong launching a new work in Pailin, I hoped the heaviness I felt for Saran would lift; rather, it seemed to intensify as the days rolled by. There was an increased awareness that we had failed to complete God's judgment on Saran. "But what is it we are to do?" I asked the Lord. "Are we hard of hearing?"

Then one night the fog lifted. I had been up late reading the Bible and praying for direction concerning Saran. Finally, I decided to go to bed. I had just stretched out under the mosquito net when all my mental energies shifted and the biblical story of Samuel and Saul was re-created before me—almost as if it were a movie. I watched Samuel take a flask of oil, pour it over Saul's head and kiss him, saying, "Has not the LORD anointed you a ruler over His inheritance?" (1 Sam. 10:1). Afterwards the Spirit of God came upon Saul and he was recognized as prophet. Then Saul disobeyed the word of the Lord and sinned—first once, then twice. The word of the Lord returned to Samuel saying, "I regret that I have made Saul king, for he has turned back from following Me" (1 Sam. 15:11). Samuel was deeply grieved and mourned over Saul, for he loved him as his own son. Then God sent Samuel to withdraw Saul's anointing—"You have rejected the word of the LORD, therefore He has rejected you. . . . He has torn the kingdom of Israel from you today" (1 Sam. 15:23, 28). Samuel was then ordered to fill his flask and anoint another.

I suddenly realized the parallel between this story and our problem with Saran. He had been anointed through our ministry; he was filled with the power of the Holy Spirit and recognized as a leader. He then sinned—first once, then twice. God's words came to us, exposing the problem and saying, "He has ceased to follow

173

me," but we had yet failed to do one thing—to exercise our spiritual authority and withdraw his anointing.

For the first time I understood what Paul meant when he said, "I have decided to deliver such a one over to Satan for the destruction of his flesh . . ." (1 Cor. 5:5; also see 1 Tim. 1:20). Also 1 Samuel 16:14 was brought out from the dungeon of obscurity: "Now the Spirit of the LORD departed from Saul, and an evil spirit from the LORD terrorized him." It was now clear to me what we had to do. In a formal way, we had to release Saran from God's Spirit into the hands of Satan that he may be taught not to blaspheme the Lord's anointing. But now the question was, how to carry this out?

I arose before dawn and anxiously paced the floor, awaiting the morning prayer gathering. As I discussed the matter with DeAnn we both felt an urgency to act on the matter as soon as possible. "Let's hurry to the prayer room," DeAnn suggested. When Thay arrived for the prayer meeting I quickly took him aside. As of yet we had told no one else about Saran except for those in leadership, and we didn't want the news to leak out unless it was necessary.

After I explained what God had shown me in the night, Thay responded very negatively. "No!" he said, "I can't have a part in that . . . I've done that before and I've learned not to . . ." his voice faded as he stood shaking his head.

"Then what do we do?" I urged.

"I don't know," he confessed. "But at least give me until tomorrow to pray about it."

The next morning seemed never to come, but I felt sure God would speak to Thay. The Scripture says, "On the evidence of two or three witnesses a matter shall be confirmed" (Deut. 19:15) and I needed Thay's confirmation. I entered the prayer room the following morning feeling more convinced than ever that we needed to move quickly. This was further established when Sam-Oeurn and Youvannette arrived.

Seating themselves on the mat next to me, they said, "The Lord has shown us that if we don't act as He has directed concerning Saran, then He will act on us and remove our work from before

174

Him.''

"Where's Thay?" I questioned impatiently. "He needs to hear this." We waited and waited until the prayer meeting was nearly over. Finally I decided to look for him in his office downstairs. I hurried down two flights of steps to the second floor and peered through his window. There he sat behind his desk with his face buried in his arms.

"Thay," I said, opening the door. "What's wrong? Why weren't you at the prayer meeting?" He raised his head, exposing his bloodshot eyes.

"You were right," he said soberly. "We've failed to carry out the Lord's judgment." He handed me his Bible, pointing to a Scripture.

"Read this," he said, "God spoke to me from my morning reading." My eyes quickly covered the passage.

"Thus says the LORD, 'Because you have let go out of your hand the man whom I had devoted to destruction, therefore your life shall go for his life" (1 Kings 20:42).

My eyes skimmed the context before replying. I was amazed how God was confirming what we must do.

"I feel that's a final warning," Thay said. "We should begin today. We can draft some letters and I'll fly up north to confront Saran and explain our decision to Kong and the rest of the Christians. You can watch over things here. If there's any problem, I'll send for you."

I agreed. We carefully drafted a letter telling Saran he was banned from fellowship until further notice. We made several copies of the letter, distributed them to church leaders explaining about Saran's excommunication. Everyone was in agreement concerning our action. Then we all laid hands on Thay and prayed for him to have a successful journey. As I watched him leave for the airport around mid-morning, I felt my concern could rest for a while. I didn't realize it, but the battle was at that moment approaching our doorstep.

Just before our evening meeting, I was sitting at the desk meditating over my Bible readings, when suddenly Sina came bursting through the door.

"Saran's here!" he said, panting from the climb up the stairs.

"What!" I exclaimed in amazement.

"Yes, he's downstairs. He's been arguing with some of the students and speaking evil of you and Thay."

A sickened feeling went through me. I was just getting ready to minister in the evening service and then this had to happen. After Sina left my office I buried my head in prayer. I felt weak and powerless.

"Lord Jesus," I cried, "I thought we had settled this affair. What do you want me to do?" Then a scene from the gospels flashed before me. I received a mental picture of Jesus making a scourge of cords and cleansing the temple. He was consumed with a zeal for God's house.

I quickly opened my Bible to my evening reading and my eyes fastened on a passage of Scriptures wherein the Lord is speaking to Joshua:

> Rise up! Why is it you have fallen on your face? Israel
> has sinned . . . both stolen and deceived. (7:10-11)
> . . . neither will I be with you any more. . . . until ye
> take away the accursed thing from among you. (7:12-13,
> KJV)

My thoughts were interrupted by singing in the auditorium above my office. I glanced at my watch; the service had begun.

Quickly grabbing my Bible, I ran up the stairs. In the evening session we had been studying 1 Timothy. I was stunned when it suddenly dawned on me that we were beginning chapter 3 that night. I gasped to myself, "This is the same chapter I was reading when the Lord first spoke to me about Saran!"

I lifted my head and peered out into the assembly. There he sat, about four rows from the back. I was dumbfounded; never had I received so much guidance and confirmation about a matter in all my Christian days. As I began to read in 1 Timothy 3 about the qualifications of a leader, I realized Saran had transgressed many, if not all the requirements. Verses 6 and 7 really stood out to me:

> And not a new convert, lest he become conceited and fall
> into the condemnation incurred by the devil.

He must have a good reputation with those outside the
church, so that he may not fall into reproach and the snare
of the devil.

I was quite prepared to expound this chapter. Before I spoke I
notified Hach and Sina to gather all the leaders and elders into my
office after the meeting and to tell Saran I wanted to see him.

As the leaders gathered together no one had to ask why we were
calling a special meeting; it was all too apparent. Once the twelve
of us were seated, Sina brought Saran into the room.

"What's this all about?" Saran questioned as he nervously
lowered himself into the vacant chair facing my desk.

"Saran," I said with compassion, "this hurts us more than you
will ever know. But unless we do as the Lord has directed, He said
He would remove us and destroy our work. Therefore, because of
our zeal for God, we are releasing you from fellowship."

With that, I handed him the letter of excommunication that we
had drafted that morning. I wished Thay were there to help with
this encounter.

"You can't do this!" he said in a sinister tone.

"Yes we can," Sam-Oeurn countered, "because the Lord has
spoken to us."

"He's right," I added. "As of now we withdraw God's
authority and the anointing of His Spirit from your life. You are not
allowed to place your foot in any of our centers of ministry unless
we notify you otherwise."

He tried to argue against our decision but we told him it was
useless. What we had decided was final, and we ended the painful
scene by dismissing him. He left, slamming the door in anger.

Though everyone was saddened by this terrible nightmare,
all of us sensed a release in our spirit. My only concern was that we
had done all that God required of us. I knew that without the
leading of the Holy Spirit I would never have had the strength to
carry out what we had just done. But I still had lingering doubts of
concern. This seemed so contrary to the Christian way of handling
things in the West.

As we stood to leave, DeAnn suggested that we join hands and commit the matter to the Lord. For the next fifteen minutes we entered into a wonderful time of prayer together. But then I became increasingly troubled by Youvannette, who had started weeping profusely.

She must really be full of remorse over Saran, I thought to myself. "Lord," I cried, "I pray we've done the right thing."

When we finished praying, Youvannette still sobbed heavily. Sam-Oeurn wrapped his arm around her and they slowly climbed the two flights of steps to their quarters. Sina, Hach, Sony and the rest of those present gradually disappeared into the night until DeAnn and I were left alone. We had such mixed emotions; the only way we could describe our feeling was confused and listless. Neither of us felt like eating, though it was long after supper time. A few moments later the dull atmosphere was suddenly shattered by a terrific ruckus coming from the stairs.

"What's that?" DeAnn gasped as we hurried outside the room. We arrived at the foot of the stairs just in time to see Sam-Oeurn and Youvannette rounding the last turn of steps before reaching us. With grins from ear to ear, their faces beamed with excitement. They trembled and shook as they laughed and chattered away in tongues. It took us nearly thirty minutes to settle them down enough to catch the whole story of what had happened.

Youvannette's weeping had not been tears of remorse as I had thought. Rather they were expressions of praise and rejoicing. While we were gathered in prayer she had seen a vision of the Lord standing over us.

"He was clothed in white flowing robes," she described, "and a crown on His head dazzled brightly. Myriads of angels stood about Him, singing and praising God more beautifully than I've ever heard. Jesus began to shower us with what looked like flowers. Then His voice resounded in words that pierced me like swords. 'Receive the Holy Spirit,' He said, as the flowers fell on us. But when I looked closely I saw that the flowers were in the shape of tiny doves, landing gently upon all of us. I'll never forget what He said next: 'I'm now coming to live with you because you have obeyed me.' "

As Youvannette related those last words my mind raced back to the final message the Lord had given me concerning Saran. "I will not be with you any more unless you remove the accursed thing from your midst." Now after obeying His voice, He tells us, "I'm now coming to live with you because you have obeyed me." Samuel's words to Saul flashed before me, "To obey is better than sacrifice" (1 Sam. 15:22). I could have shouted I was so happy.

Sam-Oeurn continued the explanation, "When we reached the top of the stairs, Youvannette spoke to me and said, 'Wasn't that wonderful?' I didn't know what she was talking about. 'I mean the Lord,' she explained, 'how He appeared to us.' The vision was so real to her that she thought we all had seen it. Then we were knocked to our knees and began trembling and speaking in tongues. After that she could hardly tell me what had happened."

Moments later Hach appeared. He, too, was excited. After he had left us he had gone to his room to pray. As he knelt near his bed suddenly a heat entered into his fingertips and rushed through his body. He, too, found himself shaking and speaking in tongues.

"Can a person be baptized with the Holy Spirit twice?" he asked.

"I don't know," I replied frankly. "I'm afraid to say anything until God finishes overhauling my theology. We are all learning together," I said patting him on the back.

But this was just the beginning. On Sunday, three weeks later, we had just had a wonderful morning service and fourteen had given their lives to Jesus. The Lord had truly moved in. There were so many new believers we didn't know what to do with them. All our churches were experiencing the same problem. Three meetings a day was hardly enough. Our weekly baptisms were times of great rejoicing.

On this particular Sunday, a baptismal was scheduled for the afternoon. In the meantime, DeAnn and I decided to rest in our one-room apartment, since this was our day of fasting. As we made our way to our quarters, we stopped at the room next to ours to look in on the five orphans.

"What do you think the Lord wants us to do with them?"

179

DeAnn asked in frustration. For nearly an hour we sat in our room, discussing the problem. Even the two families in the States and Canada were encountering all sorts of roadblocks. For more than eight months the orphans had been with us and there was no foreseeable break in the red tape that tied up their cases.

"Perhaps the Lord wants us to adopt them all," I answered DeAnn. "We might as well, they've been with us this long. But even if the visas are granted, what will happen to the work if we have to leave it to deliver these orphans? It's liable to collapse."

About an hour had passed since the morning service had ended. We decided to go for a ride on the cycle. But as we walked out the door of our living quarters, we found the building in chaos. People were running up and down the stairs full of laughter and excitement.

"Pentecost! Pentecost!" Sopha repeated, pointing upstairs, as she disappeared on the landing below.

"Wind," Sam-Bo added. "And tongues—everyone is speaking in tongues. And Peter!" he said, breathless and motioning down to the second-floor auditorium, "Peter's downstairs!"

"Pentecost . . . wind . . . tongues . . . Peter? What's going on here?" I questioned. Finally, Thay appeared and began to explain to me what had happened.

"After the service," he informed me, "about thirty people went to the prayer room on the roof. They had no more than begun to pray when suddenly a strong wind blew into the room. They said even the shutters were blown back by the force of it. Everyone began speaking in tongues—and most of them had never even heard of the experience! It was definitely the Lord. Then Somaly stood and began prophesying; she has continued now for over an hour! I've never seen anything like it!"

"But what's this about Peter?" I questioned eagerly.

"Oh, that," he said, laughing. "They're just drawing a parallel between Acts chapter 2 and what happened here. First the wind and tongues, then Peter stood and began to speak. So they've given the name Peter to Somaly."

It was more than I could comprehend. We quickly made our way down to the large hall where she was standing in the far corner of the room with her back to us, still prophesying. I could hardly believe my eyes. Several people were gathered in front of Somaly as she thundered messages to one and then another. I was astonished. She was such a meek woman and so young in the Lord. Never had I heard more than a peep out of her. But here she was, prophesying with all the authority of heaven behind her. God was speaking through her like she was His mouthpiece. Then she stopped abruptly.

"Todd Burke," she said loudly with her back still to us. "Come here, quickly."

"This has to be of God," DeAnn said as we made our way to where she was standing. Then she turned and pointed at us. "I will not have you concerned any longer about your orphans. You will take them to their new families. In three days I will give you a sign. When this happens then you will know it is I who has been working in your behalf. And when you go, do not be concerned about the work here—whether it will rise or fall without your presence. For know this: This is not your work, it is *mine*, and when you return, the church will shine like the sun."

When I opened my eyes, I saw DeAnn's face streaked with tears. God had just exposed the secrets of our hearts. No one knew of our problems and concerns over the orphans, nor of the conversation we had just had in the privacy of our room. But God knew, and He undoubtedly had spoken. He had come to live with us.

Now our question was, "What is going to happen in three days?"

181

CHAPTER 13

Shining Like the Sun

The morning of the third day after Somaly's prophecy couldn't dawn soon enough for me. I was sure the sign would be the release of the orphans by the Cambodian government. In a practical sense, the children already belonged to us, but legally the release papers would not be signed until visas were granted by the United States and Canada. The problem was a sticky one because the western countries were refusing visas for the orphans until they received documents from us certifying the release. We had been round and round, pleading and begging on our end, until the situation had reached a deadlock. Only President Lon Nol could intervene now, I was told. Dy Bellong had promised to be our mediator in this matter, but he was taking his time about the whole thing. For months now we had been waiting, praying for the future of these five beautiful Khmer babies.

But the prophecy three days earlier had sparked the dying ember of hope in me. The Lord promised a sign and we were ready for one. I went to visit Dy Bellong to see if he had indeed fulfilled his promise to us by securing the orphans' release from the president, only to find he had gone on a trip up north to oversee the dedication of refugee facilities. He wouldn't be back for several days.

I knew better than to try to approach Thach Toan, the minister of social welfare, about the problem. He was already defiantly opposed to our request, especially since the Luyendyk family in Canada wanted to adopt our four orphan boys. Many of the Khmer people feared that orphans sent to the West would end up being used as family servants. I vividly recalled our heated encounter which had taken place two months earlier.

"So, you choose to work through Mr. Dy Bellong, do you?" he had coolly remarked. "He cannot help you in this matter. The president has no authority over my department, and you will not get any help from me."

My tension rose, but I tried to remain calm. "We will get help," I said. "God will answer our prayers." I had hoped that by some stroke of divine providence he would feel compassion for our situation, but there was none to be found in him—especially since he knew of our friendship with Dy Bellong, his long-despised political rival.

Snapping back to reality, I kick-started my Yamaha and drove from the government compound. "So much for the 'sign in three days,' " I mumbled to myself. I had given up hope too quickly, however. I was about to see the Lord's words come to pass in a way I had least expected.

Nearing the American Embassy I decided to turn in and check our mail. It was still mid-morning, but I thought there might be something there already. And there was—a telegram and a letter. "Who would be sending us a telegram?" I asked myself while ripping the envelope open. It was from the Canadian High Commission in Singapore: "Authorization for four children to be placed with Luyendyk received today. Visas being sent to you via British or American diplomatic bag soonest."

I reread the cable, fearing I had possibly misunderstood the message. This was totally incredible that visas would be issued without the release form from the Khmer government. 'Impossible!' I told myself. But here it was . . . officially acknowledged by the Canadian immigration office in Singapore. My emotions soared as I quickly slit open the other envelope. It was a letter from the Warners—the American family that was to adopt Tevi, our only girl orphan. My eyes fixed on the second paragraph.

"On Saturday, July 6th we received our approval from the office of immigration on our petition for relative immigrant visa for Tevi. Since it was our understanding that this would not be granted until the release form was sent by you, we were a bit surprised to receive this approval. I checked and they said they went ahead and gave approval even though they did not have the release form." I later learned this visa would be forthcoming via diplomatic bag, the same way as the Luyendyks' visas. This meant the visas would come from these foreign governments directly to the embassy without going through the Cambodian postal system.

I could scarcely hold back the tears that stung my eyes. After so long, finally God was answering our prayers. His "sign" had indeed come to pass on the third day. This was further testimony to the Khmer believers, and also to the Warners and Luyendyks, that these children had been selected and appointed by God for them. I rushed home with the news and DeAnn and I began preparations for our flight to the States to deliver the orphans.

In a matter of weeks all papers were in hand, passports issued and vaccination requirements complete. I had cabled the families to inform them of our arrival time. I also advised them the amount of cash to have on hand to reimburse us for airfares and for nine months of care for the children. Both families had agreed from the outset to completely finance this endeavor, as we did not have sufficient funds to cover these expenses from our own pocket.

In calculating the cost for each family, DeAnn and I had decided to split the cost of our return flight between them. "It's only fair," I rationalized. "After all, we have to get back to our work here, and we're actually going out of our way to bring their children to them." But we had no peace in our hearts after sending the telegrams. DeAnn was especially troubled about this, so we decided to seek the Lord about the matter.

From the moment we determined to ask God's counsel, He clearly revealed to us His mind. We were bombarded in every Scripture reading that day. "Let no one seek his own good, but that of his neighbor" (1 Cor. 10:24). This one really hit us hard, especially when we took into account that the Luyendyk family would be covering the expenses for four children. But the verse that gave us joy to fulfill this command from the Lord was found in DeAnn's reading: ". . . for you were called for the very purpose that you might inherit a blessing" (1 Pet. 3:9).

"It's a promise from the Lord," DeAnn reasoned, "that if we

will obey Him in this, He will provide a great blessing for us. Who knows, maybe He will cause the funds for our return passage to come from elsewhere. After all, if He wants us back here, it's His problem—not ours.''

The matter was settled. I immediately wired the families again to inform them of the reduced amount. "Lord," I prayed, "you've shown us your will through your word today; we saw your hand work in our behalf the third day after Somaly's prophecy. Now I want to see the church 'shine like the sun' as you promised. We trust you to bring us back to this land. I believe you for it, Lord.''

Our visit with the children's adoptive parents was a joyous occasion. They were so thrilled to at last fondle and caress the beloved children they had waited more than nine long months to receive. After delivering the orphans we traveled to the Midwest where we visited our families and shared with friends what God was sovereignly doing in war-torn Cambodia. In the most miraculous ways, the Lord fulfilled His promise of granting us a blessing. We were invited to share with groups we had never known before, and they showered us with gifts for the Lord's work in Cambodia.

One evening we met with a large charismatic group in Lawrence, Kansas. At the close of the meeting a middle-aged lady approached DeAnn, hugged her and pressed an envelope into her hand. As we were about to drive away, DeAnn opened the envelope and was shocked to find a check for $2,000.

"I expected it would be twenty dollars or so," DeAnn cried. "Can you believe this!" But it was only the beginning. By the time we boarded the flight heading across the Pacific toward Asia, we had inherited a blessing of more than thirteen thousand dollars. During the first year in Cambodia, we had barely made it each month, stretching the offerings to feed ourselves and five other families, as well as carry the work of the church.

"Now we can get the guitars we need for the different churches!" I shouted.

"And a portable P.A. system for the evangelism team!" DeAnn added.

"And a Honda bus to carry them from village to village!"

"Praise the Lord!" we rejoiced together.

Our six-week stay in the United States passed all too quickly, but we were anxious to return to our brothers and sisters in Cambodia. We longed for the intimate fellowship we had experienced with our Khmer family there, and by this time we realized Cambodia was home for us. We had excitedly recounted to our friends the Lord's last words to us, "The church will shine like the sun." We were eager to see this prophecy fulfilled firsthand.

As our Air Cambodge Caravelle jet neared Phnom Penh, DeAnn looked out the window, commenting, "I never saw it like this before. Those craters left from the B-52 bombings make the countryside look like the surface of the moon."

I leaned over to see what she was talking about. "Hey, you're right," I replied. "Only those craters are full of water. They look like huge ponds."

It had been over a year since Congress had ordered a halt to the United States bombing of Communist sanctuaries in Cambodia, but the horrible scars remained.

DeAnn shook her head sadly. "It's such a beautiful country to be torn up like this. And the people have suffered so much."

We sat silently while the plane landed and taxied to the terminal. The airport seemed quiet because the Khmer Rouge had withdrawn during the monsoon season; but in a matter of weeks, the dry season would come and the attacks would resume.

The drive from Pochentong Airport into the city brought tears to our eyes. Coming from the land of plenty to a country so destitute was sobering and once again we felt the ache in our hearts for the Cambodians' inescapable plight. "This is where we belong," I whispered to DeAnn. She nodded her head and smiled in agreement. The cool breeze off the small lake nearby blew gently through the taxi as we made frequent stops along the way. When we arrived in front of our building the scene came alive with students, children and neighbors rushing out to see us unload our things.

"Oh, it's good you come back!" Sam-Oeurn's father shouted. Others joined in the chorus of greeting, sweeping us up the stairs to

186

our room. With all this help we soon settled in, changed clothes, and took a tour of the work. On the surface, the church did shine; the building was spotless, walls had been whitewashed, tile floors waxed, even the pots and pans in the kitchen reflected our image.

"Well, Thay, what's been happening?" I asked anxiously.

"I hardly know where to begin," he laughed easily. "So much has happened—I guess I'll start at the beginning."

Thay proceeded to unfold countless stories of those who had turned their lives over to Jesus. We now had hired two of the best carpenters in all of Phnom Penh and they were working full-time constructing benches for new fellowships that had started while we were gone. An added blessing was that they and their families were now believers, too.

"You received a letter from Oddvar Johansen," Thay said, handing me a letter across the desk. "He has offered to help us with funds for aid work among refugees if we need it. Also, he says Pastor Stanley Sjoberg from Stockholm, Sweden, is coming to Phnom Penh for a week and will be available for special meetings."

I noted the contacts Oddvar suggested for securing blankets, mosquito nets and meager necessities for refugees. "There are a lot of needs for leprosy work where Kong is located in Pailin," Thay suggested.

"Yes, I may have to make a short trip up that way to see how he's doing," I said. "What else has been going on around here?"

Thay grinned broadly, "It looks like we might start a new church in Battambang!"

"Really?" I was surprised at his statement.

"You remember Ang?" he questioned. "Well, he was recently transferred to Battambang and wrote us a couple of weeks ago about a group of new believers meeting in his home every evening. He said he felt too inadequate to pastor them, and asked if we would send Sam-Oeurn and Youvannette to launch the church."

"That's right," I recalled aloud. "Sam-Oeurn was the one that led him to the Lord, wasn't he? What does Sam-Oeurn think about the idea?"

Thay laughed heartily. "Well, now he's ready and willing to go!

187

You wouldn't believe how the Lord has spoken to him, confirming this move. He just wanted to wait until you returned before leaving.''

Thay went on to explain how Solomon Church had been growing steadily and Dana, who took over the church when Kong left, now had a group of devoted elders to stand with him in shepherding the flock of God. One of these leaders, Maran, had been praying many months for his sister, Channa, to come to the meetings. One humid Sunday morning he was genuinely surprised to see her sitting near the back.

"Good morning, sister," he said, sitting down beside her. Noticing tears welling up in her eyes, he tenderly asked, "What is wrong?"

Breaking out in sobs she explained her difficult situation. A once-wealthy friend, now a refugee, had entrusted to her his last prized possession—a costly emerald that was a family heirloom. "He begged me to sell it for him so that his family would have money to live on," she told her brother. "The value of that one stone is more than my house! I accepted the jewel and told mother about it. Together we decided on a safe place to keep it until I could find a suitable buyer."

She went on to explain that one day while she was gone to market a man visited her mother. He had a notorious reputation for stealing and gambling. "Mother didn't know about him—if I had been there I would never have shown the stone to that man! But she showed it to him, and he took it, offering to sell it. Mother thought she was helping me, so she willingly let him take it. Now we haven't seen him in over a week! And today my poor friend came, desperate for money. I don't know what to do!" she cried, hiding her eyes in her damp handerchief. Channa had resigned herself to the fact that she would never see the stone again. She had already placed her home up for sale so she could reimburse her friend.

"If your Jesus really loves me as you have said, will He help me?" she sobbed.

"Of course. He will help if you ask Him," Maran declared confidently. "Come, let's pray together," he said as they walked to the front of the church. She was overcome with emotion as the entire congregation joined together in praying for her. For the first time in days she felt a stir of hope within her heart.

Walking home after the service, Channa noticed a motor scooter parked outside her house. "Who could that be?" she wondered, not recognizing the vehicle. She stepped up her pace.

Waiting inside the doorway was the man who had taken the precious stone. She looked at him in stunned silence.

"I . . . I brought this stone back to you," he replied, groping for words. "I was going to sell it and keep the money for myself, but I couldn't do it. I felt so terrible I knew I had to give it back to you before I could have peace of mind again. Here it is." He gently rolled the sparkling emerald into her hand and quickly left.

Flying back to the church as fast as her legs could carry her, she burst through the door. "I believe, I believe!" she shouted. To the amazement of all within earshot, she shared the immediate answer to her prayer. And now, because of the proof of God's great love for her, she yielded her life to Him and signed over a priceless love offering to the church—a beautiful piece of village property on the outskirts of the city with a barn-like structure.

"It is already being used as another meeting place for believers," Thay said enthusiastically. "And they named it Emmanuel Church—God with us!"

"Not only that, but several other house churches have been started since you've been gone. One in particular was spurred by the salvation of Nahvi and Somaly. Now their mother has come to know the Lord, along with three other sisters, Sida, Sidara, and Kannitha. They have opened their huge home for meetings every night and Sina and Hach are leading them in Bible study and prayer. It's really been a blessing for all of them!"

"I can hardly believe it!" I exclaimed, shaking my head. "It's as if this whole work has exploded since we've been gone. Maybe we ought to leave more often," I joked.

"But we have good news from our trip," DeAnn exclaimed. "The believers in America have given money to help us in the work. Now we can buy some vehicles for the evangelism teams, and install a telephone in the building."

Our afternoon passed quickly as we shared fellowship with the board members and elders of the other Phnom Penh churches. The evening meeting at Maranatha Church was cut short by the newly-imposed seven o'clock curfew, but we enjoyed a blessed reunion. God was doing so many wonderful things in our midst, constantly assuring all of us of His presence. Every heart was full of excitement and joy was bubbling forth with inspired psalms, hymns, and spiritual songs. DeAnn and I had both waited eagerly for this and now we were seeing it. Over thirty songs had been written during our absence and new ones were being composed every day. Nothing short of a baptism of music was sweeping all our churches. With full hearts, we gratefully sank into bed that night.

"Do you hear that?" DeAnn whispered as she lay in bed.

"Yes, that's the song Youvannette wrote for the children in Bible class here at Maranatha," I whispered back. Echoing faintly through the night we could hear the tender voices of children singing behind the closed doors of their individual homes. As the sound drifted through the neighborhood, we could hear other young voices joining in the melody.

"The whole neighborhood is being evangelized by our kids!" I said, laughing.

"It's like an angelic chorus lulling us to sleep," DeAnn sighed drowsily.

When Pastor Sjoberg arrived from Stockholm, Sweden, about three weeks later, he was utterly exhausted. Yet within only a few hours he managed to preach the evening service at Maranatha Church.

When we took him out for dinner afterwards, he told us, "I've been preaching and traveling for about a month now, and I had become so tired I didn't think I could possibly go ahead with these meetings. But after tonight—seeing the hunger of your people and witnessing their responsiveness to the Spirit—I felt new strength enter my body. They revive me!"

Before the week was over, dozens of people had come to the Lord and many more were filled with the Holy Spirit. Pastor Sjoberg shared accounts of his visits to believers in Iron Curtain countries who were suffering persecution for their faith. As he related miraculous ways God had protected and strengthened them, our people were encouraged to trust God to sustain them through the difficulties of the war. Only later did we realize how timely this encouragement really was.

During his visit, we gave Stanley a grand tour of our work at Maranatha Church and the other congregations scattered throughout Phnom Phem. He was effervescent as he expressed his desire to financially sponsor our literature projects. "I want to help you print this," he declared in his Swedish accent, commenting about the translated excerpt of the book, *The Martyr of the Catacombs*—a beautiful novel about the struggles of the early Christians under government persecution. "And that one for new believers you showed me."

"*Food For Spiritual Growth*—we're still working on that," I explained.

"That's a worthy project, too! Let us help you with that. And how about help for refugees? Could you use funds for that?"

Thay was thrilled. He had secretly been hoping we could help the plight of the hundreds of people streaming into the capital city daily. Later that day we introduced Stanley to Dy Bellong and together we outlined a proposal for a refugee resettlement camp that would house more than three hundred families, with plans to have a Christian supervisor for each fifty houses.

In His own sovereign way, God was causing the shining church of Cambodia to continue to penetrate the darkness surrounding her.

One rainy morning as I sat in my office, Hach appeared at the door carrying an envelope. "Here is a letter for you, Brother Todd," he said, placing it on the desk in front of me. "It's from the Bible school across town."

This was the third letter I had received from the director of the Takhmau Bible School which had been established by the other missionaries working in the country. Their two previous letters had begged me to come and help. One of their church workers had apparently become demon possessed and he had everyone literally scared to death.

"He never sleeps," the Khmer director wrote. "And he keeps telling different ones of us that we are going to die soon. When we try to pray for him he spits on us. We are frightened—please come!"

Their letters broke my heart, but I knew I couldn't go. The school was sponsored by the other missionaries and every time I did something that spilled over into their camp, I was accused of sheep stealing.

"How can one of their Christian workers get demon possessed?" I asked Thay in amazement.

"That doesn't shock me," he replied. "In fact, it was that kind of thing that made me hungry for more of God's power. I was sick of seeing people come to church on Sunday wearing devil strings, then going home and burning incense in their spirit houses. They know very little about spiritual warfare or being led by the Holy Spirit."

I returned a note explaining why I didn't feel I should come. But I did give them some basic instructions on how to deal with the possessed man. "If you still have trouble," I wrote, "contact one of your missionaries."

Now, two days later, I was eager to find out what this third letter had to disclose.

"He has become worse," the man wrote. "The demon screams and laughs at us when we try to pray or cast it out. He has me convinced that I will die soon. We've contacted the missionary and have done everything you suggested, but he shouts back at us and says, 'I'm not afraid of you or anyone else except Todd Burke.' You are the only one the demon will listen to. Please come and help us."

"Why me?" I swallowed.

"Like I said before," he replied, "they know little of spiritual warfare. But when they get desperate enough they'll bring the possessed man to you." Thay's words were prophetic.

It was about an hour before curfew that evening. DeAnn had just cleared the table and we were standing around talking with stragglers leaving the evening service. Suddenly, we heard what sounded like an army of footsteps climbing the stairway.

"It's the Takhmau Bible School," Thay yelled up to us. The next thing I saw was a crowd of Khmer students flooding into the auditorium where we were standing.

DeAnn pointed to a man who was tightly restrained by two of their instructors. "He must be that possessed man," she said moving to the side.

Then he began squirming and screaming, "I'm afraid! Let me go, I'm afraid!" With little effort he broke their grasp and rushed towards me, stripping off his clothes. "Todd Burke," he yelled, bowing at my feet with gestures of worship.

"Oh no you don't," I said, jerking him from the floor and shoving him against the wall. "Only Jesus receives worship around here—no one else is worthy." Thay quickly grabbed the man's sarong and retied it about his waist as I pinned his arms against the plaster. He was bare-chested and had no shoes on his muddy feet. His eyes were fixed in a blank stare as he mechanically nodded in agreement. Unshaven, he looked like he hadn't slept in a week; dark circles bagged under his bloodshot eyes.

"I'm a demon from Satan," his voice shrilled suddenly. "You—"

"Shut up demon!" I spoke firmly, interrupting him. "In Jesus' name I command you to be quiet. We aren't going to stand here and listen to your babbling lies that you've been telling all these people. We don't put up with that."

"Don't say anymore," the demon pleaded. "I'm afraid of you—leave me alone."

"We bind your power and influence over this man," I continued confidently. "No longer will you torment these people—you are bound in Jesus' name. We will say no more." I motioned for the Khmer Bible school instructors to escort him away.

"But aren't you going to finish?" they questioned.

"We're finished," I assured them. "For that kind of demon, that's all that is necessary."

"He's right," Thay added. "From our many encounters with demonic power we've learned that, next to trying to worship and appease them, the worst thing you can do is to allow them to occupy your time with their lying. They'll detain you for hours and fill you with fear. You just have to let them know that you're confident in Christ and speak the word."

"But what should we do about those prophecies of death?" one Khmer instructor asked sincerely, mopping the perspiration from his brown face.

"Rebuke them!" I answered forcefully. "You don't want to believe a lie, do you? You'll fulfill it yourself!" The students were somber, seemingly concentrating all their attention on our instructions.

Then they filed out silently and I wondered how they were going to make it back to their compound before curfew.

"They don't have a pass do they, Thay?" I asked, concerned for their safety.

"No, not that I know of. We'd better pray they don't get arrested or shot."

The following afternoon a letter was delivered to me from one of their missionaries. That morning the man who had been possessed was found well and in his right mind. "We want to thank you," their note said humbly, "for the lesson our students learned from you yesterday. We'll never forget it."

Within the next week I planned a short excursion up north to accompany Sam-Oeurn and Youvannette to Battambang. We flew in an embassy plane and Ang joyfully met us at the airport. Leaving them to settle into a small apartment that Ang had secured, I hurriedly joined the early morning caravan to Pailin to see Kong. I was excited to see what God had done there since he had replaced Saran. Little did I know what a harrowing experience awaited me.

This trip over pocked, dusty roads usually took about five hours and the cars were packed tight with eight to ten passengers each. The caravan always ran at top speed, never stopping except at government-protected checkpoints because the area was frequently occupied by the Khmer Rouge. After leaving at nine o'clock with truckloads of military escorts, we traveled west for three hours until we were suddenly halted by the explosions of hidden mines ahead of us. Rockets exploded not far from our caravan and the atmosphere was showered with rifle and machine-gun fire and the blast of grenades. Car doors flew open and the passengers dived out, hitting the dust and searching for cover from the vicious attack. Some found refuge underneath the vehicles as they frantically grasped their devil strings and fetishes. The volume of chanting and prayers, mixed with cries of children, was drowned out by the continued noise of firing and explosions.

At first I remained seated in the car, frozen by the sudden attack. Then, frantically ducking down, I grabbed my Bible and quickly sought for my afternoon reading, Deuteronomy 2. I skimmed the chapter which told how the Israelites were passing through the lands of many peoples and kings, but when they came to Sihon, king of Heshbon, he would not let them pass. Moses sent messengers to plead with him, "Let me pass through your land, I will travel only on the highway. I will not turn aside to the right or to the left" (v. 27). I uttered those words out loud as if they applied to our situation right then. Reading on, I saw where they fought one battle and the Lord delivered them, allowing them to pass. Then suddenly the firing ceased. The immediate silence was almost as alarming as the onslaught had been! Within a few minutes a head count revealed no dead, no wounded—everyone completely protected—and we resumed our journey, arriving in Pailin shortly after two o'clock.

Kong informed me that six people had been killed just the day before when a car was hit on the way to Battambang. This narrow escape assured me all the more of the serious condition of the war, but it rightly pointed my confidence to the Father, in whom we live and move and have our being.

Kong's fellowship in Pailin had grown substantially and the Lord was pouring out His Spirit among them. He took me to visit Ton Kham, a Thai Christian living in Pailin, who had an interesting story to tell.

He received us in his home, then began to relate what God had done for him. "The doctor issued a statement advising me to set my house in order and distribute my estate," he said. "He gave me only one month to live because tuberculosis had filled both my lungs. My legs were also paralyzed. I immediately shared this distressing news with Pastor Kong and he was deeply disturbed."

I looked at Kong, and he confirmed his anxiety. "I grew upset in my spirit because I knew the Lord could heal Kham. The doctor's report was true, but I felt the sickness had come from Satan. I prayed and begged the Lord's answer. Then I felt faith to pray for Kham.''

Kham continued, ''Pastor came to my house and laid his hand upon me and since then I have been completely healed!'' He raised his hands into the air in praise to God.

''He has gone with me into the mountain villages,'' Kong added, ''and we preach to the people together. Kham speaks Thai, and very often we meet people who also knew the Thai language.'' His eyes twinkled as he broke into a smile. ''He has been well now long past the doctor's predictions, and we trust the Lord for many more years of service for Him.''

Back at Kong's house, San had prepared a delicious meal of rice and sour fish stew, and we enjoyed fellowship together before retiring. I lay awake long into the night, listening to the orchestra of bullfrogs and crickets, and repeatedly thanked God for His life in these faithful believers. ''You have done so much, Lord,'' I prayed, ''so much independent from our efforts—that is what blesses me the most.''

The next evening Kong gathered many of the townspeople and I spoke to them about the man who found the pearl of great price. Knowing the occupation of the residents of Pailin was that of mining precious stones, I purposely directed my message to them.

''Like Jesus told the woman at the well, 'If you drink this water, you'll thirst again,' '' I told the miners. ''No matter how many times you dig and find, you have to dig again.'' Then with reference to Jesus' parable of the kingdom in Matthew 13:44 I asked them, ''How would you like to find a field that possessed a precious stone so big that upon finding it you could cease from your labors and never have to toil again?'' Their faces lit up with the prospect. ''Would you sell everything you own to buy that field?'' They nodded their smiling responses with hands waving in the air.

I proceeded to introduce them to Jesus, the Rock of salvation, and to my great delight, dozens came forward to surrender their lives—to sell all they had in a sense—to gain the Pearl of great price. After praying with each one, Kong beamed with happiness.

"I've never seen the people here so responsive to the gospel," he shared with me later. "It's as if Cambodia is ready to meet Jesus!" he said enthusiastically.

"What do you mean?" I perked with interest.

"I remember before the war began in 1970," he continued, "there wasn't but a handful of Christians in Cambodia and we knew very little about the power of the Holy Spirit. Buddha was the Khmer's god. Life was entrenched in Buddhism, revolving around the myriad of pagodas and their saffron-robed priests. Missionaries labored for years and saw no results. You're lucky you weren't here then," he said seriously. "It was difficult to be a Christian, much less share Jesus with others. We were ridiculed, scoffed at, accused of importing a foreign god—some would even react towards us violently."

"He's right," San interjected. "Even when the war first began, the people's attitude didn't change but hardened more with the intoxication of war."

"Yes," Kong continued. "They were preoccupied with the excitement of a cause to fight and shed blood over. But as the war dragged on, their intoxication turned into a hangover. Everyone began to lose. The smell of death had touched every family and Buddhism offered no comfort. When you arrived in 1973 the spiritual temperature began to change drastically. For the first time my people's heart began to open to receive the message of Christ."

Kong's words sank deep into my spirit confirming what DeAnn and I felt about the miraculous experience that consummated our call to Cambodia—not that the outpouring of the Holy Spirit which was taking place was necessarily contingent upon our presence, but that God's timing was perfect in sending us when conditions were most opportune for the establishing of His kingdom.

The next morning I returned to Battambang by the taxi caravan, then caught a cargo plane to Phnom Penh. "Your church is shining, Lord," I prayed silently on the flight. "Thank you for letting me witness your glory—"

CHAPTER 14

Love Your Enemies

Early one morning as I sat in my office for prayer and Bible reading, I was particularly drawn to the passage in Matthew 10:16-23. Speaking to His disciples, Jesus tells them they will be persecuted, even delivered up to courts and brought before governors and kings as a testimony for His sake. I reflected on the testimonies we had heard from Pastor Sjoberg of the persecution of Christians behind the Iron Curtain and wondered if it would ever come to that in Cambodia.

About a half-hour later, Thay came rushing into my office, a look of consternation on his face and an official-looking paper in his hand. "Look at this," he said breathlessly, shoving it before me. I could tell it was important by all the seals, signatures, and official writing, but I couldn't decipher the script fast enough to satisfy my curiosity.

"What is it?" I asked impatiently

"It's a summons," he replied. "It was delivered to my house last night and I have to appear before the governor of my district for questioning tomorrow." He plopped into one of the chairs in front of my desk, wiping his brow.

"Questioning? About what?"

"About the church at my home," he responded. "Evidently some of my neighbors who have been giving us trouble about our meetings have taken their gripes to the authorities. We're accused of spreading foreign propaganda, among other things. I must answer to these charges tomorrow at nine o'clock in the governor's office.''

"Are you worried?" I probed. He sat up straight.

"Not for my sake," he said, "but I don't know how I'll answer them. I want to protect the church. Who knows? They have the power to ban our meetings or do whatever they want. I'm really concerned—a lot depends on tomorrow." As he talked I recalled the Scripture in Matthew.

"Listen to this, Thay—I just read this in my morning Bible readings. I believe it's for you: 'Do not become anxious about how or what you will speak; for it shall be given you in that hour what you are to speak' " (v. 19).

"Praise the Lord!" Thay exclaimed, as joy replaced the worry in his eyes. "That's encouraging—especially since you just received it." We joined hands and prayed for God to overrule in the affair and work it out for good and His glory. Thay went on his way, confident the matter would be resolved.

At nine o'clock the following morning he found the Spirit of the Lord had indeed gone before him and prepared the situation. An old friend of the governor was visiting with him when Thay entered the office.

"Nou Thay!" the governor's friend blurted out. "Is that you?" Thay was taken aback. He wasn't prepared for a friendly greeting. Then he recognized the man who was speaking. Being totally ignorant of the purpose of Thay's visit, the old man began bragging endlessly to the governor about Thay's fine qualities.

"Why I've known Nou Thay since he was just a young fellow," he exclaimed proudly. "Even tried to arrange his marriage to one of my daughters—wish now I had been successful!" he laughed, winking at Thay.

By the time they got around to discussing the summons, Thay had already shared with the governor and his friend about the Lord. "I will serve the Lord or die," he boldly declared. The governor was deeply impressed by what he heard. Their meeting ended with the governor's written permission for Thay to continue holding meetings in his home, and the rekindling of one forgotten friendship.

Another problem facing our workers was the military draft. It seemed that the ones who had the most trouble with this were the pastors of our outlying churches. One afternoon Sophal preached from his Bible about Jesus in the garden of Gethsemane and how he was apprehended by soldiers and led away to His death. On his way home from the meeting he, too, was apprehended by soldiers, put in a truck, and hauled off to army headquarters. As the war progressed the government couldn't spend much time in training their recruits—they just grabbed them off the streets, gave them a gun, and took them to the battlefield. Fortunately we got word about Sophal soon enough to arrange for his release. We persuaded the government that he was essential for our humanitarian work among the orphans and building refugee camps. We had to be alert and prayerful about our enemy's schemes to make crooked the Lord's straight ways.

A short time later I realized that persecution was indeed coming to the Cambodian church and it was becoming more severe. One day on our way to the morning prayer meeting, Thay and I met Sokun, a new believer, just outside the door of the prayer room. "What's wrong?" I asked, noticing he seemed upset.

He silently unbuttoned his bloodstained shirt and began to expose his back. I cringed, hardly believing what I was seeing. Sokun's eyes filled with tears before he could say a word.

"Oh, Lord!" I said, gasping. "What happened to you, Sokun?" He had uncovered a mass of welts, bruises and scabbed-over lash marks. Some wounds were still oozing blood.

"My father," his voice quivered. "He did it last night."

Thay interjected, "The other day his father stopped me outside in the street and warned me to leave his son alone. He accused me of brainwashing him and said if I continued he would call the police. I didn't know what to do. We don't force anyone to come to our meetings. I figured he was bluffing, but he must be serious!"

"He's serious all right," Sokun continued. "Last night he was furious. I told him I had decided to follow Jesus and that nothing would every change my mind. He slapped my face. 'We're Buddhists,' he screamed at me. 'No one in my house is going to follow Jesus!' I tried to explain to him, but he became more violent. I think he had been drinking.''

By this time, Hach had joined us to find out what was happening.

"He grabbed my wrists and tied my hands to a pole outside,'' Sokun continued, sobbing. "He tore my Bible to shreds and burned it before my eyes. Then he grabbed a bamboo stick and started to beat me with it. 'I'll drive this Jesus out of you,' he yelled over and over. I screamed for help until I had no more strength. Nearly the whole neighborhood came out to see what was happening but no one would dare help me. Finally, my mother stood between my father and me and pleaded for him to stop. He threw the stick on the ground and stormed inside the house while she quickly untied my hands and told me to leave home until things cooled down.''

"What did you do then?'' I asked, trying to control the anger I felt rising within.

"A friend let me sleep at his house last night, but now I've come to get your advice.'' His dark eyes pleaded for help.

"You can stay here until we find a believer's home where they can take you in,'' I replied.

Hach took Sokun downstairs to help him wash the blood off his back and find a clean shirt.

All the Khmer believers understood very well what Paul meant when he said, "All that will live godly in Christ Jesus shall suffer persecution" (2 Tim. 3:12, KJV). We always had at least one or two living in the building who had been forced to leave home because of their faith, but we finally had to stop allowing them to stay at the church. Not only did we want to keep it from becoming a hostel, but when the families of these young people threatened to prosecute us—even for kidnapping—we realized the best place for them was in the homes of fellow believers. When Sokun's plight became known to the church, several offered to take him in. But we stressed that we didn't want to know who was staying where, just in case we were questioned by police or hostile family members.

Sokun's experience encouraged others to stand strong in their testimony, and in that respect it was timely. Little did we know that his beating was going to usher us into a period of severe persecution.

Only a few days had passed when Bopha, another of our faithful believers, was brought to our building. Her name meant flower, which was fitting because she radiated the fragrance of Christ. She had a special place in all of our hearts.

"What's wrong with her?" Thay called over the balcony railing as we watched two young men carrying her up the sidewalk.

"She's badly hurt," Nahvi answered, who was walking alongside Bopha. They quickly carried her up three flights of stairs to the room where we had once kept the orphans.

"Lay her down there," I pointed to the bed. Bopha was conscious, but seemed to be in a daze. "What happened?" I asked Nahvi.

"I went home with her after the early morning prayer meeting," Nahvi related. "As we ate breakfast together, a Buddhist monk stopped in front of the house, chanting for his daily offering. Bopha's father demanded that she give an offering, knowing she would have to refuse because of her faith in Jesus.

" 'You know I don't follow the Buddhist way anymore,' Bopha answered. 'I follow the teachings of Jesus and to do what you ask would be denying my testimony.'

"Without any warning he screamed like a madman," Nahvi went on. "It was almost as if a demon had entered him! Bopha's grandfather, who is a witch doctor, often goes crazy just like this. In a rage he reached for a log of firewood and slammed it into the side of her neck. As Bopha lost her balance and stumbled outside to escape from him, he threw the log, hitting her here," Nahvi pointed to her lower back.

"When the log hit her she cried out once and fell in the dust, and her father turned and stormed back into the house. I quickly helped her to her feet and brought her here in a cyclo, and two young men carried her in. I'm afraid she is seriously hurt," Nahvi added, deeply concerned.

Sidara was bathing Bopha's forehead in cool water, washing off the dirt from her tear-streaked face. She was seriously hurt, as Nahvi feared. By noon she had lost all feeling in her legs and was drifting in and out of consciousness. She was suffering intense pain in her back; then the convulsions started. I grew terribly worried, but was afraid to move her. We gathered a group of faithful workers and joined hands around her bed. First we commanded Satan to remove himself, then we prayed for her healing. Though she didn't regain consciousness immediately, a peaceful calm replaced the painful expression that had drawn her face. The convulsions suddenly ceased. Early the next morning we rejoiced to find her in the prayer room—completely well.

Later that day her mother and younger sister came to see her. They felt ashamed when we told them how bad her condition had been.

"Please send her home," her mother begged. "This won't happen again."

"How can we be sure of that?" Thay asked, "especially since you allow yourselves to be controlled by demon power. And anyway, it is not our decision; it is Bopha's."

After a week, Bopha returned home to find her mother and younger sister had surrendered their lives to Jesus. Her sister, Thoeurn, began attending the Bible classes with Bopha, but the mother lived too much in the fear of her husband to participate regularly. Although Bopha's father never came to the Lord, he did allow his daughters to attend the Bible studies, and he never threatened them again.

As Christmas time approached, we tried to think of a way to make it Christ-centered and meaningful to the believers. During the French occupation of Cambodia the celebration of Noel had been introduced but the people knew almost nothing of commemorating Jesus' birth. We decided to have a "Jesus Birthday Party" on Christmas Day. It was to be a time of worship and praise to the Lord, then we planned to serve hot tea and birthday cake during the fellowship after the service.

"What kind of cake should we get, Thay?" DeAnn asked.

Indicating that he would check at one of the bakeries up the street later in the day to see what was available, he asked in return, "How many people do you think we should plan on?"

I left the two of them to figure out the details of our Christmas celebration and walked out on the second-floor balcony. I devoured a warm piece of cinnamon bread Sao Ha, our cook, had just baked, and watched the neighborhood kids play "Kung-Fu" out in the dirty street below. Everyone wants to be tough, I mused. Up and down every street they cavorted, arms hacking, legs flying. Karate was one of the main sporting interests among the youth in the country.

Suddenly I recognized Loeum, one of our nurses at the orphanage, making her way toward the building, dodging the children below. We had moved the babies to another rented house a couple blocks from the building, and had hired two more women so the nurses could take shifts. I wondered why Loeum looked so forlorn.

"Phally isn't doing very well," she sadly informed me, lowering her eyes. "She has high fever and shakes at times."

"What should we do?" I questioned her. Phally, six months old, was one of our newest additions, having arrived only the day before.

Loeum suggested we pray for Phally, so we gathered some of the leaders together, walked over to the orphanage and anointed her with oil. At the time we prayed, she seemed quite improved. She was able to take some milk, and the fever subsided. We were all sure the Lord had answered our prayer. He was answering, but in a different way than we expected.

I hurried back to the building in time to help put up Christmas decorations. Everyone was so excited about having a party. Since the war, most of them didn't have much amusement outside of these occasional get-togethers. Hach and Sina supervised the hanging of crepe paper, while the girls ironed the curtains and re-draped them at the windows. They apparently were doing a little "spring cleaning" at the same time. Four men scrubbed down the wooden platform and waxed it to a bright sheen. The blackboard was taken down and aluminum foil cutouts of the words **Happy Birthday, Jesus** took its place. I was amazed at their creativity.

Later that afternoon, all the benches were carried out of the main auditorium and the tile floor mopped and waxed. The room was beautiful, waiting in splendor for the party to begin.

That night I slept lightly, praying for Phally, for the meeting the next day, and for the release of the orphans. I woke up at 4:30 and recounted to DeAnn the dream I just had.

"I saw two babies' faces," I began. The first one was that of a newborn baby girl. Then I heard the same words that Job spoke, 'The Lord gave.' The next face was Phally's and in my dream I heard someone say, 'The Lord has taken away. Blessed be the name of the LORD' "(1:21).

"That's spooky!" DeAnn shivered. 'What do you think it means?"

I had some idea, but was hesitant to voice it for fear it may come to pass. By now, we were both too wide awake to go back to sleep, so we got up and readied ourselves for the day.

"Brother?" I heard a voice outside our window.

"Yes?" I responded, easing open the door to look out. It was only beginning to be daylight, but I could see Hach waiting for me below.

"There's trouble at the baby house. Come quick!" he cried anxiously.

"It must be serious if they need you at five o'clock in the morning," DeAnn reasoned. "I'm not quite ready yet, you go on without me."

The first rays of sunlight were peeking up over the tall buildings when I revved up my cycle. Merchants were already setting up their stands and a few cyclo drivers were already on the streets.

Within minutes I stepped inside the gate of the "Manger," as we called it. There in the yard, only a small distance from my foot, lay a tiny stiff form shrouded in a tattered blanket. One of the women shuffled barefoot to the door as I knelt down to uncover the baby's face.

It was Phally. Her eyes were frozen in a hard stony glare. I tried

205

to close them, but the eyelids refused to shut. "How long has she been dead?" I asked Sareoun, who now knelt beside me.

"Maybe two hours, mister," she replied, bowing her head.

"Why didn't you come and get me when you saw she was growing worse," I demanded, wishing I could have done something to avoid this tragedy.

"Couldn't, mister," Sareoun shook her head solemnly. "Soldiers patrol streets. Shot us if we go before dawn."

That's right, I thought feeling frustrated. This war doesn't allow for dealing with emergencies.

"How did she die?" I asked Sareoun.

"She breathe not too good for long time. Then tremble one last time and die." Sareoun longingly fingered the edge of Phally's worn blanket—they had all cared for her so much. I realized it was just as hard for them to lose her as it was for me.

What if the other babies get what she had, I feared. How do we even know what she had! It could have been spinal meningitis. Who knows?

"Oh Lord," I prayed silently, "protect the children from whatever this is. We can only trust in you, Lord!"

The aluminum gate creaked open and Thay appeared. "What happened?" he asked when he saw us kneeling beside Phally. I explained quickly, then asked Thay to take charge of the formalities and arrange for her burial.

"On Christmas Day," I sighed. "What a time to bury a baby." When I arrived back at the building, DeAnn informed me of the birth of a new baby girl to Sophal, a pastor of one of our neighborhood churches.

"They named her Sopheat," she said excitedly. "Sina brought the news to the prayer meeting this morning." Then sensing my depression she asked, "Is everything all right at the baby house?"

"Phally died early this morning," I answered softly. DeAnn was silent a moment, then offered her encouragement.

"Well, there's the explanation of the dream—the Lord prepared us for it, so we shouldn't be depressed. She probably was already sick when we picked her up at the state orphanage the other day,

206

and the Lord was just merciful to take her on home.''

"Yeah, I guess you're right, but still—''

I tried to forget about Phally. There was too much yet to be done for Christmas and I had to get to work. I rigged up speakers in the auditorium so Thay could play Christmas carols before the meeting. We wanted the meeting to be really special. Thankfully, the curfew had been moved back to nine o'clock so we could have an evening gathering.

People started coming as early as 5:30 just to visit and help with any last-minute preparations. We were going to have a special candlelight service, so some were tying red ribbons on candles to give to each person. One huge candle was placed at the front of the room. As seven o'clock neared, believers began crowding into the auditorium. I stepped out on the veranda to watch the people arriving and recognized a group of troublemakers who lived in the apartment building across from us. They were forever ridiculing our students, defacing the outside church property and making a general nuisance of themselves. I saw they were giving Sam-Oeurn a hard time so I sent Hach down to help him. They apparently were planning to crash our meeting because they heard we were going to serve refreshments. Thay started the meeting with singing and I joined him, leaving my worries at the door. Little did I know what trouble was brewing on the streets below.

For the next couple of hours we had a glorious time of praise and fellowship. After singing and worship, we served Jesus' birthday cake. Then the candlelight ceremony seemed to be the perfect end to a perfect evening. My message was about Jesus, the light of the world, represented by the big candle, who imparts light to His followers, represented by the small candles.

"At first,'' I said, lighting the small candle and holding it up, ''the flame is small in comparison to the darkness. But as others see the light, they are drawn to it, and their candles are lit with the fire from God.'' I reached next to me and lit Thay's candle. He lit another as I continued talking. The chain spread the light until the whole room was brightened by the warm glow of many small flames. The Spirit of the Lord drove the truth home and fixed it in the minds and hearts of all assembled. To end the meeting, everyone went quietly out the door and down the stairs, carrying his glowing candle into the night.

I watched them file down the staircase in thoughtful silence, then moved to the edge of the veranda to see them come out the front door.

Suddenly, out of the dark shadows across the street, I saw a group of people moving slowly toward our building. The kerosene lanterns some of them carried illumined the faces of a few of the troublemakers I had spotted earlier. Now some older fellows—government soldiers—had joined their ranks and were encouraging them in their mischief. One dark man shouted obscenities at the women. Teenage boys tried to molest the girls until they managed to escape their grasp. I noticed a cask of liquor in one man's hand. The women and girls scurried into the garage for safety, and I saw Sam-Oeurn and a few others attempting to reason with the crowd to let the people go home.

"*Yesu sii cowsu*! *Yesu sii cowsu*!" a thin, half-naked youth taunted loudly. Others joined the chant.

"What does that mean, Thay?" I asked. He had joined me on the veranda.

"Literally it means Jesus eats rubber," he explained annoyed. "You know, like a dog chases tires—it's sort of an idiom."

"I think we better go down, this looks like trouble to me."

Thay agreed and we headed down the stairs. Before we even reached the first-floor landing, rocks and bottles were flying in the air, breaking windows and chipping paint off vehicles parked outside. The mob chanted louder, fired by their intense hatred of the students who faithfully attended each day. Up until now, no one had suffered physical harm, but the crowd seemed intent on displaying their resentment.

A second assault of rocks bombarded our people. I called for Sam-Oeurn and the others to come back inside the church. Some retreated, but Sam-Oeurn and his brother, Sam-Ong, stood their ground, pleading with the jeering bunch.

All of a sudden a shot pierced the air, then several more

208

followed. Sam-Ong staggered and dropped to his knees, thudding hard against the cement. There were screams, then chaos reigned for a moment when time seemed to stand still. Blood spurted from Sam-Ong's head like a fountain; his crisp white shirt was quickly blood-soaked. Thay tore open the door and we ran to his side.

"He's been shot," he cried. The mob scattered, but we were too concerned about Sam-Ong's condition to notice. Some of the boys and men gently carried Sam-Ong back into the building, leaving me standing by a pool of fresh blood. I was almost too shocked to move. I overheard some of the students talking with their parents, "I don't think he was shot . . . I saw this big rock—"

There were rocks all around—maybe the students were right. I rushed into the building, hoping it was only a flesh wound from a flying rock. When we examined Sam-Ong we discovered that was the case, though by the bloodstains everywhere, one would have thought the injury to be more severe. Sam-Ong was resting quietly as two women bathed the matted blood from his face.

"Praise the Lord!" Sam-Oeurn shouted. "He's all right." Everyone was relieved, but puzzled about the gunshots. Where had they come from?

Within minutes we had our answer. Four Khmer policemen dressed in starched uniforms appeared in the doorway, accompanied by Hach and Sina. Out in the hallway I saw the cowering figure of the boy who had shouted "Jesus eats rubber." Inwardly I was glad they caught him.

"This is the one who threw the stone," one policeman explained. "We need your report so we can file charges against him."

Sam-Ong pulled himself up on one elbow. "No!" he insisted, shaking his head. "I don't want to press charges against him." The policeman was astonished, then looked to Thay for an explanation.

They spoke in Khmer for a few minutes, then the commander dismissed the young man, along with his three fellow officers. He stayed on for a long time, seemingly amazed that Sam-Ong didn't want to prosecute the boy, but forgave him instead.

Sam-Ong witnessed to the officer with boldness. "The Lord

told us never to take revenge. He told us He would repay the evil man, that we are to pray for our enemies and do good to them that hate us.''

I could hear the policeman arguing with him, but sensed the Spirit of the Lord dealing with his heart as he heard Sam-Ong's soft answers turning away wrath. I listened with awe to this twenty-one-year-old young man who knew so intimately the heart of Jesus. Again, the Lord was teaching me through those He had sent me to teach. "Thank you, Lord," I breathed a prayer.

The officer, Bun Ly, became a regular attendant at our weekly meetings, often bringing his friends and family with him. It was a blessing to everyone to see how the Lord turned even this evil of Sam-Ong's injury for ultimate good.

And He kept His word in taking revenge, too. A few days later we saw that same young man running down the street delirious. He was reportedly mad, having forgotten even his name. We never saw him again.

Another troublesome group of neighbors near our building was a gang of gamblers who had taken over an adjoining alley for their illegal dice games and other gambling activity. The rice wine flowed freely, and drunken brawls were frequently the result. The Khmers had many vices; at the top of the list was gambling. It was a source of great annoyance because the groups of men would call names and harass the women who attended our services. They hassled our workers and created such an uproar we could hardly hear ourselves think. The problem grew worse as the days went by and more joined the band. Countless times we tried to remove this thorn in the flesh by contacting the police, but we learned the police were either bribed, or were involved in the gambling themselves. Not even Bun Ly who attended our church could sway the police force to take action in our behalf.

"What are we going to do with those people down there?" I asked Thay, trying to restrain my voice from showing the anxiety I felt.

"The only thing we can do is pray," he shrugged his shoulders. "If we try to stop them physically, they are liable to get violent and then we may have the whole neighborhood on our backs. It's bad enough as it is, you know.''

The noise of their betting, arguing and cursing was loudest near our bedroom and Thay's office. "How can he endure all this racket?" I wondered.

I had mentioned these gamblers to the Lord, but had never once bothered to bring the matter before our morning prayer group. Finally I had my fill of their filthy talk and drunkenness. I silently fumed as I watched them litter our front walk with their cigarette butts and whiskey bottles. They made sure to aim their red spit from chewing betel nut (their form of chewing tobacco, which after long years of use would make their teeth black) so that it landed in front of the door.

Marching up to the prayer room, I suggested we all take hands and demand the removal of these people from our premises immediately. As we confidently raised our voices to the Lord, we heard machine-gun fire pepper the air. Hach, curious to see what happened, stuck his head over the edge of the roof. There, four stories below, the two entrances to the alley were blocked off by huge army trucks. Troops paraded the streets surrounding the alley, capturing all the gamblers who had scattered during the raid. Some were already handcuffed and were being dragged back to the trucks. One of the gamblers clutched his arm, evidently wounded from the gunfire. We were all astonished to realize the immediate answer to our prayer as we watched the last culprit being loaded onto the waiting vehicle. Peace reigned in "gambler's alley" once again.

Because of the growth of Maranatha Church, we were in the process of negotiating to rent a large building just around the corner to use for the Bible school. At the time, classes were meeting in one small room at Maranatha Church. I had made arrangements to meet the realtor early one particular morning, and since DeAnn wanted to see the building too, we took the car. After finishing our business, DeAnn went out to the car ahead of me, while I stayed a few minutes longer, talking with the realtor. When I joined her she seemed irritated. "What's wrong?" I

211

asked her.

"See that group of soldiers over there?" she replied, glancing off to her left. "That guy in front—the good-looking one—his name is Thol. He comes to my morning classes every once in a while and really gives me a rough time. He just came up to the car and asked me to give him some money and I could tell he just did it because his friends put him up to it."

"Hey," I exclaimed, "he was in that crowd of hoodlums who raised such a ruckus the night of the Christmas program."

"I know," DeAnn said. "He's picked up some English obscenities from somewhere and delights in making me look like a fool. And the problem is, I find myself resenting him sometimes. I really have to watch my spirit when he's around."

I narrowed my eyes and glared in his direction, almost feeling her resentment transfer to me. "Well," I said, "we can't do anything about it now. I've got to get to the embassy and take you to your morning class."

A half-hour later I pulled up to the building and saw that same soldier loitering around my office door. "I wonder what he wants now," I grumbled to myself, climbing the stairs two at a time. I was already hot and flustered by the hassles of the day.

I greeted him as cordially as possible. "Hi, Thol! Can I help you with something?"

His eyes were haughty as he spoke. Holding out his right hand, palm upward, he said, "I need two thousand *riel*."

I stood silently for a moment. Two thousand *riel* was only about two dollars, but for the Khmer people that was a lot. Had I thought he really needed it, I probably would have given it to him, but his arrogant expression agitated me. He was unlike any Khmer I'd ever met. Most were very humble and would never approach a foreigner in this way. I could hardly take his audacity.

"What do you need two thousand *riel* for?" I questioned. I stared at him for what seemed like forever, hoping he'd back down.

"I want two thousand *riel*. That's all," he replied without flinching.

212

"Listen," I spoke firmly, "either you go upstairs and attend the class, or please leave the building." His reply was stony silence, but I could almost hear his thoughts by reading the look on his face. It was as if he dared me to back up my words with action. I promptly accepted the challenge and forcefully helped him down the stairs and out the front door.

I closed the door behind him, then immediately wished I hadn't acted so hastily. I felt guilty and inwardly longed for some sort of cleansing to erase the resentment and anger that had surfaced.

Going back to my office, I spotted my unopened Bible on the desk. "I haven't even done my morning Bible reading yet. Oh Lord," I breathed heavily. I had allowed the pressures of the morning to crowd out my regular time with the Lord, which always strengthened and prepared me for the day. Searching on the card for the scheduled reading, I turned to Matthew. What I read for the next few minutes was humbling, as I sensed deep conviction for what I had done.

Verses pierced me like arrows—"Do not resist him who is evil . . . give to him who asks of you, and do not turn away from him who wants to borrow from you . . . love your enemies and pray . . . in order that you may be sons of your Father . . . you are to be perfect, as your heavenly Father is perfect" (5:39-48).

I felt I had failed my heavenly Father and failed this young man, but I thanked God He had spoken to me. Burying my head in my arms, I begged the Lord to forgive me and grant me another chance to make things right with this soldier. I didn't know if I would ever see him again after the way I had just treated him. Leaving the building, I walked down the street, hoping to find him, but he was nowhere in sight.

That afternoon, as DeAnn and I returned from a swim, I was amazed to find Thol back at our building, hanging around the entrance. I put the cycle away and walked toward Thol, gathering my courage as I went.

"Thol," I said to him in a friendly way, putting my arm around his shoulder, "come on up to my office; I'd like to talk with you." The serious, almost frightened expression on his face seemed to say, Oh no! What's this foreigner up to now?

Closing the door behind us I motioned for him to sit down. "Thol," I began, "I want you to forgive me. After you left a few hours ago I felt terrible. I came in here to pray and the Lord rebuked me for the way I treated you."

I handed him my Bible. "Here, read this," I said, pointing to the passage. "This was my morning Bible reading." His eyes slowly absorbed the words.

"God showed you this for me?" he exclaimed soberly.

"Yes," I replied. "He loves you so much that He scolded me for treating you as I did."

I reached in my pocket, pulling out a wad of *riel*. "Here," I said putting two thousand *riel* in his hand. "This is what you asked for, and I want you to have it." Then I put two thousand more *riel* on top of it, and said, "This is the second mile. I don't give you this because I think you need it or deserve it, but because I love you and want you to know that God loves you."

Thol's eyes filled with tears as he stared at me. Then he quietly folded the bills and walked out of my office.

We had no more trouble with him again. In fact, he began attending the Bible classes faithfully and brought his friends with him. Thankfully, he saw to it that they didn't get out of line.

The next time I was tempted to react in anger in a similar situation, I thought of Jesus' exacting words: "Love your enemies, and pray for those who persecute you in order that you may be sons of your Father . . ." (Matt. 5:44-45).

CHAPTER 15

Anointed for Burial

The dawning of New Year's Eve marked the beginning of our proclaimed three-day fast to usher in the New Year of 1975. All our churches in the Phnom Penh area participated by meeting either at Maranatha Church or at their own, depending on each pastor's plan. These were the most divinely blessed days we had ever spent with God's people. All of us sought the Lord together with a pure heart, rarely leaving one another's presence until the fast was broken.

The first downpour of blessing came to Solomon Church where Dana was pastor. Breathless, he arrived at the top of the stairs, "Brother! The Holy Spirit just visited us—some saw visions—many have been baptized in the Holy Spirit. It was wonderful!"

"Wait a minute," I interrupted, laughing from joy. "Now repeat it again, slowly."

"We were all praying together," he began excitedly, "when we all saw a bright light—even with our eyes shut. When the light appeared, nine people immediately broke out speaking in new languages of praise to God and we hadn't even laid hands on anyone to receive the Holy Spirit. Later in the afternoon one of the believers told me how one woman had seen a vision of a cross with blood flowing out from the center of it. She gave her life to Jesus because of what she saw."

"Praise God!" Sina and Hach echoed together. By now, several had crowded around Dana to hear the news of what happened.

215

"I can't stay long," he added. "I must get back to the church. I just wanted to come quickly to let you know how God is blessing us."

We, too, had experienced some of this same blessing. Earlier that morning as a group met for prayer, I briefly shared with them some of the things God had been showing me through my Bible readings. Referring to Genesis 32, I told them how Jacob wrestled with the Lord until He blessed him.

"If we expect power and blessing from the Lord, we are going to have to be willing to wrestle with Him in prayer and fasting, in self-denial, in taking up our cross," I said. Then I shared with them from a devotional book by Hudson Taylor, "An easy-going, non-self-denying life will never be one of power." With that, everyone began to wrestle in prayer, and before long, the blessing came.

Sopha came late to the meeting and quietly entered, easing the door shut behind her. Turning around to look for a place to kneel, she was startled suddenly by the sight of a huge door as it appeared on the opposite wall. Transfixed by this apparition, she watched the door ease open. Then a bright light flooded the room, revealing two cupped hands which slowly opened. The hands released a dazzling white dove, then pulled back, the door closing. I heard her gasp, and opened my eyes to see her head turning around as if watching something in motion. I later learned that she saw the dove circle the room three times, then it lit upon her head. The next thing Sopha knew, she was kneeling on the floor along with everyone else, speaking in an unknown tongue. Five people received the infilling of the Holy Spirit at that same moment.

"Fantastic!" I praised the Lord to myself. But that was only the beginning. Many others who came within that span of three days also saw visions. Some were delivered from demonic power and received Christ, and were later baptized in the Spirit.

Our hearts had been burdened for some time for a particular major in the government army. He had wonderfully come to know the Lord through DeAnn's morning Bible class, and since then had been seeking the fullness of God's blessing for his life. His

216

devotion and love for God and the other believers especially touched my heart. But Jesus had not yet baptized him with His Spirit. That first evening of the three days of fasting I prayed specifically for the Lord to once again open the door and release the dove of the Holy Spirit for the sake of Major Khoun, who sat beside me. Not less than a few seconds after breathing this prayer, Major Khoun began trembling, then burst out speaking in a loud tongue. Tears streamed down many faces that night as we all rejoiced with thanks to God.

He was so joyful that we asked him to lead the group in prayer as we offered the sacrifice of our "incense" to the Lord as the old year passed and the new year was ushered in. All of us had written a letter to the Lord and had placed it in a huge decorated box. We planned to burn the box as an offering of sweet-smelling savor. At the stroke of midnight, as we watched the smoke from our letters ascend into the starry sky, Sina jokingly remarked, "Our letters are going to God via Angel Post." It was a time of great rejoicing accompanied by profound awe of the Mighty One who had caused us to be born again to a living hope. Khoun was the most recently touched by this reality, and his fervent prayer reflected all our praise.

Another unusual visitation took place during those three days that we learned about later. It happened to Yong, an elderly woman who had given her heart to the Lord just prior to the time of fasting. She had joined us at the beginning of the fast but then almost decided to go home. "Most of these people are much younger than I," she reasoned to herself. "They are so full of faith and have so much to share from their readings in the Bible. Look at me; I can't even read. What do I have to contribute? I'll just go on home and pray there—maybe I'll fast some other time." She quietly slipped out the door and was fastening the latch on her sandal when she was startled by the presence of someone standing directly behind her. Glancing out the corner of her eye, she saw a tall man with white hair and dressed in white clothing.

"Do not wait, O favored one," he commanded her, "for the Lord is with you and has determined to bless you."

"I didn't dare ask any questions," she explained. "I didn't know who he was—I'd never seen him before—but I knew he was somebody very important and that I should obey his words. I took off my shoes again and went back into the room, thinking he was right behind me. But nobody else saw him like I did—and I haven't seen him again since then."

"That was an **angel**!" Hach exclaimed.

"That's what it sounds like to me," I agreed.

And the Lord did bless her indeed. Yong's reverence towards her Savior was seen in so many ways, especially in her giving. We didn't pass an offering plate in our services, but had simply attached a wooden box to the wall near the door. One Sunday as we were closing the morning service she got up from her seat with a wad of bills in her hand. She walked over to the box and began to worship, lifting her money as if handing it to God. Then she dropped it in the box. Everyone was so moved by the scene that a few others rose from their seats and did the same. There was soon a long line of believers in front of the box waiting for their opportunity to worship in giving. Though poor and illiterate, Yong was a constant example for all the young people to point to, for she had the word of God hidden in her heart.

At yet another church there was a visitation of His Holy Spirit upon all those who attended. A blazing bush appeared in their midst, and as they all watched, white doves flew out and landed upon the heads of each one present. At that moment they all began speaking in unknown tongues, glorifying God for His presence with them.

On January 3rd, at one minute past midnight, we broke our three-day fast by partaking of communion together, then shared a light meal of *babau*, a rice and vegetable soup. I marveled at the hundreds from the outlying churches who had participated faithfully in our New Year celebration.

"This has been the best year of our lives," DeAnn exulted when we finally went to bed in the wee hours of the morning.

With the heavy concentration of God's presence with us during those three days, we had all but forgotten about the shrinking perimeter of Phnom Penh. Talking casually with Major Khoun one afternoon following a Bible study, our conversation abruptly shifted to the topic of the war situation.

"Some of our best battalions have been wiped out along the Mekong River," he sadly informed us. "We have little hope of regaining that position until the monsoon rains begin again in May. The enemy will then be forced to retreat when the river swells from rain."

Thay confirmed his report. "The situation has grown very serious now," he said. "Since they have cut off the Mekong, we cannot last long. The Mekong River is our main artery for food, fuel and artillery."

"But what about the U.S. airlifts of rice each day?" I interjected.

"It helps some, that's true," Thay said, "but for months now the majority of people have existed on watery rice soup. The Khmer Rouge have occupied the rich farmlands, ultimately starving the masses who are flooding Phnom Penh."

DeAnn had overheard our discussion and added her comment. "Did you know that Sao Ha's neighbors killed her pet dog the other evening—and ate it! She's already had her flock of chickens and ducks mysteriously disappear!"

"That's nothing," Khoun added. "I've even heard stories of cannibalism of the war victims in some areas."

Our grim conversation depressed me. Excusing myself, I retreated to the silence of my office to seek the Lord for His answer. I distinctly recognized His still small voice as I read my Bible reading from Zechariah 2:5, " 'For I,' declares the LORD, 'will be a wall of fire around her, and I will be the glory in her midst.' " Though the message was meant for Jerusalem, I knew the Lord had given it to me as a message for His church in Cambodia. How gratifying it was when I began to see confirmation unfold before my eyes.

Early the next morning as the brothers and sisters met for prayer, there was a special message in prophecy. Narith, one of the women who had received the gift of prophetic utterance, cried out in the presence of all, "Don't worry, I'm not sending Todd and DeAnn away now. Their relatives and friends have pleaded with me to send them home, but I cannot allow that now. I have work for them to do—they must continue to shepherd you until my appointed time." The message instilled a greater measure of faith in our hearts to believe the Lord for His protection.

Later that day we picked up our mail to find letters which proved the accuracy of what we had heard that morning. Several days prior to this we had received a letter from a pastor friend encouraging us to remain in Cambodia in spite of the war. "We feel you could no more leave those churches than leave your family, for that's what they really are—your family."

Now, evidently because he realized the seriousness of the situation and perhaps felt a grave responsibility for our lives, we received a telegram from him:

"We were wrong or misunderstood about your staying. Please feel right and free before God to leave. If you need money, please advise. We love you in Christ."

"They are really concerned about us, aren't they?" we laughed for joy. Knowing that so many were praying for us brought a special comfort to our hearts.

A few days later we received a disturbing letter from DeAnn's mother. It had been especially difficult for our parents to realize we were in the grip of a desperate war. And they, being so far away, were so helpless to do anything. My mother-in-law wrote the following letter January 8th:

> For things I am about to say (if it isn't too late) I hope you will think and act immediately. The future is in God's hands. Todd, you have taken a wife. *You* are responsible for her safety and tender care. For some time I have felt you were called, but it seems your calling is more important to you than your first responsibility.
>
> De's first responsibility is to you.
>
> Both your lives are on the chopping block there in Phnom Penh. There is no hope for that country and I'm sure you are aware of that by now. You are both very

young and, may I say, "without experience and years of wisdom." You can't imagine what horrors there are in the world. Todd—could you stand and let De die while you continue to preach? Please get out of that country. You are of no use to God dead. Of what good are you a dead martyr?

There are other fields of service. Can you not stand the competition here or is it you don't want to be close to your loved ones? Tho I give my body to be burned and have not love what doth it profit?

I know this is strong, but naturally I cannot bear to see death come to you and De. There are years of service ahead for you both. Use your head.

You both may hate me forever, but as years go by you will see things you were deceived in. You can't imagine what we are going through here. You say, "Don't worry, God will take care of us." Wake up. This is man's day. The devil is going to and fro. Move quickly. God can do so much. You have to use your common sense. Please make arrangements. Leave the orphans there. Saigon is taken over and the enemy is closing in. You are breaking your parents' hearts. Please come home!

I love both and pray for your safety.

Love, Mother.

Had we not experienced the perfect peace of God in the midst of the situation we surely would have packed up and left. But the fact that the Lord continued to speak to our hearts, even through the lips of others, confirmed all the more in our minds that it was His purpose that we be in Cambodia. We weren't certain what the future held for us, but at that moment our feelings were best expressed by Paul when he told the believers in Acts 21:13, "What are you doing, weeping and breaking my heart? For I am ready not only to be bound, but even to die at Jerusalem for the name of the Lord Jesus." And this was our response to DeAnn's mother.

Little did we know that at the same time, my father, because he had not received my letters for more than a month, was investigating our whereabouts through the State Department. Just about the time he was ready to hop aboard a jet to come and check out the situation, our telegram reached him:

"Don't worry. Safe in Phnom Penh. Letter follows."

Later they wrote, "We are grateful for your Christmas letter (which finally arrived) and for your narrow escape from the Communists. We pray that God will always watch over you and protect you both."

Perceiving the hint of anxiety that lingered in our hearts, the Lord supplied further assurance of His almighty protection. One morning during our last few minutes of sleep we were startled by the arrival of Sophal, a pastor of one of the smaller fellowships in the city. The rays of the early sun were just creeping over the surrounding apartment buildings when the creaking of the front gate and voices downstairs awakened us. Sophal had set out shortly before curfew was lifted and had managed to arrive safely to tell us of the fantastic vision he had witnessed just hours before.

Wiping the sleep from our eyes, we hurried to the prayer room and sat listening to this pastor's detailed account of what God had shown him.

"Our family was praying together this morning when suddenly, I saw a huge ring of fire all around us," he graphically demonstrated with his hands. "All the believers were together inside this ring, but the same fire that protected us was consuming others. I know God is assuring us of His protection no matter how bad the situation may get."

Sophal had not even known about the Scripture verse the Lord had given me only a few days before from the Book of Zechariah. My confidence of God's protection was reaffirmed each day. But more evidence was yet to come.

The next day we received a letter from Dewey Friedel, pastor of Sayreville United Methodist Church in New Jersey, who was a close brother in the Lord and had felt a call to join us in our work. He shared how he was awakened one night and felt strongly impressed to pray for us. "I jumped out of bed and went downstairs," he related. "As I was praying I saw a wall of fire behind you. At first I felt confusion and fear, but then very calmly the Lord brought a deep peace and a Scripture that just fit. I wrote it down, but cannot recall it right now. But He is your light and your strength. Darkness disappears when there is light."

"How I wish I knew the Scripture he found that night," I said, shaking my head.

DeAnn chuckled happily, "It is probably the very one the Lord gave you about the fire."

That night following the evening service we were all gathered for our regular prayer meeting when Seng Bun, one of our recent converts, raced up the stairs excitedly.

"The Lord has spoken to us!" he panted, trying to catch his breath. "For the last several days rockets have been landing all around my house—almost hourly. My family grew more and more afraid until we made the decision to move in with some friends in a safer part of town. I had moved almost everything and was preparing to take my wife and two of the children to our friend's house. I told my eight-year-old daughter, Kany, to stay behind and I would return for her shortly."

Bun's face brightened at this point and we all sensed his excitement as he continued. "When I returned, she ran out to meet me yelling, 'Pa! Pa! While you were gone I was in the house and suddenly I saw a fire appear in and all around it. I heard a voice speaking "Do not fear, I am your protection." Pa, we don't have to leave now; we can stay here!' " Smiling broadly, Bun concluded, "I just came from moving all our belongings back into our home."

"Are the rockets still falling near the market area?" Nahvi asked him, voicing the question all of us were thinking.

"Oh, yes," he laughed confidently. "But we are not afraid any more. Though many of our neighbors' homes have been destroyed, and some people wounded or killed, we know now that the Lord's protection is upon us." His words reverberated in the hearts of everyone present as we joined together in praising the Lord for the way He continued to speak to us.

In the days to follow, however, we realized we could not become presumptuous in the matter of being protected. We had to experience the sovereignty of God in a very real way.

One morning while DeAnn was upstairs teaching her class, I received a phone call from Thay. "There's been an accident," he said haltingly, trying not to convey the fear he so keenly felt.

"Where are you?" I asked.

"I'm at Calmette Hospital; Sidara fell off the back of my niece's motorcycle this morning and injured her head on the curb. The doctors seem to think she will be all right in a few days, but they are keeping her in the emergency area because the family cannot afford to put her in a private room. Could we help them with this expense?" he asked politely.

"I'm coming over immediately and I'll bring some money with me," I hurriedly assured him. I turned and was met at the door by Sidara's mother, who had just heard the news. Her face was drawn and etched with fright. Nahvi and Sidara's other sisters stood beside her, tightly holding hands. "Is she all right?" they anxiously questioned all at once.

"I'm going over to see about her now—she should be out in a couple of days," I answered. I tried to speak with confidence to dispel their fears. Sidara's mother insisted on coming with me.

Upon arriving at the hospital I talked with a physician on the staff who had attended Sidara when she was admitted. "It's just a flesh wound," he assured us. "She's resting quietly, don't worry."

Thay proceeded to relate how it all happened. Sidara had spent the night with Rasmay, his niece, the night before. Driving on Rasmay's motorbike the next morning, they swerved to avoid crashing into a negligent cyclo driver who had darted into their path. "Since Sidara was sitting sidesaddle on back, her uneven distribution of weight caused the bike to tip," Thay explained. "She fell, striking her head against the curb. I was right behind them in the Honda truck and saw the whole thing."

At that moment we were joined by a uniformed policeman who had been on the scene at the time of the accident. By coincidence, he had gone to school with Sidara, so naturally shared our concern for her welfare. He remained at the hospital with us, gathering details to file his report.

"I've got to get back," I said, looking at my watch.

"I think we'll ride back with you," Thay said. "Is it all right to drop Mrs. Than off at her home on the way?"

"Sure. Let's go." We were all full of hope, confident that Sidara would be well within the week.

But when we arrived at the building we were met by an onslaught of mourning students. "What's going on here?" I demanded.

"Ever since the news about Sidara," DeAnn quietly explained, "everyone has been in the prayer room begging the Lord to heal her and raise her up."

"But the Lord has spoken to us," Bopha cried with a look of awe in her eyes.

"Yes," Narith's face was coldly serious, "it's true." Sidara's sisters all nodded soberly.

"What is this all about?" I asked, looking dubiously from one sad face to another. I suspected they had let their emotions run away with them.

"There were prophecies," Nahvi began. "The Lord said—" she dropped her head and stopped.

Thay turned to me with confusion in his eyes, then he spoke sternly to the students for a moment. Everyone struggled to regain their composure so we could understand the story.

"I have it all on tape," Hach pointed to the cassette recorder he was carrying. "I was up in the prayer room trying to find a quiet place to record a song I had just written, when all of them stormed in crying. Everyone began praying and when I found out Sidara had been in an accident, I just joined with them. All of a sudden the Lord began to speak—first through Somaly, then Narith, then through Sida and finally through Narithei."

"What did the Lord say?" Thay's voice was humbled.

Hach's eyes caught mine as if he feared I wouldn't believe what he was about to tell. "The Lord said, 'I am going to take her, I am

225

surely going to take her.' The other prophecies agreed with the first one and instructed us, 'Do not mourn for the dead or shave your heads as the heathen do who have no hope.' The Lord commanded us, 'Rejoice, for this will show forth my glory.' "

Hach paused, then looking down at the floor he said softly, "The final message told us it is His will that Sidara go to be with Him."

"No!" I interrupted loudly. Then softening my voice I said, "We must be sure about this. The doctor at the hospital promised me that she would be out in a few days. It's a minor injury; no problem."

Their faces silently reprimanded me. They obviously wanted to believe my report, but their experience in the prayer room affected them far more deeply than my words ever could. I searched the expressions of Somaly and Sida—two of her very own flesh and blood sisters had been among those who had prophesied. "What does this mean, Lord?"

I wanted to go check her condition, so I offered to drive them all to the hospital to talk with the physician and possibly see Sidara for themselves. Kannitha took a taxi to her home to inform her mother, saying they would join us at the hospital. We drove in silence to Calmette, having dismissed the afternoon class because of the circumstances.

Upon reaching the hospital, I learned her condition had unexpectedly weakened. In the time that had passed since my first visit, the surgeon had performed an operation to try to relieve the pressure building in the brain area. "Can we see her?" I asked the nurse, my heart sinking. She shook her head sternly, acting annoyed at the large group I had with me.

I motioned for the family and students to move outside to avoid upsetting the hospital staff. Then I quietly moved through the hospital, peering through every window and door that would open, trying to find Sidara. I finally found her. Slipping silently into the room, I almost wished I hadn't found her. She was hideously deformed, her body swollen practically beyond recognition. Half of her long silky black hair had been shorn from one side of her head, and a blood-soaked gauze patch covered her scalp. She appeared to be sleeping. I stepped to her side and whispered her name. No response. She was breathing unevenly and her face had the pallor of death.

"She's unconscious," a voice startled me from behind. The nurse briskly walked to her bed, glaring at me.

"H . . how is she? I mean is she going to be all right in a few days?" I stammered. "The doctor told me—"

She curtly interrupted me. "The doctor was wrong. This girl will be lucky to live through this afternoon."

I shuddered at her cold attitude, but then I supposed she was upset because I had broken their rules. "Now, if you'll please leave, I'll carry on with my work here," she said brusquely.

I took the hint and with a heavy heart made my way to the garden where the family and students were waiting, seated in the grass. I had to level with them about Sidara's condition, especially since the Lord had so perfectly spoken to them already. Though they had been prepared by the prophecies, they were still filled with grief at my words. The mother, who had joined the group by this time, broke into sobs. "No!" she cried to the Lord. "Don't let her die!" They continued to sit solemnly in the garden for several hours, awaiting final news about Sidara.

As five o'clock neared I persuaded them to return with me for the evening class. It was a somber group that trudged up the stairs to the auditorium. I fell on my face before the Lord, desperate for His message for them.

"Lord," I prayed, "if you indeed spoke to them this morning and promised this would be for your glory, then change their mourning into joy. Show me what I can say to them that will minister joy amidst this flood of grief." I quickly skimmed through my evening readings and in each one the Lord communicated His message of hope. The service was not accompanied with boisterous rejoicing, but each heart silently acknowledged that He is a sovereign Lord in control of every breath.

After the message, everyone filed up to the prayer room on the

227

top floor. We had no electricity, only candles and kerosene lanterns flickered as we gathered close and sat down on the straw mats for prayer. Moments later Narith appeared in the doorway. "She's gone home," she said softly. Sopha screamed and jumped to her feet, gazing at the ceiling. A handful of others also lifted their heads, as if they also saw something overhead.

"I see Sidara," Sopha said in reverent awe. "She is standing in heaven, holding a golden jeweled crown and now she is speaking. She says, 'I have finished my course and have been found faithful. Now you all must follow after me. Be faithful unto death. There is yet much work to be done for the Master. Come, I am waiting for you here with my Lord.' "

Tears flowed freely and hands were lifted in praise to the Lord for His comfort. The Spirit of God had removed the aching grief from each heart and replaced it with joy and gladness.

The mother quickly sent a cable to her husband, Than Sina, in Koh Kong province, one hundred miles west of Phnom Penh on the coast. He resided there as governor, living with his other wife. Polygamy was not an uncommon practice among those who could afford it. In the meantime, Thay and I struggled with trying to arrange Sidara's burial. Our problem was how and where to bury her.

A local contractor who was working with us on constructing the refugee camp, gave us permission to bury Sidara on a piece of property he owned east of the city. Our carpenters built a beautiful casket and inscribed on its side, "I will raise her up at the last day."

Placing her casket in the back of a truck, we formed a funeral procession and headed eastward. When we arrived at the banks of a tributary of the Mekong River, we had to transfer everyone to boats to reach the burial plot on the other side. Just as we were getting into the boats, Sidara's father, Than Sina, arrived.

His four daughters gathered around him and recounted all that had happened. Tears streamed down their faces as Nahvi told of the prophecies and how Sidara had appeared to many after her death. Holding his daughter's worn Khmer Bible, Than Sina opened it gently. "She really loved this book," he said, looking at the numerous verses she had underscored during her readings.

"Yes," I acknowledged, "she had memorized much of it. But most important, she lived it."

Tears trickled down his cheeks as he nodded silently. "I would like to know this book as she did," he said, clutching the Bible close to his heart.

The Khmer believers witnessed their first Christian burial and through the experience gained a new perspective on death. As we left the beautiful gardenlike setting, Nahvi said gently to her father, "You see, pa, because Sidara followed Jesus, her death only means she has gone to live with Him forever."

CHAPTER 16

Yet Another Door

The response of the believers to Sidara's death graphically demonstrated to all the depth of their resolute commitment to Christ. In contrast to the Buddhist's prolonged periods of mourning and superstitious traditions surrounding burial ceremonies, God had inspired these believers to accept the reality of death without fear. This experience instilled in their hearts an eternal awareness; now nothing could alter their course—not even death. They became even bolder in witnessing, and the church continued to grow as countless Khmer people sought a refuge of peace in the midst of strife.

I was encouraged by the progress we saw in every area of the work except with the handling of adoptions for our orphans. The Manger had now expanded to include fifteen infants who had been either orphaned by the war or abandoned to us by desperate relatives. One day a mother came to our door carrying her emaciated baby. She had journeyed from a small village to Phnom Penh in search of her missing husband, only to learn he had been killed in action on the battlefield. This news, added to the fact that she had no place to live, left her hopeless. She had not eaten in three days. In desperation she pleaded for us to take her listless child. Lifting her blouse she exposed her shriveled breasts. "Look, no milk!" she cried. "Please take him and feed him. Give him a good home. I can only hope for death."

"No," we replied. "We don't want to take your child. We want to feed you and the baby and provide a place for you to stay. When you become strong enough, then we can help you find work.'' She agreed to our conditions and we immediately fed her. She greedily devoured three bowlfuls of steamed rice. However, after staying for two days she disappeared, taking with her several of our nurses' skirts and blouses. We never saw her again. Now we had the task of finding a home for her six-week-old son, whom we named Sorya, ''the sun.''

Such incidents as this continued, and within a matter of months we had fifteen orphans to find homes for. I was continually having to go to the Red Cross or some other humanitarian agency to find milk, medicines and clothing for the babies. This worry, along with endless legal tangles in arranging the adoptions, three services daily, and teaching in our Bible school, left DeAnn and me exhausted at the end of each day. We had to cling to Galatians 6:9, ''And let us not lose heart in doing good, for in due time we shall reap if we do not grow weary.''

The adoption applications continued to stack up not only from the United States and Canada, but also from Britain and Sweden. We tried in vain to get the babies released for adoption; no one could help us—not even President Lon Nol. Once again we were faced with the problem of what to do with our orphans. I was especially concerned about Talvary and Sithan, whom we had promised to European families, because their little bodies were frail. Their condition would no doubt become worse if they stayed much longer in Phnom Penh. In my frustration I had almost succumbed to the thought of using bribery or even smuggling them out of the country.

Early one morning I entered our daily prayer meeting, which by this time had become the pivot point for the ministry. Not only would all our leaders join together, but as many as thirty others attended every day to seek the Lord with us. True prophets and prophetesses ministered to the body, giving clear and decisive direction. When they would prophesy, especially the women, they would first begin to weep profusely with heavy sobs. Then the prophecy would come.

On this particular morning I arrived late. Everyone was already seated on the straw mats and praying in the Spirit. As I entered the door I could see by the pool of tears under Narith's bowed head, that the Lord was probably going to speak to us through her. I had no more than quietly seated myself next to DeAnn and begun to pray when God's power began to erupt through Narith. She aimed her trembling finger at me and spoke forcefully.

"You repent and cleanse your heart. Cast off your fear and doubt, **now!** For today I'm going to help you and prosper your work. You will know that I am the Lord God and that I am with you when you see how I arrange for you today."

Thay looked over at me with a broad smile on his face. Only he knew of all the problems we had with the adoptions and of my scheming to get the babies out of the country.

"Wow!" I said to him as we walked out of the prayer room. "That was really something. But how do we act on it?"

Thay's face wrinkled thoughtfully for a moment. Then he replied, "Why don't we give Thach Toan a call and see if we can get in to see him." Under the new rulings, only Thach Toan, the minister of social welfare, could sign the release for adoptions. However, on several occasions he had dismissed us from his office, refusing to help in any way.

"Go ahead," I answered. "Call him if you think it will do any good." Thay called Thach Toan's office, but learned that the minister was sick and at home in bed. "If it's urgent," his assistant replied, "I can take you to his home to meet him." Reluctantly, I agreed.

A tall brick wall encircled the premises with chipped glass and barbed wire all over the top and surrounding the entrance. A heavily-armed soldier guarded the gateway. Once the assistant stated our business we were immediately ushered through the gate and into the house. With carpets on the floors and the rooms decked with modern furnishings, one could easily have mistaken his residence for a home in the West. "Where did he get the money for such a place?" I suspicioned aloud to Thay. Then the minister appeared wearing a long robe and smiling.

"It's good that you've come," he said politely. "But I didn't expect you so soon. Did you see that man who just left?'' He pointed toward the door.

"What man?'' I questioned, puzzled by his pleasant manner.

"I didn't see anyone,'' Thay said, shaking his head.

"Are you sure?'' he asked again. "He just left a few minutes ago and said that you would be coming to see me.''

"Who was he?'' I probed.

Thach Toan fumbled for a moment. "I'm not sure,'' he answered, "but I assumed he was with your embassy. He seemed to know much about the grave situation of our country and for this reason asked me to please assist you with your orphan work.''

Bewildered, I looked over at Thay. With the conversation in Khmer I wasn't sure whether I heard correctly. Thay laughed, shaking his finger excitedly. Then he whispered to me "Yes, he was with your embassy all right, but the one up there,'' he exclaimed, pointing toward heaven. I was speechless.

"So what is it I can do for you?'' the minister asked kindly. Barely able to collect my thoughts, I handed him the two adoption files that bore his signature with the notation "Refused.'' He immediately took his pen, scratched through his former refusals, then began signing his agreement to release on all the forms. I could hardly believe this was actually happening. When he finished, he looked up at us and asked, "Is there anything else I can help you with today?''

I told him I had additional orphans I would like release papers for, and he agreed to sign them. We excused ourselves, thanking him for his kindness. As soon as I got back to the building I took the other applications for adoption from the file.

"Rush these back to him for his signature, Thay,'' I said, handing him the files. "Let's strike while the iron is hot!''

Not only did we get the orphans released for adoption, but in a matter of hours, Thach Toan's office delivered passports, health certificates, exit visas, and entry visas into Britain and Sweden for Thalvary and Sithan. Since all commercial flights had ceased because of the airport bombings, the United States ambassador gave me special permission to fly to Thailand on an embassy cargo plane. It all happened so fast that I didn't even consider the serious implications of leaving DeAnn behind. I told her goodbye at the building and said jokingly, "Hey, when we got up this morning we never would have guessed I would be flying to Europe with two orphans today." I hurriedly made last-minute preparations and rushed to the airport.

At three o'clock that afternoon our plane raced down the runway as shrapnel from rockets pelleted the airship behind us. Out the window I saw huge black billows of smoke ascending from an ammunition dump that had just been hit. Had it not been for the U.S. airlift of rice into Phnom Penh, the capital would have collapsed months before. The airport was the city's only lifeline left, and now it was being besieged by rockets and artillery every hour. I prayed and held my breath until we had safely climbed out of artillery range. Looking down on the beleaguered capital, I wondered how much time was left before the inevitable took place. Suddenly it dawned on me that DeAnn was down there, and she was one of the last foreign civilians in the country. "Oh, God!" I prayed, "watch over her and protect her until I return."

Since there was nothing more than canvas slings for passenger seats on the plane, I had to find a way to secure the infants during the flight. Thankfully, the flight was short and both little girls slept soundly until we reached Bangkok at five o'clock. I checked into a hotel for the night, getting little sleep before having to board a commercial flight early the following morning. I was getting a good workout, changing diapers and preparing formula—and wished DeAnn could be with me. Before the plane landed in Copenhagen, one of the stewardesses kindly offered to watch the babies so I could sneak in a shave and cleanup.

Valerie Lowe flew from London to meet me in Copenhagen to receive their Khmer baby, Thalvary. It was refreshing to witness the climax of her excitement after months of waiting and praying.

I flew on to Stockholm with Sithan, where I was joyfully met by Lief and Aina Petersson. Sithan was their first long-awaited child and they broke into tears at the sight of their new baby girl. I can't remember when I had ever seen two people more uncontrollably elated in my entire life. "You've made us so happy," they repeated over and over, holding the tiny bundle close. The joy and appreciation of these two families and the loving homes provided for Thalvary and Sithan made all the efforts worthwhile.

I arrived in Sweden in the midst of a snowstorm, wearing a short-sleeved safari suit with only a small shoulder bag for luggage. But arriving in Sweden unprepared for cold weather didn't shock me half as much as learning it was "Anti-American Week." I was amazed to see giant posters pasted up along the streets of Stockholm. One depicted two Khmer Rouge soldiers loading a rocket launcher aimed at the American flag. **America Get Out** the poster read.

My friend Stanley Sjoberg asked me to speak for some special meetings at his church, and some people bought warm clothes for me so I could tolerate their cold weather. Four months earlier, after Stanley's visit to Phnom Penh, he had returned to Sweden and filled the newspaper with the story of what God was doing in that war-torn land. He further organized a massive campaign to raise funds for refugee camps and printing Christian literature. Because of this and the newspaper advertising about my speaking at the church, I realized I was already well-known in Sweden.

Gunnar Olson, a Christian businessman in Sweden, briefed me about the time Stanley went to his church in Sollentuna and shared about the revival in Cambodia. "Suddenly he stopped in the middle of his message and began to weep," Gunnar said. "Then he knelt down on the platform and cried out, 'Lord! If we don't begin to see revival like that in our country, then I must return to that land and be where you are pouring out Your Spirit!' "

As soon as word got out that I was in Stockholm I was besieged by reporters. But an American coming from Cambodia and speaking a positive message about the revival wasn't exactly what secular reporters wanted to hear. My presence seemed to dampen the fervor of their "Anti-American Week." I only told the reporters what God was doing among the Khmer people, and refused to discuss any United States involvement in Cambodia.

One evening as Gunnar was interpreting for me before his

congregation, he stopped in the midst of the message and excitedly shared a word he felt the Lord had given him for me. The word was: "I've kept you in a narrow place and you've ministered faithfully and fruitfully. Now your path is going to widen and your ministry broaden, taking in more area and more workers."

I was surprised to say the least, but I waited until after the meeting before questioning him about the meaning of the prophecy.

"I'm not sure what it refers to," he replied, "but I felt it would confirm something you were already considering." I pondered for several moments.

"I don't know what 'more area' actually means," I replied. "But it could be in reference to a country called Bhutan."

"Bhutan!" he said, surprised.

"Yes," I continued. "Several months ago a friend of mine, Larry Romans, told us about this country and asked us to pray for it. 'You never can tell,' he told me, 'you just might find yourself working there someday.' I was too busy to even consider it at the time, so I dismissed it."

"That's fantastic!" Gunnar exploded. "You won't believe this, but just the other day we received a letter from a fellow on the border of Bhutan. He asked if we knew of anyone who might be interested in launching a work in that country. We didn't know what to do with the letter," he confessed. "Now I know it was meant for you!" His excitement was contagious, but a part of me wanted to reject it as only coincidence. I rebelled against the idea that our ministry in Cambodia might be coming to an end. But the more I tried to shove it out of my mind, the deeper it lodged itself. Something within me whispered, "This matter is from the Lord."

When I got back to the hotel that evening I had an urgent telegram waiting for me. "It's from DeAnn!" I said to Gunnar, who had accompanied me to my room. I opened it hurriedly; the message left me deeply concerned. "Don't go Pailin. Come home soonest."

"I've got to get back," I said anxiously, "DeAnn's in trouble. I know her—she wouldn't send this unless it was serious." Gunnar went immediately to book my flight for the next morning. After he left I went to my knees in prayer. Opening to my evening reading in 2 Kings 4, the message I received from the chapter was, "It will be well" (v. 23).

I flew commercially as far as Bangkok, then boarded an embassy cargo flight into Phnom Penh. I had previously planned to cross the Thai border into Pailin and visit Kong and from there travel to Battambang to meet Sam-Oeurn. But DeAnn's cable urged me to forego my plans and return to Phnom Penh immediately. It had taken me two days to reach Cambodia from Sweden. As our plane circled the airport my heart churned with impatience to find out what had happened to DeAnn. The aircraft finally received clearance to land and moments later we rolled to a stop.

"Hurry," a marine guard urged, handing me a helmet and a protective vest. "Get in the hangar—quickly. It's not safe out here." The airport had become the prime target for a new Khmer Rouge offensive. All the windows in the buildings had been shattered by the incessant pounding of the rockets. A charred Boeing 707 jet lay on its side along the edge of the runway; it had been hit during takeoff after unloading its precious cargo of American rice. I put on the helmet and vest and ran into the hangar.

When the embassy van arrived the few passengers made a mad dash to board the vehicle. The trip into town seemed like eternity for me, but the van finally turned down Nehru Boulevard.

"DeAnn!" I shouted, bounding up the stairs. She appeared at the doorway and ran down, meeting me halfway.

Flinging her arms around me, she tearfully cried, "Oh, I'm so glad you're back!" Then pulling back, she remarked sheepishly, "I felt bad after I sent you that telegram."

"What do you mean? I was worried sick about you—what happened!"

"Just after you left, two Khmer Rouge infiltrators arrived at our building and questioned Sam-Oeurn's father and others who were standing around downstairs. They wanted to know where you went and why I didn't go with you. When Sam-Oeurn's father mentioned you would be coming back, they grew angry."

By this time Nou Thay had emerged from his office, hugged me, and joined DeAnn in explaining the sequence of events that had transpired just after my departure.

"They threatened her life," he said matter-of-factly, nodding in DeAnn's direction. Seeing my eyes grow wide in unbelief, he went on to explain. "There are Khmer Rouge intelligence agents all over the city; they know all our movements. They realize that when the Cambodians see all the foreigners leaving, they will likely give up hope and will settle for surrender. So these two fellows were a little disturbed when you didn't flee with everyone else. I guess they figure the best way to get you to leave the country is to threaten your lives."

I stood speechless for a few moments trying to absorb the implications of what Thay was saying. I didn't realize our movements were so well known to the Communists, nor was I aware that there were so many spies freely roaming the streets. "Thank God, DeAnn's safe!" I said as tears of relief spontaneously welled in my eyes.

"Something wonderful happened to me while you were gone," DeAnn said excitedly, grabbing my arm as we went into my office. "After the two men threatened me I became very scared and upset. I was even afraid to leave the building, so I sent Hach to the telegraph office to cable you. Later I wished I hadn't because I knew you would be worried about me.

"That evening, just before eating, I bowed in prayer and poured out my fears to the Lord. I prayed, 'Oh, God, it's only a matter of time before the Communists take over. What should we do? Should we stay through the siege, go to another country, return to the United States, what? Guide our hearts to find your answer.

"After I prayed, I settled down to have a bowl of soup. I flopped open one of those old almanacs—you remember, the ones the embassy threw out. Then I pulled over the kerosene lantern so I could see what I was reading. And you know what I had opened the almanac to?" she asked, her voice rising.

"My eyes fell right upon the boldface type **Bhutan!** She

238

pantomimed her surprise for effect. "It was just a tiny article about the country—but it was so weird, especially after I had just prayed asking the Lord what the future held for us. What do you think of *that* answer?"

My mind was reeling, recalling the unbelievable events that had so recently pointed me to consider the nation of Bhutan as our next target of ministry. "Listen to this," I laughed, growing more elated by the moment. Then I shared with her about Gunnar's prophecy and the unusual events that had taken place in Sweden. We were stunned to realize that though we had been thousands of miles apart, God had sovereignly dealt with both our hearts about this Himalayan kingdom of Bhutan. We were thrilled about the prospect of a new venture, but our hearts were torn, still not wanting to forsake our family in Cambodia.

An hour later we hurried to the embassy to pick up our mail before the offices closed for the day. Two letters and a note from the regional security officer awaited us. To our great surprise, both letters talked about Bhutan! Several months before, when Larry had shared with us about the need to pray for Bhutan, I had casually passed the word on to two other brothers who had written and asked, "What countries can we pray for?" Now, both these friends were responding at the same time, expressing interest in this tiny kingdom.

The letter from Dewey Friedel was particularly interesting. He wrote, "On my desk I have a magazine article about the country of Bhutan." He went on to explain how he had been interceding for this nation and its nineteen-year-old king, Jigme Singye Wangchuck. "And get this," he added, "last night I had a dream that we were trying to get into the country but we were having some difficulty. I awoke just before the miracle."

The evidence that was stacking up was incredible. "I wonder what magazine he was looking at?" I questioned aloud. I was itching to get any information about this country.

"We'll have to ask him later," DeAnn answered. "Look at this note from Sid Telford (the security officer on the embassy staff). He probably wants to urge us again to get out of the country."

239

We walked back to Sid's office, crossing the outdoor compound that separated the huge embassy structure from his makeshift quarters. I heard an unusually high-pitched whistle and feared a rocket was headed for the compound. I roughly jerked DeAnn and we crouched near the wall before the shell exploded directly on the other side, about thirty feet away. After the barrage had ceased we ran into the street to view the destruction. By God's grace no one was injured, but small craters pocked the pavement, and hot pieces of twisted shrapnel lay scattered everywhere. One piece had been driven into the trunk of a coconut tree. A barn was completely destroyed and a headless chicken bolted into the yard of a nearby villa; a piece of flying shrapnel had cropped off its head. A Cambodian soldier quickly jumped the fence in hot pursuit. He lunged, capturing the twitching bird. As the dust cleared, he grinned broadly. "Now we have chicken soup for dinner!" he exclaimed proudly.

Hurrying back to the embassy security office, we hoped we had not missed Sid, since it was almost closing time. We had become quite friendly over the months and enjoyed talking with him because he usually was the best-informed person at the embassy. Sid could always bring us up-to-date on the war situation.

He welcomed us into his office and proceeded to try to persuade us to leave Cambodia. "For God's sake, get out of this place," he urged, grinding out a cigarette in the already overflowing ashtray.

I looked at him steadily as he pulled another cigarette from the pack on his desk and lit it. "It's for God's sake we're staying, Sid," I said determinedly. "As I've told you before, when the Lord gives the order for us to leave, we'll go."

By this time my standard answer had become a joke with him. He laughed, shaking his head. "Well, where would you go, if you had to leave?" he asked.

Looking at DeAnn I smiled and spoke confidently, "It's funny you ask. We're getting bombarded with leadings to go to a little country called Bhutan that lies between India and China. I don't know, maybe that's the next place."

Sid took a long drag and looked off in the distance for a minute.

"Hmmm . . . Bhutan. I believe it was just last night that I was reading about Bhutan's new king in *National Geographic*."

"Which issue?" DeAnn asked quickly.

"Would you like to borrow my copy?" he offered, noticing our sudden interest.

"Boy, would we!" I exclaimed.

"Come by the house about seven-thirty and you can pick it up," he responded.

That evening after supper, we drove to Sid Telford's villa to get the magazine. Before going to bed that night we eagerly digested every word and picture about Bhutan.

"What a place," DeAnn summed up. "It looks impregnable."

"Well," I answered, "don't forget how impregnable Cambodia was supposed to have been—and we've been here for a year and a half. If God wants us there, a door will open."

Any one of these events directing us toward Bhutan wouldn't have carried much weight by itself, but all of them considered together indicated clearly that the hand of God was in the matter. We were beginning to feel about Bhutan the way we had felt when we first heard about Cambodia. However, we were still haunted with the realization that our ministry here was about to end. Our love for the Cambodians made it painful to think of leaving. "What will happen if the Communists do win the war?" we questioned. Everyone we asked had a different theory. But none of us could imagine how terrible it was actually going to be.

CHAPTER 17

The Fragrance of His Spirit

From the time we arrived in Cambodia it had been our desire to see those whom the Lord gave us grow into mature leaders. Gradually we saw them weaned from being dependent upon our presence. They had proven themselves capable of bearing the responsibility of the ministry under the Holy Spirit's direction and basically the work was now in their hands, leaving us more time for language study, writing Bible courses and teaching in the Bible school. Nou Thay, along with a board of elders, was now responsible for the leadership of Maranatha Church and the oversight of the other outlying churches and fellowships.

But our project of printing *The Martyr Of The Catacombs* and *Food For Spiritual Growth* was still frustrated. Though the finished translations had been in the hands of the printer for weeks, there was no electricity to run the presses. Stringent rationing was enforced to the point that we enjoyed only four hours of electricity each week, hardly enough to allow for the printing of these desperately needed books.

Concerning the orphans we were still caring for, release had been granted for all of them, but U.S. visas had not yet been received. We were waiting to receive the files for other orphans as well. Thinking it would be another month before visa packets arrived, I discussed with Thay and DeAnn my plans to journey north to visit Sam-Oeurn in Battambang and Kong in Pailin. But an unexpected letter changed my plans.

"It's a ticket for passage to Australia!" DeAnn read in

amazement, while I quickly scanned the letter.

"What for?" Thay asked.

"It seems I've been invited to be one of the speakers at a missionary conference there around the first of April, and they are wiring the ticket for me to come," I explained.

"Are you going to go?" Thay queried.

"I guess so—but DeAnn's coming with me this time. I'm not going to leave her alone here anymore."

Soon after the ticket to Australia came, we received visa packets for all five of our girl orphans who were to go to the United States. We decided to take them with us to Saigon, where DeAnn would wait with the children, while I went on to the conference in Australia. I would then return to Saigon, and the two of us would escort the orphans to the States to meet their new parents. In the next few days, we notified the American families, arranged flights through Pan American Airlines in Saigon, packed for the trip, and tried to wind up our affairs. Sid Telford at the United States Embassy Security Office was relieved to see us go.

"We're not running because of the war," I tried to explain when we went by his office. "We're just taking these orphans to their families—and we'll be back in a couple of weeks."

"Don't be so sure of that," he cautioned. "Since Congress has refused further aid to Cambodia we're walking on thin ice here. We've got a U.S. Navy carrier positioned in the Gulf of Thailand, ready to lift us out of here by helicopter when we give the signal. Bases in Thailand are anticipating our move any time now."

"But it's been touch and go like this for two dry seasons in a row," I argued. "If the government forces can just hold on until the rains begin, they've got it made—for another year, at least."

By Sid's manner and tone of voice, I knew the situation was grave. I also knew that when the United States diplomatic corps evacuated, Cambodia's takeover by the Khmer Rouge was imminent. But I still hoped to return.

That day I had received a Scripture from my Bible readings that gave us assurance we would return. "I am with you, and will keep you wherever you go, and *will bring you back to this land;* for I will not leave you until I have done what I have promised you" (Gen. 28:15, italics mine). I couldn't share this with Sid, though. He already thought we were crazy as it was. Though Sid was skeptical of the government forces' ability to hold the city of Phnom Penh, I was granted special permission to reenter the country using the embassy flights. We confirmed our plan to leave Phnom Penh the next day, March 29th, 1975.

We slept fitfully that night and got up hours before dawn to plan our day. My reading in the morning was unusually appropriate: "The kingdom of heaven is as a man travelling into a far country, who called his own servants, and delivered unto them his goods" (Matt. 25:14, KJV). Receiving this as a leading from the Lord, we handed over all funds, books, and personal belongings to the care of various Khmer leaders. That morning we purchased a motorcycle for use at one of the Phnom Penh churches, and I signed over the other vehicles to the board of Maranatha Church. DeAnn busily boxed up our most important files and packed one small suitcase of clothes for the two of us. "After all," she reasoned, "we'll be carrying five babies, so we can't take much baggage. And anyway, we're coming back!"

A few hours before departure time we were just finishing our packing when Nahvi interrupted us. She appeared at our door, out of breath from running. "Brother! Sister! Come quickly! Thay needs you at the new building; he says it's important!"

We immediately dropped everything and rushed over to the building we had rented for the Bible school. Thay met us at the gate.

"Hurry!" he yelled. He ran ahead of us, flinging open the doors to the main entrance hall. "Praise the Lord!" over a hundred voices joined in shouting. We froze in our steps as our eyes took in this incredible scene. It was a surprise banquet held in our honor. Several long mats had been rolled out on the floor and loaded down with food. Our churches in the area had joined together for what was to be our last fellowship meal. All the leaders and key members stood on either side of the mats, beaming with delight over our astonishment. Then Major Khoun stepped forward as their spokesman.

"You have given us so much, and have risked your lives to bring us the gospel," he said, his voice choked with emotion. "We now want to show you our love and appreciation." As different ones walked forward placing their gifts at our feet and giving the traditional *sam peah,* it was impossible to maintain our composure. Tears streamed down our faces, and we realized they were treating us as if they would never see us again. We sat down and began feasting on the meal of rice and chicken curry which had been prepared through great sacrifice on their part because of the scarcity of food. "Who's responsible for this?" I asked Thay. "We knew nothing about it!"

"Many of them worked together to do this for you," he answered. "Some of them feel you will not be able to return."

"No," I protested. "I feel the Lord has assured us of our return."

"You might return," he replied soberly, "but it may not be for a long time." His words jolted me, but I was still clinging to the Scripture I had read that morning.

Hiding their fear that we would never return, our Cambodian friends made our last hours in Phnom Penh some of our most memorable. Though they were torn by their love for us, those closest to us were relieved to see us go. They knew there was a greater threat to our lives than to theirs. As the hour neared for our departure, we gathered for prayer and they anointed us, praying for God's divine purpose to be fully accomplished through us wherever we would go. Then we quickly finished packing our things and went to the Manger to pick up our five babies.

"Please let us ride with you to the airport," Sareourn and Loeum begged. Having nursed and cared for the babies so long, they had surely earned that privilege. I waved for them to pile into the back of one of the waiting vehicles. Our final eight-mile journey to the airport began with the constant rumble of gunfire in the background. I thought of how shocked I had been on first learning the source of that threatening noise; now we were so accustomed to it we hardly gave it a second thought.

As we neared the terminal the explosions grew louder. Again, the airport was under siege. We bade a tearful though hurried farewell to our Cambodian friends, then huddled behind bunkers with helmeted government soldiers to wait for our plane. They gave us flak jackets and helmets to protect us from possible sprays of hot shrapnel. Finally, our plane wheeled near the terminal. Holding the babies tightly, we rushed from the bunker to the plane and secured the little ones with straps to the canvas seat. In a matter of minutes our nervous pilot had the aircraft racing down the runway. Once we were airborne, we watched our family waving below until they were enveloped into the shrinking landscape. We'll be back, I assured myself, trying to suppress feelings of doubt. But I couldn't hold back the sting of tears.

For fear of being shot down over Vietcong territory, our pilot flew westward to the coast, then made a circle to reach Saigon. The normal forty-minute flight took more than two hours. When we disembarked in Saigon, DeAnn carried two babies and I carried the other three, along with our luggage. A man from the Holt Adoption Agency saw us struggling in the airport and volunteered to take on the responsibility of housing and feeding our five orphans until we were ready to leave Saigon. This meant the burden would not be so great on DeAnn while I was in Australia. One of our babies, Cheata, required immediate hospitalization because of a bad respiratory condition and a high fever.

"I don't know how to thank you, Mr. Chamness," I told the director gratefully. "We really appreciate your help." DeAnn was quite relieved that she didn't have to keep all five babies in a hotel room while I was gone. In fact, her week's stay in Saigon turned out to be a restful vacation.

I located DeAnn in a hotel near the house where the babies were to be kept before reserving my flight to Sydney, Australia. I also booked our continuing flight to the United States on April 3rd.

"I'll be back as quickly as I can," I said kissing DeAnn goodbye at the hotel. I was worried about her staying in Saigon, since Vietcong troops were rapidly encircling the city. They had already occupied the greater part of the South Vietnamese countryside.

But the situation there was by far more stable than the situation in Phnom Penh, so I went on to Australia.

Seven days later I returned to Saigon. My flight had been so delayed that I feared missing connections for our scheduled flight to the States. I hope DeAnn is at the airport instead of the hotel, I worried to myself. There will barely be enough time to change flights much less take a taxi into town to get her and the babies.

When I got to the baggage claim area, I saw her tear-stained face bobbing among the hundreds of Vietnamese jamming the terminal. She was toting two of the heaviest children in slings strapped across her chest. Tim Friberg, our friend with Wycliffe, had helped her to the airport and was carrying the other three babies.

"I thought you would never make it," she sobbed when I finally reached her. The strain of the ordeal she had been through was written on her face.

"I know, honey," I cried. "I'll explain later. Come on, we're going to miss the Pan Am flight if we don't hurry." We were the last to climb aboard, waving goodbye to Tim. With weary sighs we strapped in the five girls and gratefully settled into our upholstered seats. Real seats were a luxury after traveling on cargo planes and sitting on canvas straps.

Our normal two-day flight ended up being a four-day ordeal because the plane developed engine trouble. We stopped first in Guam and stayed overnight in a hotel while they overhauled the engine. Then we had to stop again in Hawaii for the same purpose. Caring for the five little girls under these circumstances and hustling back and forth between airports and hotels was exhausting. In Guam some Red Cross workers helped with the babies so we could get a few hours of sleep.

Meanwhile, our parents and the adoptive families of the orphans had all met in Oklahoma City, thinking we would be stepping off the plane on Friday, April 4th, as scheduled. When news reached the States about the tragic crash of a plane outside Saigon carrying orphans and their escorts, our party was sick with worry, thinking we may have been aboard. With great fanfare they excitedly welcomed us two days later.

For days we were being showered with attention from relatives, friends, and reporters, but all we could think about was Cambodia. We lived from one news broadcast to the next, anxiously hoping Lon Nol's forces could outlast the Khmer Rouge offensive. DeAnn was physically exhausted from the strain and tension of the preceding weeks.

"You can't go back now," my mother warned. "DeAnn's resistance is low and she's so weakened—you'd be asking for trouble, believe me!" So we decided to wait for DeAnn to regain strength before trying to travel further.

Then on April 7th we received a telegram from Thay: "Received six more babies and nine family files. Please wire director general authorization for me to sign adoption contracts for you. Church all right and prospering. Praise God. Thay." I immediately wired my approval, hoping these files would be processed and ready when we returned. But in the next few days the situation in Phnom Penh worsened. The Khmer Rouge were gaining more control each day; the fall of the city and its government was imminent.

In desperation I wired Thay: "Send out orphans any way possible. Fast and pray for your country and for our return. Devote yourself to ministering and prayer. Work while it is day. Love and miss you much. Todd."

We had no way of knowing if Thay ever received that cable. The day after sending it, we viewed on television the final helicopter evacuation of remaining embassy personnel. All telephone and telegraph lines were cut, preventing our contact with anyone in the country. Four days later on April 17th the government forces gave way to the Khmer Rouge invasion. Our hopes fell, knowing that now our return could in no way be guaranteed.

We were puzzled by the seemingly festive mood of the Khmers: "Peace at last!" they shouted in the streets. We watched the video news reports with mixed emotions. We couldn't imagine the ruthless Communists giving humane treatment to those who had been involved in Lon Nol's regime. The first few days of occupation seemed bright for the Khmers, but almost overnight the horrors of the predicted blood bath began. When reports of the new regime's atrocities began to filter out of Cambodia, the western world was numbed with shock.

Although we couldn't return to Cambodia, our stay in the States was brief. The new call to Bhutan compelled us to journey into northeastern India to spy out the land around this Himalayan kingdom. We left the United States on April 27th and flew to Stockholm, Sweden. Stanley Sjoberg had asked us to stop there for a visit to minister in a charismatic conference before going on to India.

But this time there were no anti-American posters and demonstrations as I had encountered in Sweden three months earlier. Reports coming out of Cambodia had silenced the revolutionaries. Their Communist counterparts, the Khmer Rouge, weren't the peace-loving nationalists they had been built up to be. On the contrary; their thirst for blood was far from quenched when so-called "peace" came to the country on April 17th, 1975.

In spite of the turn of events, I found I was still in the spotlight in Sweden—only this time I was on the defensive. Reporters were constantly calling me or sending messages requesting interviews. One fellow managed to corner me in my hotel and I surrendered a few answers to loaded questions.

"Now what about your revival in Cambodia?" he asked cynically. "It's all gone down the drain, hasn't it? All that time you spent there has been wasted." He eagerly waited with pad and pencil for my answer.

"No," I protested, "I don't believe the Lord is finished with Cambodia."

"Let's be realistic," he argued. "The Khmer Rouge aren't going to let Christianity continue. They're going to wipe out everything that smells of foreign influence."

"You're probably right," I answered, "but I don't believe God's power is limited by an atheistic political system." I stopped him before he questioned me any further. "Listen," I added, "I can give you my opinions but let me seek the Lord and give you His answer to these questions."

He looked a bit startled at that idea. "I know the Christians here in Sweden will also want to know what I think about the situation of the church in Cambodia now that the Khmer Rouge are in control," I continued. I gave him the name of the church where I would be speaking that evening. "Please attend," I urged him. "You can print my whole message in your newspaper."

After he left, his words rolled over and over in my mind—"All that time you spent there has been a waste, down the drain." I began to pray and seek the Lord about what to say that evening. Then in my Bible readings I came to the story where the woman emptied an alabaster vial of costly perfume over the head of Jesus. As the fragrance filled the room the disciples became indignant. "What is the point of this waste?" they complained. "This perfume might have been sold for a high price and the money given to the poor."

"Why do you bother the woman," Jesus rebuked them. "For when she poured this perfume upon My body, she did it to prepare Me for burial . . . and wherever the gospel is preached in the whole world, what this woman has done shall also be spoken of in memory of her" (Matt. 26:6-13).

Suddenly, as I meditated upon this passage of Scripture, I felt the Holy Spirit speak to me in words I'll never forget:

"The time you spent in Cambodia has not been a waste! I sent you there not only to raise up a body of believers, but to anoint it and prepare it for its burial—for a time when it would have to go undergound. But know this, wherever they are scattered, the fragrance of my Spirit will be upon them. And when you do receive word concerning the church, you will not be hearing of a buried body of believers—but of one that is resurrected and walking in the midst of impossible conditions."

A warm rush of excitement filled me as the impact of this message soaked into my spirit. I could hardly wait for the meeting that evening. When I stood to speak I glanced around the auditorium in search of my reporter friend, and spotted him near the back. I then proceeded to deliver the message in all the fervor in which it had come to me.

"Many Christians will die; some may already be dead," I informed my listeners. "But God is alive and so is His church. I know of no other people who are better prepared for whatever may lie ahead than those believers in Cambodia."

After the meeting I met the same reporter in the lobby. "It's not what I wanted to hear," he said smiling, "but I did hear something." I never found out if he had printed my message, but I believed it was printed on his heart.

The following morning Gunnar Olson came hurriedly to our hotel room. "Brother Todd," he shouted excitedly, "Oddvar Johansen just contacted us relaying the message that Pastor Kong has escaped from Pailin! He's now located in a refugee camp on the border of Thailand."

"What?" I said, amazed. "Are you sure?"

"The message seems to be quite positive," he exclaimed.

Knowing Kong was safe in Thailand heightened my hopes for finding other members of our Cambodian family. We cut short our visit in Sweden and immediately exchanged our tickets to India for tickets to Bangkok, Thailand. Upon arrival there, we endured a grueling five-hour bus ride to Chanthaburi, where we spent the night with Jakob Aasebo, a Norwegian missionary, and his family. Jakob, who had met Kong in Pailin months earlier, had first spotted his face among the hundreds of escapees during one of his trips to the Pong Nam Ron refugee camp. Jakob was unsure of my whereabouts, so he telegrammed Oddvar Johansen who was temporarily living in Oslo, Norway. Oddvar had in turn contacted Stanley Sjoberg and the message finally reached me. Jakob was thrilled to see us.

"Is Kong all right?" I asked him, eager for any news.

"Oh, he's fine," he assured me. "He has some wonderful stories to tell you, but I'm going to wait and let him tell you himself in the morning."

I hated to have to wait that long, but we needed a good night's sleep.

When the following morning finally dawned we piled into Jakob's car and headed toward the Cambodian border. I had traveled this route many times before when taking supplies from Bangkok to Pailin, and from there on to Phnom Penh. As we climbed out of the car near the camp's entrance, eager Khmer children pressed against the barbed wire barricade separating them from the outside world. Among the inquisitive faces I saw Kong's youngest son, Joseph. Before we could be checked through the guard post, Kong and his whole family pushed through the crowd of refugees to greet us with open arms.

"Oh, brother! Brother Todd!" he cried, running towards me. With heavy sobs he held me tightly for several minutes, unable to speak. San and the children hugged DeAnn as they chattered in Cambodian. Kong showed us to their makeshift quarters which consisted of nothing more than sheets of plastic draped over poles.

"Kong, how did you escape?" I questioned him eagerly, impatient to find out what had happened in those closing days.

"At first I didn't know what to do when I heard over the radio from Phnom Penh that the Communists had taken over," he began. "Their words were harsh and threatening. I was deeply troubled and began to ask the Lord for direction. I then heard clearly the same words that God spoke to Philip, "Join this chariot" (Acts 8:29). I looked out at our jeep and knew the Lord was telling us to flee to Thailand. So I planned our escape.

"I quickly gathered all the believers and neighbors who would go with us, packed a few belongings, then traveled the rough road across the border into Thailand. Not many came with us at first. Thinking we were crazy, they laughed at us when we urged them to come along. 'Peace has come' they said confidently. 'One flees from war, but not when the war is over. Why flee now?' I told them they might not like the Khmer Rouge version of peace."

I looked over at DeAnn in amazement. San, with a solemn face, confirmed Kong's account with her nodding.

"Only a few hundred of us left Cambodia at that time," Kong continued. "When we arrived, we waited in this area sectioned off for us by the Thai government. It was almost like being imprisoned. After two days we began to wonder if we had made the right decision. Some grew impatient and went back. But on the third day we began to hear of total tragedy that had overcome our city. News came from refugee stragglers who managed to escape the Khmer Rouge attack. We learned we had escaped only a few hours before the Communists overran Pailin. The reports that new arrivals continue to bring with them are terrible. By now there are more than three thousand refugees in this camp alone.''

By this time others had gathered around and began giving us their version of what had happened. I talked with first one and then another. "They're killing everyone," a young man told me. "See this," he pointed to a soiled bandage wound crudely around his thigh. "The Khmer Rouge loaded hundreds of us into trucks and told us they were taking us to Battambang for a celebration of the new government. But once they drove us out of the city, we were ordered to get off the trucks. Suddenly soldiers emerged from the jungle and began to mow us down with machine-gun fire. I escaped and ran into the tall grass. It was fortunate that I only got hit once—the shell is still in my leg. I walked three weeks through the forest to reach Thailand.''

I listened to stories like this until I couldn't bear to hear another word about the Khmer Rouge. What could make anyone so bloodthirsty? I wondered.

"Brother Todd," Kong said as his countenance brightened, "I want to tell you about something wonderful that happened. You remember Ton Kham, don't you?"

"Sure," I replied. "He's the elder in your church who was healed of tuberculosis.''

"Well," Kong continued, "on a Sunday morning, eleven days before the fall, there was a loud bang on our door before the sun had dawned. I hurried out of bed, and as I unlocked the door of the church I heard someone weeping. There stood Kham holding the lifeless body of his thirteen-year-old son. He had died in the night after having suffered more than a week with a severe fever. Later that morning as the believers gathered for our meeting, they were broken-hearted when they learned of the boy's death. His body had already become cold and stiff. When it was time for the service, the congregation joined hands in prayer to commit the boy's spirit to the Lord. Suddenly, my wife pierced the air with a frightening scream—"

"His fingers began to move!" San exclaimed, finishing the story. "I rushed over and placed my hand underneath the blanket. His chest was growing warm and began to rise and fall as he started to breathe. Within moments he was sitting up and praising the Lord with us!"

"Fantastic!" I shouted.

"That's incredible," DeAnn said.

"Yes," Kong added. "It really happened. God raised him from the dead!"

I was jotting down the details of these stories as fast as I could. For a moment I forgot all about the atrocities of the Khmer Rouge.

"There's something else you should know," Kong interrupted my writing. "Two days after this happened I went to Battambang to pick up the motorcycle you bought for me. While I was there I met with Sam-Oeurn and Youvannette. I was amazed to see all the new believers; their work had grown so fast! I shared with them the miracle of Ton Kham's son and they all rejoiced. Then Sam-Oeurn got real serious. '*Kruu*,' he said soberly, 'the other evening as I was praying I had a vision.' He went on to describe how he felt he was lifted up where he could see all of Battambang. Suddenly the Khmer Rouge overran the city, burning the buildings and driving the people away. The city was in flames when a voice spoke to him saying,

'This will happen soon; it will happen very soon. You must prepare your people.'

"When I first heard this I was shocked," Kong continued. "I tried to reject it, but because it came from Sam-Oeurn I figured it might be true. I returned to Pailin, and in less than a week it happened just as he said."

Tears of joy filled our eyes as we listened to this amazing account.

"Wow!" DeAnn exclaimed with excitement. "That sounds

like the dream Dullah shared with us before leaving Phnom Penh.''

''What's that?'' I questioned as Kong and San gathered close to listen.

''You remember,'' she continued, ''Dullah saw a large dove circling over Phnom Penh while guns below tried to shoot it down. Suddenly, the dove was hit and exploded into hundreds of smaller doves that scattered over the country.''

I was beginning to understand that God had caused such things to happen because He knew they would need strength for what lay ahead.

''What about Nou Thay, Dana, or any of the other believers of Phnom Penh?'' I asked Kong. ''Have you heard anything about them?''

''No, I haven't,'' he shook his head sadly. ''I'm really afraid for them. We pray for their safety every night.'' We were all silent for several minutes. Then I shared with Kong some of the other visions and miracles that God had given the believers in Phnom Penh in the last days before our departure.

''They, too, have been prepared for the worst,'' I assured Kong. ''I'm sure that even while we talk some have gone to be with the Lord; others may be receiving unusual divine protection. It's all in God's hands now.''

Then I asked him, ''Have you seen or heard anything about Saran?''

''No,'' he answered. ''I haven't heard anything about him since he left Pailin ten months ago.''

I was quiet for a moment, thinking about Saran. ''I hope somehow he comes back into fellowship with God,'' I said.

Later I met a young man named Heng Sambo who had become a Christian after arriving in Thailand. Someone had helped him write out his testimony in English:

''When I was a student in Battambang Province, I saw a Christian going everywhere and telling everyone who was living in the town about the New God. Afterwards, my friends and I wanted to protest against him. We started to look for his mistakes but we could not find any, because he was a real Christian. He had a quiet character and respected all the messages of God. I didn't know God then—''

My heart rejoiced when I later learned that the ''real Christian'' Sambo mentioned was my dear friend Sam-Oeurn.

DeAnn and I spent the rest of the day talking with other refugees who had trekked through the forest into Thailand. We gathered gruesome reports of mass executions, brutal beatings, stabbings and cruel torture of those whom the Communists considered their enemies. Our hearts became heavy as we viewed the refugee's unsanitary and cramped living conditions—they were existing almost like animals under the constant surveillance of Thai military guards. Many begged us to help them emigrate to western nations. But Kong wanted to stay in the camp to spread the gospel. Already he had a nucleus of strong believers besides those he had brought with him from Pailin. I promised I would try to get permission for him to float along the Thai/Cambodian border, visiting all the refugee camps to preach the gospel. I didn't realize it then, but hundreds would soon come to know the Lord through his ministry in these camps. He had already held some large meetings and over three hundred copies of the *Tuk Rueh* Bible course that we had left in Bangkok had been distributed.

As darkness approached we were urged by the police to vacate the premises. Only refugees were allowed to spend the night within the confines of the camp.

We drove on north a distiance, then stopped and took one last look across the dirt road leading into Cambodia. I had crossed this road so many times before—free to come and go as I pleased. Now, as if with invisible chains, we were held back from entering this once gentle land. As I gazed over into Cambodia, my mind raced over the events of the past two incredible years. I thought of the two closest friends I had ever had—Nou Thay and Sam-Oeurn. Tears streamed down my face as I wondered if I would ever see them again.

''Oh, God,'' I prayed, ''please protect them wherever they are.''

We drove silently back to Chanthaburi. Arriving at the Aasebos' home, we went to our room, but neither DeAnn nor I could sleep. We talked for long hours, sadly wondering about the fate of those we loved. When we finally went to bed I slept fitfully.

I dreamed I was searching throughout Cambodia for our beloved family. I went to all the familiar places, but I could find no one; I could only hear their voices. Then for some reason I realized I was carrying a huge piece of lumber wherever I went. Suddenly some Khmer Rouge soldiers spotted me. I was running along a railroad track trying to escape. The piece of lumber was slowing me down, but I was afraid to let go of it. As I neared a bridge, I was startled by a tall, glistening angel standing below in a ditch. "Hand it to me," he said. "I will keep it for you until you can return and build again—"

I awoke from the dream with a start and suddenly sat up in bed. DeAnn woke up, too, and I began to share with her what I had dreamed.

"Todd," she said incredulously, propping herself up on her elbow in bed, "that dream must be confirmation of the Scripture the Lord gave you about going back to Cambodia!"

"It could be," I responded. "But since I've studied that passage more carefully, I realized that after God originally gave the promise to Jacob it was more than twenty years before Jacob actually returned to the land. We'll just have to put our timetable into God's hands."

"Well," DeAnn said thoughtfully, as we lay down again in the early morning darkness, "at least the Holy Spirit was not forced to leave. I know He must be working in miraculous ways through the lives of the believers."

"Yes," I answered. "God assured us from the beginning that this was His work. But I'll never forget the sight of that angel holding the piece of lumber and saying, **I WILL KEEP IT FOR YOU UNTIL YOU CAN RETURN AND BUILD AGAIN.**

To receive a newsletter which reports on continuing developments in Todd and DeAnn Burke's ministry, and to inquire about the sequel to *Anointed for Burial,* please write:

Todd and DeAnn Burke
P.O. Box 20123
Oklahoma City, OK 73156

EPILOGUE

Now two years have passed and an estimated two million people have died since "peace" came to Cambodia on April 17, 1975. As the Khmer Rouge's genocidal measures are steadily grinding the hope of the Cambodian people to dust, God's Spirit has caused some to be born again to a living hope.

On frequent visits to the various refugee camps along the Thai/Cambodian border, I saw Kong's ministry there blossom. At one time I witnessed one of his baptisms of as many as 143 new believers. The devotion of these who have lost everything in terms of this world's goods, but are rich in Christ, deeply stirred my heart. I strangely found myself praising God for the Khmer Rouge because in His wisdom He chose them to bring the hearts of the people to Himself.

The copies of our "Tuk Rueh" Bible course that were left behind in Bangkok, Thailand, became one of the primary tools of teaching for the new believers. Copies were immediately exhausted in the refugee camps, requiring reprints of more than 15,000. The last printing has not only been used along the border, but also has found its way to many other nations where Cambodian refugees have now resettled. What a blessing it has been to see God's purpose for those long-awaited Bible courses I couldn't carry back to Cambodia.

Though the nation of Democratic Kampuchea (as Cambodia is now referred to by the communists) is still closed off to the world and we have heard nothing from our family there, we trust in God's promise that His Church is resurrected and is walking in the midst of impossible circumstances. The tragic account of the blood-bath which Cambodia is still experiencing is well portrayed in a new book by the *Reader's Digest* recent publication of **Murder Of A Gentle Land**.

I often think of our brothers and sisters there as being like the three Hebrew children who were cast into the fiery furnace by King Nebuchadnezzar. Strangely, instead of only three walking unharmed in the midst of the fire, the king saw a fourth figure with them, and His form was like the Son of God (Daniel 3).